# Motorin' Along!

A hundred years ago, the
automobile was little more than
a noisy curiosity—some 50
years later, it had changed the
face of North America forever.
These are memories of that
leisurely yet adventurous
journey, fondly recalled by folks
who were along for the ride.

*THE CAR THAT MADE WALKING A PLEASURE?* Not really. Although the clever sayings these New York State teenagers painted on the side of their Model T poke fun at this little vehicle, chances are they were delighted with their Lizzie. When this photograph was taken in 1929, Model T's were no longer being made, but these tough, versatile machines would continue to travel the nation's roads for decades to come. Simple to operate and repair, although not particularly fast, they were the ideal car for kids who were strapped for cash but wanted their own wheels.

**Editor:** Michael Martin
**Contributing Editor:** Clancy Strock
**Assistant Editors:** Deb Mulvey, Kristine Krueger, John Schroeder, Mike Beno
**Art Director:** Maribeth Greinke
**Art Associates:** Jim Sibilski, Gail Engeldahl, Linda Dzik, Stephanie Marchese
**Photo Coordination:** Trudi Bellin, Mary Ann Koebernik
**Editorial Assistants:** Blanche Comiskey, Joy Bartol-Snyder
**Production Assistants:** Claudia Wardius, Ellen Lloyd, Barb Czysz
**Publisher:** Roy J. Reiman

© 1998 Reiman Publications, L.P.
5400 S. 60th Street, Greendale WI 53129

**Reminisce Books**
International Standard Book Number: 0-89821-232-4
Library of Congress Catalog Number: 97-76274
All rights reserved. Printed in U.S.A.

Cover photo of Illinois family and their new 1939 Plymouth was shared by Mollie Miller Plush of North Randall, Ohio. Mollie, her brother, Dan, and their parents, Sennet and Gladys, posed on Chicago's South Side.

Photo above and on back cover by Brown Brothers (hand-tinted by Melissa Burghart)

For additional copies of this book or information on other books, write: Reminisce Books, P.O. Box 990, Greendale WI 53129-0990. **Credit card orders call toll-free 1-800/558-1013.**

# Contents

Brown Brothers (hand-tinted by Melissa Burghart)

*"PUTT-PUTTING" INTO A NEW ERA.* Early autos like this one were not particularly speedy (although, over longer distances, they were faster than horses). Engines weren't strong or reliable and—even if they had been—roads were unsafe at speeds over 10 or 15 miles per hour. Chances are, these ladies' big hats would have blown away, even at lower speeds.

# Prologue

*By Clancy Strock, Contributing Editor, Reminisce Magazine*

ince the day the first automobile appeared on the road, it has drawn controversy the way a cool pond draws children on a July afternoon.

It's been blamed for everything from frightening horses to poisoning the air. But try to imagine life without it.

Nothing so well fit the itchy feet and unquenchable curiosity of Americans as the automobile. And nothing else could have tied this sprawling nation together as did the "horseless carriage".

When the first cars were invented in Europe, they were regarded as fancy toys for the wealthy, and dangerous diversions for the speed-addicted young. But to create the world we know today, cars (and their lumbering cousins, trucks and buses) were a *necessity*.

After all, you could hike or travel by horse across most countries in Europe in a day or two. But not here. Yes, Daniel Boone did leg it from Missouri to Yellowstone while in his 70s just to see if the tall tales about the place were true. But we didn't produce many Daniel Boones.

### What an Innovation

What we did produce by the millions was a dandy means of getting from here to there comfortably and speedily, whether to take our crop to market or visit Aunt Mae in Miami or see the Golden Gate Bridge or just go out for a Sunday drive.

And that's what this book is about —the first half of the 20th century, when automobiles became the magic carpet for rich and poor alike, almost in the blink of an eye.

To be historically correct, the Era of the Automobile dawned a few years before the new century began. Gottlieb Daimler and Karl Benz were tooling around Germany in their "Patent Motor Car" as early as 1886.

The French and English were busy at work in *their* garages, too. Word of all this reached the other side of the Atlantic and soon dozens of mechanically talented men were creating their own versions of automobiles. Bicycle manufacturers and carriage makers especially were drawn to the new field.

And why not? Go back to that term "horseless carriage". It's precisely what those early cars were...a buggy minus

> "My dad vividly recalled the first car he encountered..."

the horse, but with a crude tiller for steering and a putt-putt gasoline engine linked to the rear wheels with bicycle chain.

Hey, just about anyone could build a car! C'mon, Bill, let's make one of our own.

In 1897, the Stanley brothers developed their "steamer", and Alex Winton produced a car that hit an astonishing 33.7 miles per hour over a 1-mile test. R.E. Olds formed the Olds Motor Vehicle Company (later putting his initials together to create a name for the Reo auto).

My dad vividly recalled his first encounter with an auto. It probably was around 1904, when he was 8 years old. One afternoon, he and his younger brother heard a noise like nothing they'd ever experienced before. Someone had unleashed the Hounds of Hell!

They sprinted across a field to hide in the bushes beside the dirt road at the north edge of the family farm. The noise drew closer and closer.

*And there it was...an automobile!*

The driver—hopefully human—was covered in a "duster" coat that reached to his ankles. Enormous goggles shielded his eyes and a cap was pulled down to the tops of his ears. (Today he'd probably be hailed as a space alien.)

And that's how most people met the future in the first decade of this century. Little did they know what marvels lay just ahead.

Meanwhile, the prevailing wisdom was that automobiles were an odd fad that soon would pass away because:

a.) Only the ultra-rich could afford them.

b.) The human body could not long endure speeds as high as 20 mph.

c.) Cars would never be able to go where horses could go.

d.) Sensible people wouldn't stand for the terrible racket, and soon cars would be outlawed everywhere.

The total U.S. population at that time was 76 million. Today the United States has nearly four times more people. Personally, I'm happy that cars replaced horses.

Yes, I know cars pollute the air something awful and use up our precious petroleum resources, but think about the mess we'd be in if 270 million people were depending on horses for their transportation. Whew!

What the automobile did was provide a magic carpet for the masses, as the stories in this book make clear. It ♂

**CLANCY STROCK is a retired professor of journalism at the University of Nebraska. He is a book author, free-lance magazine writer and Contributing Editor of *Reminisce*, North America's most popular nostalgia magazine.**

ended our "horizon-to-horizon" lives.

Visionary men like Henry Ford quickly understood the coming demand for automobiles. New brands of cars proliferated like rabbits.

There were Chandlers and Jordans and Hupmobiles and Durants and Stanley Steamers and Willys-Overlands and Packards and Kissels. And let's not forget the Pierce-Arrow and Allstate and Nash and Graham-Paige, as well as the DeSoto, Chrysler, Chevrolet, Reo, Plymouth and Essex.

For the upper crust, there were Lincolns and LaSalles and Oaklands and Buicks and the top-of-the-line Locomobiles. If you were a movie star, you flaunted your success with a snazzy Stutz Bearcat, Duesenberg or the ultra-posh 16-cylinder Cadillac limousine.

The car that drew throngs of admirers in our town was the racy Cord…a car so sleek and sculpted that it still awes crowds today.

Later came the American Austin and the Cunningham (only 28 built in 2 years—and the inventor lost money on every single one!), the much-hyped but short-lived Tucker and the post-World War II Kaisers and Frazers.

### They Carried a Car

At my high school, the local "rich kid" turned up with a new American Bantam, a midget car that was 9 feet long. A group of frivolous students managed to move it to the top of the school steps, tucking it into an alcove from which there was no easy escape. (Envy is a wretched vice!)

The proliferation of cars, each quite distinctive in appearance, made for a fine game while traveling. The rules were simple: The first person to correctly identify an oncoming car (by both make and year) won a point. Whoever had the most points at the end of the journey was the winner.

My mother had scant interest in autos and was the official scorekeeper. Today, alas, all cars look pretty much the same whether coming or going.

Besides wiping out a good game on boring trips, this dreary sameness also accounts for all of us bewildered people peering helplessly around large parking lots, wondering which car is ours.

Various brands had their unique personalities and special audiences. The Buick became known as "the doctor's car". Bankers favored the Packard, an appropriately solid, respectable and un-flashy vehicle.

Rural mail carriers were partial to Model T (and later, Model A) Fords, because they were durable, dependable, and unfazed by rain, snow, sleet and mud.

Well-to-do farmers in my part of the

Charlie Heidecker

*SYMBOL OF SPEED.* **This popular hood ornament from the '30s hints at how far autos had come since the era of the "horseless carriage".**

world drove Dodges, because they had the power to slog through gooey roads rutted by spring rains, as well as the gumption to conquer deep snowdrifts.

While the automobile created an entirely new form of recreation, travel was definitely for the brave and adventurous, as you'll learn in this book. There were few paved roads.

Worse yet, there were no highway markers or signposts. When you came to a crossroads or fork in the road, lotsa luck! You could as easily end up in Pittsburgh as Poughkeepsie.

Many early roads were created by

wagon convoys headed west. Some had been trails for cattle drives. They meandered over hill and dale, forded creeks and rivers, and most certainly hadn't been laid out by surveyors.

Out there in the wide-open spaces, you might come to a gate that blocked the road. You got out, opened the gate, drove through, went back to close the gate and then drove on.

When a tire blew out, you jacked up the car, pulled off the wheel and tire, patched the inner tube, inflated the repaired tire with 200 thrusts of the hand pump and put the tire back on the car…a dirty 20-minute job under the best of conditions.

If you became stuck in the mud or slid into a ditch, you hiked to the nearest farmhouse, hoping to find an obliging farmer who'd hitch up a team of horses and pull you out.

When you faced major mechanical difficulties, you legged it down the gravel road and hoped to find an auto dealer in the next town. And even if you did, it might take him a week or more to get the necessary replacement part.

### Legendary Lincoln Highway

But help was on the way, and from an unexpected source. In 1912, Carl Graham Fisher, a headlight manufacturer, assembled a group of auto, tire and concrete manufacturers. America needed a coast-to-coast highway, he said. It would be good for car owners and for all businesses.

They raised private money to improve and link up existing roads into a

*"DEMOCRATIC" FLATS.* **Whether poor or wealthy, all car owners had to deal with the occasional flat tire.**

H. Armstrong Roberts

J.C. Allen and Son (hand-tinted by Melissa Burghart)

Archive Photos/Hirz

remedy was to remove the gas cap, take a deep breath and blow air into the gas tank.

To get the picture, you might imagine a red-faced man trying to play a four-wheel, 2,000-pound tuba. Mom would lean forward, cock an ear and report the good news when she could hear gasoline trickling into the carburetor.

Then we could continue…but only for another 6 to 8 miles. We measured distances in terms of how many "blows" were required. Sterling to Rockford, Illinois was a daunting eight huffs-and-puffs journey.

### Better and Better

Slowly but surely, automobiles improved. Engines became more powerful and reliable. Self-starters replaced arm-busting hand cranks. Roll-up glass windows replaced side curtains. Mufflers hushed engine roar. Heaters outmoded lap robes and heated bricks. Dashboard gauges reported on speed and the engine's vital signs. Tire blowouts became rare.

Through it all, the industry sorted itself out and the Big Three (General Motors, Chrysler and Ford) became the dominant car producers.

America's annual Big Event was not when the circus came to town or the latest Bing Crosby movie opened. Instead, it was the autumn debut of the new model cars.

Dealership windows were masked with butcher paper. Splashy, teasing ads hyped the wonders soon to be unveiled. When the big day arrived, throngs gathered to get their annual injection of the dreaded "new car fever". The objects of our affection were here at last—new cars!

Whether you're an automobile enthusiast or not, you're in for some fascinating reading in the pages that follow—personal memories of the invention that profoundly changed our lives forever. ❧

**BUSINESS AND PLEASURE.** By the '20s, businessmen like those pictured above had adapted the automobile for all kinds of uses, from simply getting to the job to, as in the case of traveling salesmen, *doing* the job.

**NOT A T.** As engines got more complex, many drivers longed for the simplicity of those trusty old Model T's. It became harder and harder to understand what went on under the hood.

transcontinental highway 3,348 miles long. Not a cent of federal or state money went into that visionary project.

The monumental job was completed in 1920 and designated U.S. Route 30. It was later named the Lincoln Highway. Portions of it were rough, and pavement was still a few years away. But Americans now had a well-marked route from the Atlantic to the Pacific.

Three thousand Boy Scouts were recruited to put up concrete markers along the route—a few of those pylons still stand today.

It didn't take long for automobiles as well as freight trucks and buses to crowd the highway, creating a demand for fuel stops, restaurants and motels. The small towns along the way pros-

pered from the steady stream of travelers in need of supplies.

Up until World War II, autos were reasonably simple to maintain, and every man was his own mechanic. My dad spent hours tinkering under the hood until a balky engine once again was purring smoothly.

### Our "Huff-Mobile"

That lasted until he bought a 1947 Oldsmobile. Lifting the hood, he took a long look at the automobile's innards, shrugged with incomprehension and announced, "It appears I've worked on my last car."

Only one of his earlier cars—a 1930 Willys—thwarted him. The gas line regularly plugged up, causing the car to gasp and shudder to a stop. The only

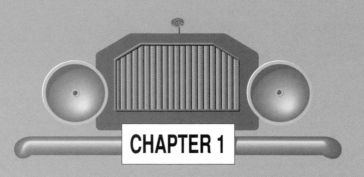

# CHAPTER 1

Brown Brothers (hand-tinted by Melissa Burghart)

***CHAUFFEUR-DRIVEN SMILES.*** The expressions on these women's faces suggest that this may well have been the first time they'd ever ridden in an automobile. And, it's likely that the woman behind the wheel was there strictly for the photo (in the early years, only men drove). Without a windshield, goggles were a necessity for drivers of vehicles like this.

# Steamers and Screamers

Close your eyes. Now try to picture a world without automobiles…without trucks or buses…without gasoline engines of any kind. Unless you've already celebrated your 100th birthday, it's nearly impossible.

So you can imagine the excitement and controversy at the beginning of this century when men began tinkering with the machines soon to be known as "horseless carriages".

Like anything new and revolutionary, autos were greeted with massive skepticism. Most of them neither worked very well nor for very long. Their inventors were lumped into the same category with those goofy Wright brothers down in North Carolina who were actually trying to fly, for pity's sake!

There were lots of failures and precious few successes. But the true believers were stubborn rascals. In Massachusetts, for example, two twin brothers named Stanley were experimenting with a steam-driven car.

A man named Ford in Detroit thought a gas engine was the answer. Another visionary saw electricity as the way to go and came up with a car powered by nearly a ton of batteries.

### Boiler Required Watching

Steam was especially attractive, because steam engines had been around for a long time and engineers knew how to build them. The only drawback was the boiler—the size of the boiler a car could carry, and the fact that boilers had a nasty habit of blowing up if they weren't watched carefully.

**STEAM TEAM.** Francis and Freelan Stanley, pictured below in their famed 1897 steam "runabout", were identical twins.

Brown Brothers

But steam could generate a lot of speed. In 1901, a steam-driven car hit the incredible speed of 78 mph (a bigger problem was that there were few, if any, roads safe enough to drive that fast). American George Cannon developed a steamer that went like the dickens but required two men to handle it—one in front to steer and one in back to operate the boiler.

Even though gasoline engines eventually became the popular choice, engineers continued tinkering with steam cars until 1932. Over 100 different makes appeared during that period.

### Gas Not Needed

Far and away the most successful models came from the Stanley brothers. Their speed and reliability made them popular with fire and police departments. And why not? They didn't use gasoline and could travel 50 miles on one fill of water. Not only that, the boilers didn't explode.

You'd think a car with all those virtues would have captured the auto market. But it had its foes, primarily because it was too quiet! Unwary pedestrians couldn't hear it coming.

I'm sure that was a problem with electric cars, too. An elderly lady in our town owned one…a tall black machine that looked like a phone booth on wheels.

She regally stepped into it after church every Sunday and noiselessly glided away. (And to think that now, 70 years later, electric autos may again be in our future.)

Those early days of this century were exciting indeed. While the traditionalists sat on the bench in front of the grocery store and cackled "Get a horse!", the adventuresome were bragging about their trips to far-off places…even as far as 40 miles away!

But neither the scoffers nor the dreamers could foresee the day when there would be 176 million of those infernal machines on our roads by the mid-'90s. As someone pointed out, that's 53 million more motor vehicles than there were *people* in the United States back in 1930.

Now turn the page and read early memories of the time when America's romance with automobiles was still in its puppy-love stage.

—*Clancy Strock*

# Whitney's Wagon: 'A Menace to Life and Limb!'

*By Elinor Whitney Butterfield*
*Las Vegas, Nevada*

My grandfather, George Whitney, was a lifelong tinkerer and inventor who could tell fascinating stories about the early days of the steam-powered horseless carriage.

In 1896, he built his first workable model of what was then called a "motor wagon". I have a copy of a 1925 newspaper article, in which he recalled the thrills of those heady days:

"My first idea was to use two bicycles propelled by a motor," Grandfather explained. "I went to work and built my 98-pound motor, but discovered that the bicycle wheels were too light. The wheels I finally built were more like wire buggy wheels, the front ones considerably smaller than the rear.

"I did my experimental work in Boston and had the devil's own time to get through the crowds that gathered around me! The police department had evidently been notified that I had a queer-looking vehicle, and I received a legal notice saying that I had to be preceded by a man waving a red flag!

"It had been reported to the chief that I had a machine that ran like the deuce. They considered me a menace to life and limb, so they dug up some old law originally intended to apply to road rollers and construed it to apply to my case.

### Pulled a String

"I knew a fellow who was in the Massachusetts legislature at the time, so I got him to take me up to the State House and introduce me to the members. Among them were Henry Cabot Lodge and Calvin Coolidge.

"I showed them my automobile and invited them to take a ride with me, which they did, expressing amazement at the smoothness and speed, and prophesying that there would be thousands of them on the road before long. The result of that interview was that I was given the freedom of the streets.

"As far as I know, I was the first man to travel by automobile from Boston to New York. I made regular trips in that first car from Boston to Providence, Worcester and Newburyport. One time, my uncle, Amos Whitney, accompanied me on a trip from Boston down to the Pratt and Whitney plant at Hartford.

"Back then, horses were frightened by automobiles even if they stood still! It was almost unheard-of to pass a horse in the road without it shying.

"My uncle was a horse lover who kept stables of his own and was a very conscientious man. So, every time we passed a horse that shied and broke out of his harness, my uncle would get out,

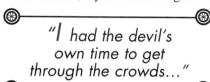

*"I had the devil's own time to get through the crowds..."*

talk with the driver, present his card and ask to have the bill for any damages sent to him at his factory.

"His cards ran out before he got to Worcester, and I venture that more farmers in that section had new harnesses than ever before!"

Grandfather's strange vehicle attracted attention wherever it went—so much so that he had to devise a strategy to complete his trips on time. Unfortunately, it didn't work very well.

"Wherever I stopped," he once explained, "crowds gathered around me so densely I had difficulty getting started again. I soon learned there were a dependable set of questions that would be asked. For my own protection, I had a little folder printed containing answers to the average questions.

"I passed these around wherever I went, exactly as a quack doctor passes out his circulars. But they failed to achieve the looked-for result—folks simply stuck them in their pockets and proceeded to stand and question me just as before!

"Everyone who saw my motor wagon wanted one like it. I built 16 of them, each one different. Then I entered into a contract with A.L. Barber, who bought my patents and formed the Locomobile company." (*Editor's Note: Locomobile eventually sold Mr. Whitney's patents to the company that built the Stanley Steamer.*)

During the early part of this century, Grandfather helped manufacture over 5,000 cars for Locomobile. But steam engines were always his first love, so when the company began switching over to gasoline engines, he went on to other ventures.

George Whitney lived to be 101 and was tinkering and building right up until his death in 1964. He held over 300 patents, but none had a more revolutionary effect on the 20th century than that little "power wagon".

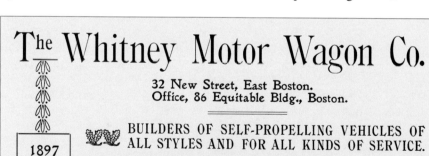

**CARD GAMES.** Folks asked inventor George Whitney so many questions about his "power wagon" that he had to hand out cards like this one.

*WATCH YOUR STEP.* These ladies had to climb into this early-model automobile from the back. With luck, the fenders kept the mud off their fancy clothes.

### He Was a Speed Demon on Foot

MY MOTHER told me about the first horseless carriage her father ever saw. Grandpa Potras was French Canadian, lived in the United States and spoke very little English, so news of these newfangled contraptions had completely bypassed him.

One memorable evening, he was walking home from town when he heard a strange noise behind him. Turning, he saw this thing popping, banging and belching smoke. It was only a 100 yards away and gaining fast.

Now Granddad was a little guy—not more than 5-foot-4—but he decided he'd try to outrun whatever it was. He was still ahead of it when he reached his house, but the yard was surrounded by a 6-foot-high board fence and the gate was down at the far end.

Granddad decided he couldn't chance going through the gate, so he shinnied over the fence and dashed into the house, absolutely terrified. He was so wild-eyed and out of breath that it took three of his daughters and Grandma to calm him down and convince him that what he'd seen was an earthly object.

As he said at the time, "I think sure it was the devil!"

He wasn't kidding either!

—*Frederic Hemenway*
*Ryderwood, Washington*

### Fire and Brimstone Could Wait

A TALE I've heard many times, repeated by family members as well as friends, concerns my grandfather, a Baptist minister during the early part of this century.

The story goes that one Sunday, while he was in the midst of a fiery sermon, a horseless carriage could be heard approaching outside the church.

Grandfather stopped preaching and shouted, "Let's go see the automobile!"

So the entire congregation, along with their preacher, got up and rushed out of the church to stand in awe as the marvelous invention drove through town, scaring every horse in sight.

When it finally disappeared down the road, everyone trooped back to their seats and Grandfather picked up with his sermon right where he'd left off.

—*Montie Odom, Abilene, Texas*

*WHERE'S THE HORSE?* It must have been one exciting day when this strange-looking homemade "buggy" emerged from Joseph Neff's workshop near Butler, Pennsylvania in 1900. Albert Slater, also of Butler, says his Grandpa Joseph was quite an inventor around the turn of the century. That's his wife, Kate, beside him, while four of their 10 kids are standing at a safe distance.

**ROAD TO REO?** Arthur Blake Jr. of Tucker, Georgia says this Reo was likely the first auto in the county. That's Arthur's grandmother and her nephew, Bob Bowden of Greensboro, Georgia. Although the Reo didn't have a hardtop, it certainly looks like Bob did!

## Her First Reo Ride Rocked the Countryside

IT WAS a beautiful summer day in 1905 at our quiet country home near Edgerton, Kansas when we heard the "chugchug" of a gasoline engine. As a child, I didn't know what a gasoline engine was—to me, it was just a terrifying noise.

The noise grew louder. Something was coming down our country lane, moving fast and creating lots of dust along the way. Our horses ran snorting to the back of the pasture while the chickens squawked and ran frantically in all directions. Then a big cloud of dust with a metal monster inside it turned into our driveway and came to a halt in front of the house.

So this was the horseless carriage we'd heard so much about!

After Papa and the driver made sure that no animals had been injured and no fences were torn down, we were offered a ride in this strange, new kind of buggy. The men sat in front while Mama, my little brother and I occupied the backseat.

Mama put her arms around us to keep us from falling out as there were no doors on that Reo (and no top either).

The horseless carriage rolled noisily along, bumping over the dirt roads and creating general havoc throughout the countryside.

Other peoples' animals were just as frightened as ours had been—and it sounded as if every dog in the county had heard the commotion and was broadcasting at the top of its lungs!

Still, I had a wonderful time and have never forgotten my first automobile ride in that riotous Reo.

—*Dorothy Halladay, Wichita, Kansas*

## Horseless Carriage... Or Satan's Steed?

MY MOTHER, Nettie, grew up in the little town of Factoryville, Pennsylvania. She was the youngest of three sisters and two brothers but also the bravest of the girls—the one who hitched up the horse and buggy and drove it herself.

At the time, her German family had heard of the automobile, but none of them had ever seen one. Then one day, Nettie and her mother were out driving in the buggy when they saw a peculiar-looking "thing" approaching on the road.

"Ach du lieber!" cried my grandmother. "It's one uf dem plack deffils—let me oudt!"

So, Mother stopped the horse while Grandma hid behind the buggy. Until that "black devil" passed by, Mother had her hands full with her rearing, frightened horse.

Eventually, Nettie was the only one of the girls who drove a car, went to business school and even owned her own home. She never looked back, but she was always ready for what the future would bring…even "plack deffils"!

—*Josephine Dunn Newark Valley, New York*

### What'll They Think of Next!

*Editor's Note: This item appeared in a magazine called Leslie's Weekly in 1905.*

For the coming winter, side doors on the front seats will be the proper thing in motorcar equipment. They have been made popular in Europe, and one of the prominent American cars has a new design of body which includes this feature. These doors will keep out cold, mud and water.

—*Contributed by Loring Bigelow Laguna Hills, California*

**BACON AND A LITTLE STEAM.** That's Charles Bacon posing proudly atop his 1903 Stanley Steamer. Charles' grandson, Lawrence, of Winchester, Massachusetts says his grandfather told him that not long after he'd sold the car to another man, the steam boiler overheated and blew up!

# Foresight Wasn't Grandfather's Forte

*By Dorothy Sidney Smith*
*Hanover, Indiana*

**W**illiam E. Sidney, my grandfather, was in at the very start of the automobile industry. And, although his career was short-lived, it certainly was spectacular!

In 1900, Grandfather Sidney gave up a good job in Michigan to bring his homesick wife back home to Indiana. Although he was only 20, Grandfather had strong mechanical know-how and was soon hired by the Haynes-Apperson Automobile Company in Kokomo.

Haynes was just starting the manufacture of autos, "a contraption then in crude form," wrote Granddad in his memoirs, "and selling for $10,000 to $15,000.

"The shop was small and production amounted to about two machines per month. There were no two machines exactly alike and absolutely no such thing as interchangeable parts."

Pioneer automaker Elwood Haynes had begun working on the idea of using gasoline to power a "horseless carriage" back in 1891. Three years later, he hired the Apperson brothers, Elmer and Edgar, to help build the automobile he envisioned.

## Joined Fledgling Business

After his car had its famous run on the Pumpkinville Pike east of Kokomo on July 4, 1894—at an amazing 6 to 7 miles per hour!—the three men formed a company and started production. It was this fledgling business that my grandfather joined in 1900.

With his background as a machinist, he soon caught the eye of Elwood Haynes, who placed him in charge of developmental engine work.

One afternoon, Grandfather was sitting on the floor making adjustments on an experimental two-cylinder engine when a workman approached with an open can of gasoline.

Noticing some oil on the engine, the workman thoughtlessly extended a piece of gasoline-saturated cotton to wipe it away. Flame from hot metal ignited the waste, then jumped from there to the can he was carrying in his other hand.

The workman panicked, and instead of throwing the can out the open window behind him, he threw it toward

**A FACE-SAVING MANEUVER.** William Sidney narrowly averted tragedy while working in his engine shop.

Grandfather, instantly setting his hair aflame!

What saved him, Granddad later related, was that he remembered the location of a quenching tank nearby. He dove in, leaving the surface of the water

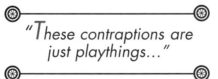

*"These contraptions are just playthings..."*

burning. Coming up for air, he submerged again as other workers grabbed expensive lap robes from an auto and smothered the flames.

The fire department was prompt, and damage to the shop was not extensive, but Granddad did suffer burns. Fortunately, he'd kept his face covered with his hands, so he wasn't scarred—although his skin was so tender that, for years afterward, he wore a Vandyke beard.

There was a humorous side to the incident that Granddad loved to relate to us. After the can of gasoline ignited, the workman, realizing that his clothes were on fire, pulled off his pants, threw off his jacket and ran up the street for a distance of two or three blocks.

When he finally stopped to catch his breath, he looked down to see that he'd discarded not only his pants, but his undershorts as well!

As Grandfather put it, "Witnesses stated that, if possible, his speed *returning* to the shop was in excess of his previous run!" For years afterward, locals enjoyed recalling that memorable sprint.

Actually, it wasn't the shop accident that discouraged Grandfather Sidney from pursuing a career in auto manufacturing so much as it was one of the company's customers.

## Talked into a New Job

A very wealthy man was having an auto built and he often dropped by the shop to see how the work was progressing. He watched young Sidney at work and one day, as his auto neared completion, he asked my grandfather if he'd be interested in a position as master mechanic at one of his plants.

He pointed out that there could be no possible long-term future in auto manufacturing. "It's just a fad," he said. "These contraptions are just playthings for wealthy men."

At the time, those arguments seemed convincing to Grandfather. So, he gave up his career in the "fad" industry and went to work for a new boss. Years later, he told us grandchildren about the men he'd worked with at Haynes-Apperson.

Many of them eventually moved to Michigan and either sold their inventions or joined large firms like General Motors and became quite wealthy.

Granddad cheerfully admitted he'd thought the automobile had little future. He chuckled at his lack of vision but never seemed distressed that he'd lost his big opportunity in the automotive business.

For him, it was just a part of his total education that led him to become a highly respected civil engineer. Grandfather lived to the ripe old age of 90 and loved talking about his adventures back in the days when automobiles were only "rich man's toys". 🕮

**FIRST AND FASTEST.** Author's Grandpa Benoit (at left with wife Emma and their children) not only built the first gaso-line-powered vehicle in Swift County, Minnesota, but he won the county's very first auto race with it.

# Grandpa's Homemade Auto Was a Fairgrounds Flash

*By Annette Benoit, Clifton, Colorado*

I only knew my Grandfather Benoit in his retirement years, so I was unaware of his previous celebrity status in our part of western Minnesota. To me, he was the kindly gray-haired grandpa with the crew-cut, mustache and small spectacles that covered twinkling brown eyes.

Many an evening, he could be found smoking his pipe and playing solitaire under the soft glow of the dining room table's lamp. Because of complications following an illness, Grandpa had lost his hearing when he was young and was unable to communicate verbally with his grandchildren. We had other ways, though.

We'd stand at the table where he played cards and smile up at him until he'd put down his worn cards. Then he'd get up and go over to the big buffet, where he kept a jar of striped pink and white peppermints.

Holding the jar at our level, he allowed us to take one or two pieces. Smiling our thanks, we'd follow him back to the table, where we stood amazed at how quickly the cards flew into their respective places.

Grandmother Emma, a petite lady, sat nearby in her rocking chair, fingering "sign" messages to Grandpa, telling him of the latest adventures of his grandchildren. He'd reply in French, the only language he spoke. His voice was rather squeaky and high-pitched because he couldn't hear himself, so Grandma was his spokesperson at home, just as she'd been for the business he'd begun in 1895 in Benson, Minnesota.

Grandpa specialized in repairing bicycles and selling bicycle supplies, but he possessed an exceptional mechanical genius that enabled him to repair many other things. After a while, his bicycles became known far and wide.

## Even Bigger Than a Bike

Then, according to *The Swift County Monitor*, "In February 1901, he purchased a turning lathe and began manufacturing an automobile in his spare time.

"All the parts were turned out of wood, then the patterns were sent to Minneapolis to be cast into iron. When the molds were received, Mr. Benoit polished and finished them and put them together."

The auto was completed in April of 1902 and was completely homemade, including the gasoline engine. It was Swift County's first automobile.

Equipped with a 6-horsepower Dyke engine, it was a powerful, lunging, plunging one-cylinder creation with no brakes that, with a bit of a tailwind, could tear down the pike at the heartrending speed of 20 miles per hour!

Its first run to the town of Clontarf, a distance of about 6 miles from Benson, was completed in only 28 minutes. That summer, the highlight of Benson's Fourth of July celebration was a race between Grandpa Benoit's homemade auto and one recently purchased by A.C. Rosetter of Appleton. Mr. Rosetter's vehicle was the only other horseless carriage in Swift County.

The big event was the first automobile race ever held in the county...and in the state, so it was said. It took place at the 2-mile track at the Benson fairgrounds in front of more than 5,000 spectators. I'm happy to report that, according to accounts of the day, Grandpa won by a "wide margin".

Inevitably, over subsequent years, Grandpa's bicycle shop was transformed into a modern garage for servicing automobiles, and my father and an uncle joined him in the business.

They're all gone now...that special car... my grandparents and their children. Now and then, I see traces of his mechanical abilities in us, his grandchildren, and realize that his gifts have passed on to a new generation. And then the memories run warm...of a little Frenchman who loved his grandchildren, peppermints and ingenious ideas. ❧

## From the Beginning, Dad Was an "Olds Man"

I USED TO work with an older man who told me about the time his dad rode a mule into town and saw his first car ever (a 1908 Oldsmobile). Mistakenly, he assumed that all horseless carriages were the same.

When he returned home, he gathered his children around and explained the error of their ways to them. "You kids have been reading those books all wrong," he said. "It's not called an *automobile* at all—it's an *Oldsmobile*!"

—Dale Eldrege, Pasadena, Texas

## Sunday Drivers Steamed Grandpa

WE LIVED on a farm in Warren County, Ohio, on a dirt lane about a half mile off a gravel road. There were nine of us then—my parents, grandparents and five of us kids.

Every Sunday, Grandpa would take us kids in a horse-drawn surrey (with a fringe on top) to a church about 3 miles from our farmhouse. I can remember him saying, as we got into the surrey, "I hope we do not pass one of those 'machines' today."

If he ever saw a cloud of dust in the distance, it meant that one of those dreaded "machines" was coming. Grandpa would climb down from his seat, grab the horse by the head and lead him and the surrey off the road into a rail fence corner.

He'd wait there, holding the horse firmly, until the automobile, racing by at 20 miles an hour, was safely past.

Invariably, his disapproving comment was, "There they go! Out to kill someone on a Sunday morning! They should be in church!"

—Roger Cornell, Hamilton, Ohio

## They Scare Horses, Don't They?

*Editor's Note: This letter appeared in the Lewiston, Maine Journal in the spring of 1907.*

Concerning the automobile question, I think 5 miles an hour too slow, but 8 miles an hour should be the limit for the safety of all concerned. And from every Saturday noon until Monday at 6 a.m., they should not be allowed to run. The penalty for violating this law should be $100 and 60 days in jail.

We find throughout the state of Maine perhaps one automobile to 500 teams. The people who own and use teams are the ones who have built and keep the roads in repair, and I believe they ought to have proper protection.

Maine is utterly unfitted for the rapid running auto. Its roads are narrow with many hills and sharp curves, which give anyone with a nervous horse no chance to turn out.

It is my opinion that if the voters of Maine had the privilege of voting on the speed of autos, they would either limit them to 5 miles an hour or exterminate them from the state.

There is not any commercial benefit derived from the automobile—they are only a source of pleasure to the few who are able to own them, I most sincerely hope that this present legislature will not adjourn without giving the people of Maine some better protection against the automobile.

—Contributed by Loring Bigelow
Laguna Hills, California

*SUNDAY SPIN.* Fashionable foursome was out enjoying the Connecticut countryside when this photo was taken around 1910, says Margaret Ellert of Lake Worth, Florida. Margaret isn't sure exactly who these folks are, because the picture was salvaged from an old photo studio in Queens, New York.

**MISSISSIPPI MARVEL.** This 1910 Mitchell was the first car in Booneville, Mississippi, says Booneville resident W.T. Rutledge. That's his grandfather behind the wheel (with Grandmother directly behind). Some folks pleaded for a ride—while others didn't dare come close for fear it would explode!

## To Great-Grandfather, Glide Was a Real Mystery

I'LL NEVER FORGET the time my dad took the train 60 miles east to Peoria, Illinois and came home in a new chauffeur-driven car. It was a Glide, made right there in Peoria and shown at the New York Auto Show of 1908.

Dad was so thrilled with that car! It was Brewster green with thick leather seats, and it had kerosene lamps and a brass whistle that sounded like a steam train's. Since it was the first one in the area, all the neighbors came around to see it.

I'll never forget my Irish great-grandfather's reaction to the new car. He was very impressed, but greatly puzzled, too.

"Behures alive, boy," he'd say to my father. "What makes them go?"

Dad would try his best to explain, but the conversation inevitably ended with my great-grandfather exclaiming, "Saw me leg off, boy—I don't understand it!"

Every day for 2 weeks, Dad had a driving lesson (that's what the chauffeur, Archie, was for). There was a "hollow" about 2 miles from us with steep hills, and Dad told Archie that if the Glide could go up that hill, he'd be convinced of the car's worth.

Archie looked it over and said he could do it easy. "In fact," he said, "I'll do it backward!" And, with a lot of neighbors watching, that's exactly what he did.

Dad was so impressed that he took Archie back to the train station the next morning. We were building a garage for the Glide, but in the meantime, Dad kept the car in the barn. The barn had sliding doors on opposite ends and a ramp leading up to them.

The first time Dad drove alone, he told Mama to open up the front doors, but just to be on the safe side, she opened the doors at the opposite end as well. A little later, here came Dad with a big smile on his face.

He waved happily as he came through the gate. Then he drove up the ramp, went into the barn...and right out the other side!

Eventually, Dad did learn how to stop that Glide where he wanted to.

—*Alene Kirch, Larned, Kansas*

## Town Doc Got Dunked

MY UNCLE MARK was a doctor and among the first residents of Springville, New York to own an automobile. But the transition to a horseless carriage took a bit of getting used to.

Not long after Uncle Mark purchased his car, this item appeared in the local newspaper:

*While driving his automobile on Woodard Avenue Monday afternoon, Dr. M.N. Brooks lost control of the machine and ran it into the village pond south of the fireman's building on Buffalo Street. Dr. Brooks manfully stuck to the throttle until he was thoroughly immersed. Assisted by many friends, the automobile was taken from its watery grave, but not until after the doctor had tried to walk to the shore on a plank —unsuccessfully.*

To make matters worse, the above item was accompanied by a long poem that poked good-natured fun at the town's distinguished man of medicine. Although the poem's a little too lengthy to quote here, the last stanza will give you an idea of its tone:

*And now, when the doctor
appears on the street,
His friends seem to think
it's time for a treat.
They fiendishly ask,
as the sidewalk they block:
"Oh, have you watered
your auto this morning, Doc?"*

—*Lela Fennell, Wilmington, Delaware*

**GARAGE? WHAT GARAGE?** This scene was common in the early days of the automobile. Matt Roswell of rural Kansas had only two choices when it came time to decide where to park his new vehicle: the barn or the lawn. Matt's granddaughter, Lenore Stephens of Ralls, Texas, shared the photo.

## Dad's Maxwell Made Grandma a Bricklayer

ONE of my earliest and most pleasant memories concerns the car my dad bought in 1909, just before he and my mother were married. It was a Maxwell with right-hand drive.

They'd planned to drive it to Colorado for their honeymoon, but they only got about 18 miles before flat tires and dusty roads cooled their ardor for a long automobile ride (they took the train to Denver instead).

While we all enjoyed that first car, it posed challenges when going more than a few miles. It performed fine on a flat surface, but climbing a hill was another matter. That's why Daddy always kept two bricks in the car.

If the car started to stall and roll backward, Grandma would get out and place the bricks behind the back wheels so Daddy could get a fresh start. The other passengers would walk up the hill while Daddy and Grandma (moving the car and the bricks a few feet at a time) finally got the vehicle to the top.

I was especially impressed by the Maxwell's horn, a big rubber bulb placed near my dad's right elbow but outside the chassis. That bulb seemed huge to me—honking it was more than my childish hand could manage. But Daddy had no trouble with it, and the noise it made sounded like the honk of a wild goose.

We seldom went out at night, but sometimes we'd be late getting home

**VISIT TO DEVIL'S DEN.** The Civil War had only been over for about 50 years when Howard Smith's mother and father (in the front seat) visited the Gettysburg battlefield in their 1905 Maxwell. Howard, of Williamsport, Maryland, says this photo was taken at a place called the Devil's Den.

from an afternoon jaunt and caught out as dusk fell. That's when Daddy would use a match to light the carbide lamps on the front of the Maxwell.

—*Naomi Richwine, Lincoln, Nebraska*

## They Probably Put on Clean Underwear, Too

MY DAD purchased his first car about 1910. He'd never driven a car before, and after the 20-mile drive from Buffalo, his hands were full of blisters from holding so tight to the steering wheel. The road was full of ruts, and it took plenty of force to keep the car going straight.

That night after he'd finally gotten home, his supper was interrupted by a loud bang. One of the car's tires had blown!

Such incidents did little to inspire confidence in the new vehicle. Not long

afterward, Dad invited all his nieces and nephews to go for a ride with him. They couldn't resist his offer, but, before getting into the car, they all made sure their feet were washed—just in case any of them were killed on the way!

—*Arlene Pfitzinger Marilla, New York*

## The Mechanic Rode a Pony

IN THE EARLY part of this century, my uncle worked for his father in a blacksmith shop. Around 1909, he started working on Mitchells, Chalmers, Hupmobiles and other early makes of automobiles, learning by trial and error.

When emergency calls came in, he would answer them riding on a Shetland pony. If he couldn't get the car fixed on the spot, he'd get a sturdy team of horses and tow it back to the shop.

—*Keith Eyler, El Cajon, California*

**A GREENVILLE GREAT.** This photo of a 1908 Great Smith was taken in Greenville, New Hampshire in 1910 by Charles Ruckstuhl's grandfather, the town dentist. Charles, of Groton, Massachusetts, notes that his grandmother is behind the wheel with her 3-year-old daughter beside her, and his great-grandfather is in the backseat. The Great Smith was built in Topeka, Kansas and had a 50-horsepower engine.

# Stanleys Were the Strong, Silent Type

*By Bert Guenther, Lakeland, Florida*

I will never forget the 1913 Stanley Steamer my father owned. The power, of course, was supplied by a two-cylinder steam engine, and underneath the boiler was a round metal housing that contained the burner.

It usually took us 20 to 30 minutes to build up enough steam pressure to get the car moving. There was no clutch or transmission—all you had to do was push the throttle lever and the car moved forward, smoothly and silently.

Since early models of the Stanley Steamer didn't have a condenser, they used lots of water. The water supply was in a 30-gallon tank—enough for 30 to 50 miles. If your trip was longer than that, you used the hose that was standard equipment on those vehicles.

It was let down into a stream, lake or watering tank while a suction pump (run by steam, of course) siphoned wa-

## "It was like floating on a cloud..."

ter into the tank 'til you were good for another 30 to 50 miles. About 300 to 350 pounds of steam pressure was sufficient to give good performance under average driving conditions. When pressure reached the maximum desired, a valve automatically shut off the flow of kerosene to the burner.

If pressure dropped beyond a certain point, the valve would reopen and the burner would come back on. One of the most frequent complaints heard from Stanley Steamer owners was that their pilot lights would blow out on windy days!

And, depending on how brisk the wind was, relighting the burner could be a daunting task. Still, I have many fond memories of that car.

The kerosene burner had a distinctive odor that let me know Dad was firing up the boiler. To this day, whenever I smell a kerosene burner, it takes me back to those happy days riding in the old Stanley.

Like most Stanleys, our car had good springs and genuine leather seats with cushions that were thick and soft. If the roads were reasonably good, the ride was so smooth and quiet it was like floating on a cloud.

Acceleration was fully as brisk as any production car today. In fact, as far as speed is concerned, legend has it that the Stanley Company made a standing offer: Anyone who could hold the throttle open for 5 minutes could have the car for free!

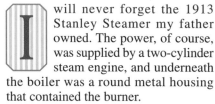

Back in the early 1900s, a daredevil reached speeds of 125 miles per hour driving a special Stanley with extremely high boiler pressure. Unfortunately, before the end of his run, the boiler exploded and he was killed.

### There She Blows!

To guard against explosion in regular Stanleys, a fuse plug in the boiler would blow and let the pressure off. As you might imagine, 400 pounds of pressure blowing through a quarter-inch hole can make an unbelievable noise. If you met a team of horses just about this time, you could be absolutely certain of causing a runaway!

The longest trip we made with our Stanley was in Wisconsin, from Ripon to Mondovi, when I was about 5. I don't remember much about this 200-mile journey, but my mother told me that after 19 hours on the road, I still wanted to ride some more—I was a nut about cars even then.

But the trip was an ordeal for my parents because the roads were so bad. For most of the way, we drove in sand almost up to the axles. In order to keep us moving, the engine had to be lugging under full power almost the whole time.

Once, when we stopped at a restaurant, the owner asked my dad what kind of car he was driving. Ours was the first vehicle they'd seen in 2 weeks.

The improvement of gasoline-powered cars and the high cost of keeping the Stanley running eventually convinced my dad to sell the old girl to someone who knew very little about steam power.

A year later, the new owner lit the burner and went into the house to have lunch while it built up steam pressure. But the burner went out and fuel spilled all over the floor. When the man attempted to relight the burner, the fuel on the floor ignited and burned down his barn with the car in it. It was a tragic end to a great automobile. ❧

**BLAZING BEAUTY.** One of the reasons Donald McCoy loved this 1911 Stanley Steamer was because it would "go like blazes". From the way her father's hair appears to be blown back, Joan McCoy Mears of Saluda, North Carolina suspects this Stanley was indeed a real "speed burner".

**STEAM WAS A DREAM IN THE MOUNTAINS.** When Clinton Atkinson wanted to impress people with his Stanley Steamer, he'd take them to the White Mountains of New Hampshire. As his son, Richard, explains below, a steamer could go just about anywhere.

### Dad Was a Steam Lover Supreme

MY FATHER, Clinton Atkinson, had the first Stanley Steamer in East Concord, New Hampshire (see the photo above). He used it to take people on excursions to the White Mountains.

Few vehicles then could tolerate the pockets of thin air common at high altitude. But the steam car had no problem. Dad would just stop beside a brook or a stream, fill the boiler with water, fire it up and be on his merry way.

In fact, a steam car was the first vehicle to climb to the top of Mt. Washington on the carriage road. Even back then, steam cars could get up over 100 miles an hour—if anyone was foolish enough to go that fast!

My father loved steam cars and owned 13 of them during his lifetime. He worked as an engineer on a locomotive and remained a steam lover to the end. I can still recall his comment years later when he watched two diesel engines pulling railroad cars.

"Look at that!" he'd sputter. "It takes two of these newfangled engines to pull what a steam engine could pull all by itself!"
—*Richard Atkinson*
*Concord, New Hampshire*

### Was Big Brother a Clod?

IN THE DAYS of my youth, the roads in South Carolina were dirt, mostly red clay—and those were the main roads!

One very rainy day, we were riding along on one of those deeply rutted red clay roads. My father had the driver's windshield removed so he could see out (no automatic windshield wipers back then).

I was sitting in the front seat and my youngest sister, Margaret, was in the middle of the rear seat. As a car approached from the opposite direction, a big clod of mud came through the window. Naturally, I ducked—but my sister didn't and was plastered all over with wet red clay.

It's easy for me to remember this incident. That's because I was reprimanded for ducking and not protecting my little sister!
—*Walter Noland*
*Charleston, South Carolina*

### Absence Did Not Make Aunt Mary's Heart Grow Fonder

MY UNCLE WILL, a plumber in upstate New York, owned a well-maintained 1916 Stanley Steamer open touring car. Even by today's standards, the Stanley Steamer had tremendous acceleration.

One afternoon, Uncle Will, Aunt Mary and a friend had driven to Keuka Lake (a distance of about 10 miles) and were about to head back home. They were just starting to climb the steep hill from the lake when Aunt Mary stood up in the open backseat to adjust her skirt.

It was at that precise moment when Uncle Will gunned the throttle to climb the hill. Aunt Mary went right over the back of the seat in a somersault and landed in the dirt road!

Meanwhile, Uncle Will was engaged in "man talk" with his friend. They were almost home before he looked back to say something to Aunt Mary and realized she wasn't there. Hurriedly, he drove back to the foot of the hill as fast as he could. That's where he found Aunt Mary, unhurt—but not a happy traveler, either.

She wasn't upset so much about being dumped out. What *really* bothered her was that it had taken her husband 20 minutes to even realize she was missing!
—*James Angliss*
*Bellevue, Washington*

**MOM BECOMES A MOTORIST.** Edna May Ogle of Vevay, Indiana won this brand-new car on a trip to Colorado sometime prior to 1915. Her son, Dudley Lasseter of Austin, Texas, shared this photo of her sitting proudly behind the wheel of her prize—wearing a hat that would no doubt have blown off at the first opportunity!

**BUSMAN'S HOLIDAY?** In 1908, this bus took riders from Lockport, New York to Lake Ontario, where they either caught the boat to Canada or the train to Buffalo. Jane Erickson of Honeoye Falls, New York notes that her father, Thomas Whitmore, was one of the regular drivers on this route. That's him in the white shirt seated behind the driver.

## A Lady Behind the Wheel? Never!

AROUND 1912, my mother was principal of a school in her hometown of Kincaid, Kansas, a thriving farm community.

She'd recently purchased a new car, and she was quite proud of it. Then, one spring evening, she was called in before the school board to discuss salary and hiring for the next year.

The three members of the board were friends of the family, so she was quite shocked to learn that, in order to be rehired, she had to get rid of the car. When she asked why, they told her that they wanted a "lady" for a headmistress, and it was their opinion that no lady would ever own or drive a car!

They were a bit surprised when she then informed them that, the evening before, she'd taken a ride to Mildred, a town 6 miles away. The school board there seemed to like cars (the members had all taken rides with her). And, since they needed a principal, they'd offered her a job for the following year at a $30-a-month increase.

Since she knew the Kincaid school board had never given that large a raise, she'd taken the job in Mildred—*and* would be keeping her car!

Years later, when she told us this story, she'd always laugh and say, "I wonder what they would have said if they had known that, for 2 years before that, I owned a motorcycle that I kept on my dad's farm!"  —*John Cundy, Garnett, Kansas*

## Grandpa's One-Car "Pileup"

MY IN-LAWS had never owned a car, but they finally got the urge and purchased one. One afternoon, my wife's father and grandfather were practicing driving around the barnyard. After figuring they'd learned all there was to learn about driving a car, they decided to put it into the barn for the night.

With Grandpa behind the wheel and his son reminding him just how far into the barn he needed to go, Grandpa forgot how to stop the car. He drove right through the double doors at the back of the barn—and out a 20-foot drop to a manure pile below!

Fortunately, he wasn't injured, but we eventually had to hitch up a team of horses to pull him off of that manure pile.

—*Roger Cornell*
*Hamilton, Ohio*

## He Got "Up to Speed" Quickly

MY GRANDPA, Edwin Brightbill, loved automobiles and the speed they provided. That's him in this photo (at right) with his family outside their home in Frystown, Pennsylvania. The occasion is the arrival of Grandpa's first automobile, a 1911 International touring car.

Years later, my boyfriend (who eventually became my husband) and I were driving on a highway when a car swerved around us and left us in the dust, even though we were going the speed limit.

My boyfriend exclaimed, "Look at the old pappy go!"

To his amusement, I glanced over and blurted out, "Hey, that's my grandpa." It was, too!

—*Marian Boltz, Jonestown, Pennsylvania*

**"TOURIST" TIME.** When this 1911 International touring car arrived at the Brightbill farmhouse in Frystown, Pennsylvania, the whole family turned out for the occasion. And, chances are, there was probably some "touring" done that day.

## Dad's Sales Made Him Cream of the Crop

PRIOR to World War I, my father was a salesman for the Creamery Package Manufacturing Company of Chicago, selling machinery to creameries and ice cream factories in northeastern Wisconsin.

In 1913, the company sponsored a contest among their 40-some salesmen scattered over many states to see which one could sell the most machinery that year. The winner would receive a seven-passenger Paige touring car.

My father put forth a great deal of effort and, at the end of the year, was notified that he'd won the contest and the automobile. You cannot imagine how delighted we were!

The picture (at right) shows the car near our home in Berlin, Wisconsin with our whole family—including "Old Don" asleep on the running board.

—*John Purves*
*Sturgeon Bay, Wisconsin*

*A PAIGE FROM THE PAST.* It's not every day that you get to have a new car delivered to your house absolutely free. That's what happened at the Purves residence in Berlin, Wisconsin when John Purves (far right) won a sales contest. John Jr. (far left) recalls this car spending winters up on blocks in the barn.

## Field of Screams

BACK IN the teens, when autos were fast replacing horses, the Stelzer Brothers hardware store in Mishicot, Wisconsin sold everything from hardware to farm equipment to automobiles.

My grandfather, who lived on a farm near there, bought a silo from the Stelzers. One day not long afterward, two employees were installing it from high platforms while an interested 10-year-old spectator (me) looked on.

Just about then, a

neighbor, Mike Sonnenwald, passed happily by on his way home. He was coming from the Stelzers' store, where he'd just bought his first automobile, and he gave us an enthusiastic wave as he drove past.

A few minutes later, Grandfather's phone rang. It was Mrs. Sonnenwald frantically calling for help. Mike was driving in circles in a field next to the house because he'd forgotten how to stop the vehicle!

The two silo men quickly climbed down from their platform, raced to their truck and drove the half mile up the road to the Sonnenwalds'.

Once there, one of them chased Mike and his new vehicle around and around the field 'til he was finally able to jump on the running board and turn off the car key.

—*Ray Schwerzler, Sheboygan Falls, Wisconsin*

*MAXWELL MEN.* Charles McCullough (behind the wheel) and Lloyd Cotterman owned a car dealership in Lima, Ohio, where they sold Maxwells and other types of cars. This picture, says Lloyd's daughter, Nellie Louise Lacey of Cridersville, Ohio, was probably taken around 1910.

## Mom's Mind Made a Turnaround

MY FATHER'S FASCINATION with motorcars began with the first ones that were available. Shortly after his marriage in 1915, he decided to buy one, an Overland.

A four-door sedan with curtains instead of windows, it caused quite a conflict in his marriage. In fact, Mom told him she wouldn't ride in it.

Within a couple of months, however, she was not only riding in it—she was driving it! This photo (at right) shows Dad with his car decorated for the Fourth of July.
—*Iris Swenson*
*Moorhead, Minnesota*

## Family Trip Home Was A Regal Ordeal

DURING A VISIT to see my father's family in Burlington, Indiana back in 1915, someone suggested we drive the 50 miles to Cicero to visit my mother's parents. In those days, an extended motor trip was not casually undertaken.

There were no paved roads, only gravel roads with soft spots that turned into mud holes with rain and a little traffic. Most turns were essentially right angles, suitable for horse-drawn vehicles, but a little difficult for motorcars.

After considerable discussion about the route and the roads, it was decided, with some misgiving on the ladies' part, to make the trip. We'd travel in Grandfather's Regal.

As some old-timers may recall, the linkages between the hand throttle and carburetor in that car had a number of ball-and-socket joints.

When word got out about our trip, there was considerable speculation (and I'm sure some wagering) among the townspeople about the probable success of our venture.

But, although we did run off the road once or twice at some of the square corners, we made it to Cicero without any disasters. Once there, we had a pleasant visit between the two sets of grandparents (who otherwise felt their children had married the wrong person).

The return trip was another matter, though. Around dark, one of the ball-and-socket joints linking the throttle to the carburetor broke. Consequently, Grandfather no longer had direct control over the speed of the engine.

After some discussion of the alternatives, my father suggested a relatively simple solution. The hood would be removed from the engine and he'd ride on the fender. Grandfather would yell instructions up to Father, who would then manipulate the carburetor to increase or reduce our speed.

This wasn't exactly a comfortable arrangement, but it was the only way we were going to make it home. I don't know what time of night we finally arrived back in Burlington, but we felt we'd set some kind of endurance record for a cross-country motor trip.

After that triumph, all bets were off regarding the success of any other motor trips the Redding family might undertake.
—*J.W. Redding*
*Dallas, Texas*

**AN OUTING IN THE OVERLAND.** This car was among a group of eight Overlands shipped to Kalispell, Montana in 1908. It was taken out only when the weather was good and the roads were dry, says Violet Yates of Pullman, Washington. That's Violet sitting on her mother's lap in the backseat in this 1911 photo. Her aunt and uncle are in the front.

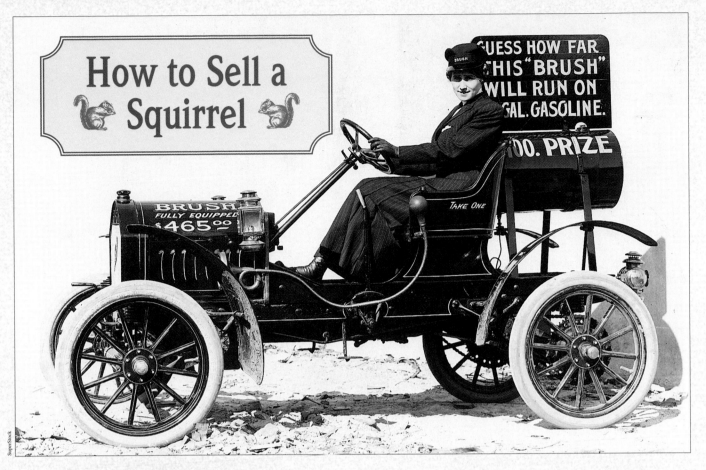

# How to Sell a 🐿 Squirrel 🐿

SuperStock

**BEAUTIES AND THE BRUSH.** Verl Beach of Corvallis, Oregon says that one of these two young ladies in their summer finery is an older sister and the other a family friend. The picture was taken in Genoa, Nebraska about 1910. Verl remembers riding in this chain-driven Brush on a toolbox set behind the driver's seat.

**BIG DEAL IN ST. BERNARD.** This Brush (at right) was the first car ever seen in St. Bernard, Nebraska, reports Florence Saylor of San Marcos, California. That's Florence's mother in the center, peering out between the friends who owned the car in 1909.

BACK BEFORE the days of assembly lines, there were literally thousands of car manufacturers. The Brush Runabout Company of Detroit was one of the most successful of them, despite the fact that its product had only a 6-horsepower engine.

From 1907 to 1911, Brush dealers sold cars with promotions like the one shown above. But, given the small size of their car's engine, perhaps their most successful sales gimmick was to ask potential buyers to think about the reason a squirrel can climb a tree better than an elephant.

It proved a persuasive argument, and the little two-seater Brush became one of the best-selling cars of its kind.

Certainly, the folks seen on this page seem pleased with what was probably their first "horseless carriage". 📯

# 'Grandpa' Was a Small-Town Speed Demon

*By Marjorie Wartchow*
*Idaho Falls, Idaho*

e wasn't a relative, but kids in Avoca, Nebraska called him "Grandpa" anyway. A short, heavy man, he looked much like Santa Claus with his snowy white hair and steel-rimmed glasses resting on a bulbous nose. He also had a booming voice and a sneeze that could be heard for miles!

Grandpa's garage was across from our side porch, and whenever he took out the "Auto" (as he called it), it was a production not to be missed.

First he removed the big duster "Grandma" had made out of feed bags. Next he filled the radiator with water from a sprinkling can and crawled up in the seat to adjust the throttle. Then he returned to the front of the car and, with a couple fast turns of the crank, had her running.

That was followed by a mad dash up to the seat again, where he managed to keep the engine running while he backed out at top speed in an explosion of flying dirt and grass.

After Grandma climbed aboard, Grandpa proceeded down the street and, as was his custom, immediately began honking the horn. Those honks weren't little "beep-beeps" either, but a loud "ACHUGA! ACHUGA!"

By the time he turned the blind corner up the street, all of Main Street had cleared for him, and he sailed over the bridge and railroad tracks at 35 miles per hour. Someone had once told Grandpa to "hold her speed steady at 35" and that's exactly what he did. His speed never varied.

They told the story around town of the day he went to get his car serviced. Luckily, the mechanic saw him coming and jumped into the grease pit while Grandpa came to a screeching halt directly above!

After Main Street, Grandpa took the hill out of town (at his usual 35 miles per hour). Just before dark, we'd hear him coming back home. Then he'd cover his "Auto" with the duster, and the big day's outing would be over.

Grandpa died one night in his sleep. Now I imagine him floating around among the clouds in his beloved "Auto" while he waits for St. Peter to open the heavenly gates wide so he can go sailing in, still "holding her steady at 35". 📯

*PLEASURE TRIP.* Members of this "touring group" were obviously well-prepared for an automotive outing when the photo was snapped around 1911. David Dorflinger of Berlin, New Jersey shared the photo and, although he isn't able to identify the vehicle's occupants, he notes that it has carbide headlights and Pennsylvania license plates.

*A SUNDAY AFTERNOON OUTING.* The streets in Beverly Hills, Illinois (then a part of Chicago) weren't even paved when this photo was taken about 1912. Eleanor Dougherty, now of Brooksville, Florida, is sitting on her mother's lap in front. Eleanor says she well remembers having to stop whenever it started to rain so the isinglass windows could be put up.

**THE CREAM RISES AT THE BACK.** The vehicle on the right had a unique feature, says Alan Page of Denver, Colorado. Yes, that's a cream separator mounted in back! Alan's grandfather (the man in the center wearing the bowler hat) sold milking machines and cream separators for the De Laval Separator Company and used this apparatus for demonstrations. Photo was taken in front of a hardware store in Corry, Pennsylvania in 1914.

## Uncle's Winton Packed in The Picnic Bunch

IN THE SPRING of 1916, when I was in first grade at the District 57 school in Linn, Kansas, my uncle was driving a Winton he'd purchased in 1909.

As the end of the school year approached, our teacher informed us that our annual last-day-of-school picnic would probably have to be held on the school grounds.

Normally the picnic was held along a creek a couple miles outside of town, but the man who had previously furnished his hayrack for this auspicious event was not going to be able to accommodate us this year.

That's when I took it upon myself to tell the teacher my uncle would be glad to take us. Fortunately for me, when I told him about my unsolicited offer, he was flattered to be asked.

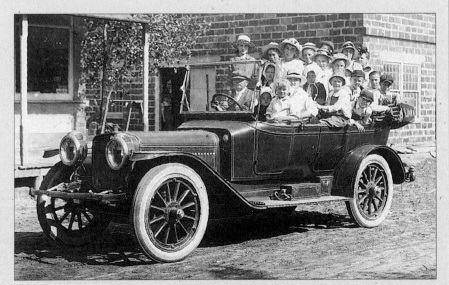

As you can tell from the photo (above), when the big day finally came, about 25 excited youngsters (everyone in grades one through four!) were packed into that Winton. For many of them, it was their first automobile ride ever. —*Naomi Richwine Lincoln, Nebraska*

# Grandma's 'Hummer' Was A Silent Runner

*By Wallace Webster, Kirkland, Washington*

The year was 1916 when Grandmother took delivery of her Detroit Electric car in Minneapolis, Minnesota. There were at least a dozen other electric vehicles on the market in those days.

They were quite a favorite among older people because they were so easy to drive and made almost no noise, just a nearly inaudible hum when the car was in motion.

Grandmother's new vehicle seated five adults, three in the backseat. In front were two swivel-chair seats. They could be faced forward or swung around toward the passengers in the rear. The car could be driven from either the left front seat or the left rear seat.

There was no steering wheel, but rather a horizontal steering bar about 2-1/2 feet in length. It extended just above knee level from a vertical bar attached to the steering mechanism beneath the body of the car.

The steering bar was controlled by the driver's right hand, while a shorter bar for the left hand was the "power bar" (corresponding to an accelerator on a gasoline car). The power bar had five settings.

When that bar was pulled all the way back, the car remained stopped. The first position would bring the car up to 5 miles per hour, the second to 10 miles per hour and so on, all the way up to the maximum possible speed of 25 miles per hour.

Opening the front or the back deck, you might expect to see a motor, but there was none, only two battery compartments with eight or 10 batteries in each. The strong and powerful electric motor that drove the rear wheels was located in the middle of the car, underneath the floorboards.

The Detroit Electric had a range of 60 to 75 miles before the batteries needed recharging, which my grandmother did every night. At the back of her garage was an electric motor-generator set that took the alternating house current and changed it to direct current to recharge the batteries.

Grandmother drove that car until her death in 1926. It was fun to drive since it was so different from driving a gasoline-powered car.

The last time I drove the Electric was in the spring of 1927 when, at my father's direction, I took it to a dealer to be sold. I certainly wish that quiet beauty was still in our family's possession. ✒

**BACKSEAT DRIVER.** Believe it or not, this is an electric taxicab, one of the first in New York City during the early part of this century. Not only were they very quiet, but the cab-driver must have had a great vantage point to look at the road ahead!

Taxi Stand

## Great-Grandma Was a Sunday Show-Off

THIS photograph of my great-grandmother, Emma Jane Phillips, and her daughter-in-law, Louise Phillips, was taken in Browntown, Wisconsin, probably about 1915.

Louise and her husband, Alva, lived in Freeport, Illinois, and every other Sunday, they would get an invitation to drive up to Wisconsin to enjoy one of Emma Jane's home-cooked meals.

Emma Jane claimed that she invited them because she missed them so much, but my Grandmother Rosa (Emma Jane's daughter) told me that she may have had ulterior motives.

It seems she greatly enjoyed being seen riding around town in her son's fancy new automobile. My uncle told me that people in Browntown were in awe of Alva when he'd drive around the streets backward.
　　　　　　　*—Esther Betker*
　　　　　　　*Beloit, Wisconsin*

*"LIKE A THUNDERBOLT FROM A CLEAR SKY."* That was the slogan for the Vulcan automobile, which is what Esther Betker believes her great-grandmother, Emma Jane Phillips, is riding in above. Emma Jane loved being seen in this car so much that she would sometimes ask her daughter-in-law, Louise (at the wheel), to drive very slowly. That way, all her friends would be sure to see what a success her son had become.

*SEATTLE OR BUST!* Flags were flying and spirits soaring when this carefree group of Washington State youngsters made their first trip to Seattle in the summer of 1914. The picture was sent by Walter Taubeneck of Marysville, Washington. Walter's father, Al, missed out on the trip—and was probably sorry he did when he saw this picture!

## Steamer "Stumped" Grandpa

MY GRANDFATHER made his living operating a sawmill and a threshing machine, both powered by steam. So, when he decided to get a car, it was probably natural for him to buy a Stanley Steamer.

He had it delivered to my dad's home, but when it arrived, there were no instructions how to operate it. Assuming he'd be able to figure it out, Grandfather fired up his new vehicle and started driving it around the yard.

Unfortunately, the only way he could think to stop the thing was to head straight for a big oak tree! When the collision occurred, a number of parts flew off the Stanley, but, thankfully, it did come to a stop.

When I grew older, all that was left of that Stanley were the brass headlights and some other small pieces. Sometimes I'd ask my grandfather about them, but, for some reason, he never wanted to talk about it.

—Malinda Bowles
Baltimore, Maryland

*MACHINE FOR A MANSION.* Joseph Lindgren (above) was the chauffeur for William Beach Olmstead, headmaster of the Pomfret School in Pomfret, Connecticut. This picture was taken about 1914 in front of Olmstead's summer mansion in Gloucester, Massachusetts. Joseph's grandson, Craig Lindgren of North Reading, Massachusetts, provided the photo.

*FIRST CHEVY EVER!* When the first Chevrolet rolled out the door of the plant in Detroit, Michigan, the production "gang" was all there, says Mary Ann Roberts of Beloit, Kansas. Mary Ann's father (the man without a hat just to the right of the driver) helped build the bearings for this vehicle. Auto historians still dispute the exact date the first Chevy was built, but it can safely be said that this picture was taken in either 1912 or 1913.

# Fence-Bustin' Mom Had Farmer Fuming

*By Muriel Winters, Phoenix, Arizona*

On the summer day my mother was driving our Elcar touring car with my two grandmothers and me as passengers, she learned an important lesson: Never take your eyes off the road.

We were driving merrily along and Mother was talking to her mother, who was sitting beside her, when suddenly she looked up and saw grass in front of her—the road had turned, but she hadn't.

She went to step on the brakes, but those older cars didn't have rubber pedals, so her foot slipped off and hit the gas pedal instead. The car flew across a ditch, through a fence and into a farmer's yard.

My Grandma Wilson and I were in the backseat, and every bump we made in our flight caused my head to bounce up and hit Grandma in the eye. Luckily, her black eye was the only injury sustained by any of us.

When we came to a stop and my mother settled down, she asked the farmer if he had a driveway she could use to get out of his yard.

"Nope, you'll have to go out the same way you came in," he insisted.

Well, we soon found out that going back down and then up through that ditch was a lot more difficult than flying over it.

We finally made it back up on the road. As we drove past the farmer's yard, we discovered he *did* have a driveway. We figured he must've been so mad at Mother for wrecking his fence that he wouldn't let her use it! ✒

**SHAKE AND BRAKE.** The woman standing in the back of this 1913 Studebaker is shaking out sand and crumbs after a picnic at Sylvan Beach in upstate New York in 1916. Robert Hollenbeck of Columbia, Maryland tells us the car belonged to his father (with his back to the camera). Robert's mother is in the passenger seat and his grandma is smiling at the camera. The lake was 20 miles from their home in Munnsville, so the family probably wouldn't have been able to enjoy pleasurable outings like this without their trusty Studebaker.

## Roadside Repairs... While You Wait!

IN 1921, my grandparents and two of their children were on their way back home to Colorado after an extended stay near our home in Bremerton, Washington.

They'd purchased a new Dort for the trip, and my Uncle Ray, who was about 14 then, drove most of the way. Grandpa had nearly had an accident when the Dort blew a tire and never drove again.

Near Red Desert, Wyoming (just a stop in the road), a wheel came off their car. This posed a real problem since the nearest town, Rawlings, was a good 50 miles away.

As there were no other cars passing by, Grandpa set off down the road carrying the busted wheel. Eventually, whether by walking all the way or by hitching a ride, he made it to Rawlings. But the garage there didn't have the proper replacement parts, and sending to Denver for them meant a 4-day wait.

This was a ticklish situation since Grandpa knew his family back on the roadside had very little food.

So, he bought a bag of groceries and stood out in the street until someone finally came along in a car that was headed toward Red Desert. He asked the driver to take the groceries to his family while he remained in Rawlings, waiting for the wheel parts to arrive.

When the wheel was ready, Grandpa went to the train station to get a ride back. He discovered there was no stop at or near Red Desert, but, after much haggling, the engineer agreed to slow down the train enough so that Grandpa could throw the wheel off, then jump off the train himself.

That was exactly how it happened and, after another long walk back to the Dort, repairs were made and the family resumed their journey home. Thankfully, there were no further mishaps.
—*Bernice Buckner Bremerton, Washington*

# Grandma's First Ride Sparked a Family Feud

*By Bernice Chappel*
*Brighton, Michigan*

Like most of our rural Michigan neighbors, we used a buggy for transportation. Then, one never-to-be-forgotten day in the summer of 1915, things changed forever.

After a 20-mile drive behind "Old Molly", we arrived at Grandpa and Grandma Avery's farm near Perry to discover a shiny new Dodge car in the driveway.

"Grandpa's got an auto!" I yelled. "He said he might get one!"

"It's beautiful," murmured Pa, "but I'll bet Mother Avery won't ride in it."

Jumping from the buggy, I ran toward the back door. Grandpa, his chest-length white beard blowing in the breeze, laughed as he came down the steps, then grabbed me and tossed me above his head.

Breathless, I grabbed his arm and squealed, "Will you take me for a ride?"

"After dinner," he promised, before putting me down and going to greet my parents.

While Grandpa showed the Dodge to Ma and Pa, I ran into the kitchen. Grandma was draining a kettle of potatoes into the black iron sink. Setting them down, she gave me a big hug.

"Grandpa's going to take us for a ride after dinner!" I exclaimed. "I can't wait!"

"Humph!" she snorted as she shuffled over to the cupboard.

For me, the dinner hour seemed endless—all I could think of was riding in that new Dodge. At last, dinner was over and the dishes were done.

### Grandma Got Stubborn

Grandpa was eager to show off his new purchase. "Come on, Lucy," he called. "Get your hat and let's go."

"I ain't going," said Grandma, dropping wearily into her rocking chair.

"Doggone it, Lucy! Why are you so obstinate?" he lamented.

Ma tried a different approach. "Come on with us," she urged. We don't want to leave you here alone."

"Grandma, please?" I urged.

Reluctantly, she followed us outside. Ma, Grandma and I climbed into the back and Pa sat up front. Meanwhile,

**GRANDMA WASN'T HAPPY.** James and Lucy Avery (top) didn't see eye to eye about the shiny new Dodge that showed up in their driveway one day, says granddaughter Bernice Chappel. But Bernice's parents, George and Gertrude Klein (above), were so impressed they went out and bought a new Reo the next spring. Portrait of Bernice below was taken in 1914, a year before the memorable ride described on these pages.

Grandpa went to the front of the car, grasped the crank and spun it in a clockwise direction.

After several failed attempts, the motor sputtered feebly and stopped as Grandpa jumped back. "She kicks like a mule!" he exclaimed. "Guess the spark's set too high."

After moving a lever slightly, he cranked again to no avail. At this point, Grandma reached for the door handle. "Jim, I'm not going," she announced. "I can't stand to sit here and watch you break your arm."

"Stay where you are, Lucy—and stop sniveling!" Grandpa shouted.

Sliding back into her seat, Grandma covered her eyes with her hands. "I don't know why I have to be tortured with this dad-ratted contraption!" she complained. "Just because you ain't got no sense…"

"Lucy, hush up!" Grandpa commanded. "I've got enough on my mind without listening to your complaints." He returned to the crank with renewed energy born of anger and frustration. Suddenly, the motor started with a roar that rocked the car.

### The "Fun" Began

Adjusting the gas lever before he climbed in, Grandpa turned to us with a triumphant smile. "Sometimes she's a little ornery. Ready?"

"Yes!" I squealed in anticipation.

After much grating and grinding of gears, we were on our way at last. As we sped along at almost 15 miles per hour, the wind whipped through our hair and clothing. Grandpa turned to look at Grandma. "Now ain't this nice, Lucy?"

"Watch the road!" she screamed. "Or we'll end up in the ditch!"

"You'll get used to it," Mother said soothingly. "Then the two of you can go for drives in the country." Grandma shook her head but didn't speak. Her jaw was set, and she grasped the top of the door so tightly that her knuckles were white.

Grandpa chuckled. "It's funny how people are so scared of new things. The other day, Jack Finch was walking to town, so I stopped and asked him if he wanted a ride. Know what he said? 'No thanks, I'm in a hurry!'"

We all laughed…except for Grandma. Then Grandpa turned onto a narrow

**TOURING WITH THE FAMILY.** This Stevens-Duryea must have been an impressive presence in the tiny town of Warrens, Wisconsin back in 1914. Mary Barber, now of Orland Park, Illinois, is the little girl sitting on her mother's lap in the front seat. Mary's father, Fred, is ably handling the driving chores (note that the steering wheel is on the right side of the car) with the rest of the family in the backseat.

trail-like road. "No, Jim!" Grandma gasped. "We'll all be killed on these hills—I just wish I'd had the sense to stay home!"

"Dad blast it," Grandpa bristled, "so do I!"

I'd never seen Grandpa so upset. Then I remembered hearing Ma say that his hair and beard once were red and that he had a temper to match.

As we bumped down a small hill and up a larger one, the Dodge lost momentum, then jerked to a stop halfway up the hill. Grandpa nervously fussed with the gear shift and we heard him mutter, "Neutral—can't start the motor when she's in gear."

Then the car began rolling backward down the hill. Grandma screamed and reached for the door handle. "Stop!" she wailed.

**Ride Went Downhill Fast**

As we picked up momentum, Grandpa became even more confused. It was a long way to the bottom of the hill and there was a big drop on the right. "Don't turn the wheel," cautioned Pa.

Meanwhile, Grandma had the door open and was heaving herself toward it. "Ma! Don't jump!" my mother shouted as she pulled Grandma back into her seat. Pa suggested that Grandpa put

on the brakes, but by then, it was too late—the left rear wheel dropped off the road and we banged to a sudden stop against a large elm tree.

Grandma's hands were over her eyes. "I knew it," she sobbed. "An old duffer like him ain't got no business fooling with these things."

Grandpa's patience had run out. "Hark your clack, Lucy!" he yelled as he opened the door and climbed out.

Grandma pulled herself out on the other side of the car (I'd never seen her

---

*"It was a long way to the bottom of the hill—with a big drop on the right..."*

---

move so fast!) and the two of them met behind the car.

"Look at that fender!" Grandma scolded. "That's what you get, you mutton-headed old duffer! You and your fine new contraption! You just had to spend money on this, this *thing*. And now you've gone and smashed it!"

As the argument behind us grew louder, Pa grinned at Ma. "Looks like my cows won't get milked on time tonight," he said.

After the argument subsided, Pa offered to go to the nearest farmhouse. Soon, he returned with a farmer and his team. A log chain jingled behind the whippletree.

"Having a little trouble here, Jim?" the farmer asked.

**Gave Welcome Advice**

Grandpa nodded and explained he'd only had the car for a few days. "Put her in low at the bottom of the hills, then she won't stall halfway up," the farmer explained.

After the Dodge had been pulled back on the road and the farmer thanked, we tackled that hill again—this time in low gear. Halfway up, Grandma looked to the right over the steep, unguarded bank. She gasped and closed her eyes. I looked over at Ma and she smiled at me.

The motor roared and snorted, but soon we broke over the top of the hill. "I'll just leave her in gear," Grandpa said to Pa. "Don't want to stall her again and throw Lucy into another fit."

He glanced back at Grandma, who ignored the remark. The rest of the way home, she remained silent with closed eyes, as though she couldn't stand to view the danger we were in...or maybe she was praying for her life. ✎

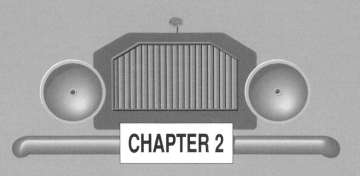

CHAPTER 2

Brown Brothers (hand-tinted by Melissa Burghart)

**A FLIVVER MEANT FREEDOM.** These folks enjoying a picnic on a pleasant Sunday afternoon would probably have been much closer to home if it weren't for that Tin Lizzie behind them. The Model T greatly expanded people's horizons, allowing them to venture much farther from their immediate surroundings than ever before. Delays might be likely, but Lizzie would get them there somehow.

# We Loved Lizzie

f ever an invention perfectly captured the personality of its creator, it was the quirky, cantankerous Model T Ford. The "Tin Lizzie" made its debut in 1908 and was destined to become the American Volkswagen.

At 8 feet long and 7 feet high, it initially sold for $850, but by 1915, a runabout cost a mere $440. Henry Ford modestly called it "the most perfect automobile in the world".

Well, perhaps. But consider: It was started with a hand crank that had a nasty habit of breaking wrists and thumbs (an injury so common in those days that it was known as the "Ford fracture"). And, instead of a gearshift, the car was operated with three foot pedals—one for forward, another for reverse and the third to stop.

## Speed Was an Unknown

There was no gas gauge, and the fuel tank was under the front seat. Nor was there a speedometer or any other gauge on the dashboard. Speed was controlled by one of two levers on the steering wheel.

You didn't "own" a Model T—you had a complicated and unpredictable relationship with it. One Ford owner expressed his feelings thusly:

*The Ford is my auto; I shall not want another.*
*It maketh me to lie down beneath it; it soureth my soul.*
*It leadeth me into the paths of ridicule for its namesake.*
*Yea, though I ride through the valleys, I am towed up the hill.*
*For I fear much evil, thy rods and thy engines discomfort me;*
*I anoint my tires with patches; my radiator runneth over'.*
*I repair blowouts in the presence of mine enemies.*

*Surely, if this thing followeth me all the days of my life,*
*I shall dwell in the bughouse forever.*

Model T owners celebrated their love-hate relationship with their vehicle in thousands of jokes, too. A popular one making the rounds about 1916 told of the farmer who was tearing the roof off an old barn. After pondering what to do with all that tin, he decided to crate it up and send it to the Ford Motor Company, thinking they might have a use for it.

## A Tough Repair

About a week later, he received a letter in the mail: "Your car," they wrote, "is one of the worst wrecks we've ever seen—we should have it fixed for you in a week to 10 days."

Despite its rattletrap construction, Lizzie was a howling success. And Henry Ford continued to improve it, adding doors, a horn, a trustier radiator, a quieter muffler, a self-starter and an improved engine.

He even bent to popular demand and, in 1926, made the car available in colors besides black. During the 19-year life of the Model T, more than 15 million were sold, the last one rolling off the assembly line late in 1927.

Of course, that was far from the end of the line for Lizzie—Model T's continued in service for many more years. Farmers often cut down and altered them to make serviceable pickup trucks. We had one on our farm, and long after Dad stopped using it, the feisty little vehicle sat in our garage—he just couldn't bear parting with an old friend.

Today, of course, a Model T in mint condition is a treasure that will fetch many times its original cost. It's a precious piece of American history: The vehicle that gave ordinary folks their introduction—bumps and all—to the world of auto travel.

—*Clancy Strock*

# First Lizzies Weren't Tin

*By Lulu Leitgen, Garnavillo, Iowa*

In 1910, my father bought the first Ford in Clayton County, Iowa. He took a train to Monona to pick it up and had to learn to drive it before he brought it home. We waited all day for him to return.

I was only 5, but I still remember how thrilled we were when we saw that shiny black car come down the driveway. The body was all wood except for the fenders. There were no front doors.

### Tossed the Top

The radiator, lights and other trimmings were made of brass. The top could be folded down, but we ended up removing it because there was too much wind resistance (that car needed all its power just to keep moving).

Several of my uncles later bought the tin Fords known as Tin Lizzies. For any trips of great distance, we traveled in a caravan of four or five cars.

In 1911, we all went to Dubuque and saw our first airplane. On the return trip, we found ourselves driving in the dark. All the drivers stopped to light their carbide lights, but soon we were hopelessly lost, trying many different roads before getting back home.

Another time, we visited the Galloway Implement Company in Waterloo (the first time I ever ate in a restaurant). It was almost daylight the following morning when we returned because an 80-mile trip was terrifically long

**ONLY THE FENDERS WERE TIN.** This Ford was one of the first ever in eastern Iowa.

then—especially at 25 miles an hour.

On trips to visit relatives in Manly and Mason City, we took turns driving in the lead position, because the dust was unbearable for those in the rear.

In later years, whenever we stopped at car museums, I always looked for the wooden-bodied Ford but never found one. I began to think I'd been mistaken about its construction.

### Confirmation at Last

Then we visited the Ford Museum in Dearborn, Michigan. I approached a museum worker and told her my story. "Most certainly there was a car like that," she said. "Just go up the stairway and see what you can find."

At the top of the stairs sat one special circular room with only two cars on exhibit. One was the first car Henry Ford ever built. The other, in all its black-and-brass glory, was a wooden-bodied car just like the one that came down our farm driveway in 1910. ✆

**READY TO RIDE.** The Hamptons of Whittier, Iowa were probably about to head out for a Sunday drive in their 1912 Ford when this photo was taken. Lillian Miller of Birmingham, Iowa points out her grandparents in the backseat and Uncle Floyd behind the wheel of the family's first car.

# Horses Had the Last Laugh

*By Dorothy Clanton, Harrison, Idaho*

y parents homesteaded 180 acres on the Oregon-Idaho border in 1906. Eight years later, lured by a promotional gimmick offering each buyer a $50 rebate if sales topped $300,000 the following year, my father bought a Ford touring car.

As it turned out, sales that year totaled $308,218, so Dad got his rebate. But the first time our horses, "Ol' Doll" and "Sport", got a look at "Betsy" clattering into the farmyard, they made a dash for the far end of the corral.

Farmers who bought Fords usually expected them to do everything their horses and wagons did. Some were even modified to pull plows, saw wood and pump water.

## A Bright Idea Gone Bad

With such a versatile vehicle, Dad decided one day that he didn't need to go to the trouble of hitching up the horses to haul a wagonload of hay to the barn. He'd just tie the wagon onto Betsy.

As Dad drove through the pasture toward the haystack, Ol' Doll and Sport (who by then had become more or less accustomed to Betsy) stood in the corral, idly chewing on some hay and eyeing the procedure with interest. Dad got the hay loaded and started back to the barn. Basking in the euphoria of his success thus far, he made a too-fast turn around the pond. Betsy made it—the hay didn't!

The entire load slid off into the water, and for years, my

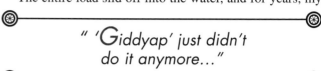

" 'Giddyap' just didn't do it anymore..."

brother insisted that he'd heard a pair of horse laughs coming from the direction of the corral.

There were three major areas in which my father and his new motorized form of transportation had trouble. One was getting it started ("Giddyap" just didn't do it anymore).

Adjusting the spark and throttle took practice and patience (not Dad's long suits). If they weren't set properly, the car "kicked" when cranked. For a while, as farmers in the area got used to this contraption, our doctor did a booming business mending broken arms.

The business of steering was a problem, too. Ol' Doll and Sport were so accustomed to Dad they almost knew what he wanted before he did. He could meander along, visiting with passengers and pointing out items of interest, with full confidence that the rig would stay on the road.

## Betsy Was No Mind Reader

With Betsy, when Dad turned to talk to someone in the backseat or to better see how his neighbor's crop was progressing, he usually leaned on the steering wheel—and it turned, too. Many a time we had to pull Betsy out of the ditch.

The third area was more Dad's passenger's problem than his. In summer, Betsy was very much an open-air rig and Dad chewed tobacco, which, of course, involved spitting.

You can probably imagine what that combination meant for my brothers in the backseat. For years afterward, they'd remind Dad of the torture he'd put them through.

Like everyone else who owned a Model T, we found Betsy to be cantankerous, uncooperative, unpredictable and sometimes just plain ornery. On the other hand, she was built so simply that most people could eventually get the hang of driving and repairing her.

The old saying that you could fix a Model T with baling wire and a good hairpin wasn't far off. The motorized era wasn't to be denied—even Dad finally made his peace with Betsy.

However, for the duration of their time on the farm, Ol' Doll and Sport maintained their aloof attitudes.

*LOST BUT LOVING IT.* For couples like this one, the Model T provided undreamed-of mobility. It turned Sunday drives into leisurely explorations and, if folks got lost (as most usually did), there was almost always someone around who could point the way home.

*HOW MANY EARS TO THE GALLON?* Resourceful farmers found innumerable ways to take advantage of the Model T's incredible versatility. This Lizzie is helping to shell corn on an Indiana farm.

J.C. Allen and Son

## Too Much "Yumpin' "

IT WAS always a good idea to pull up on a Model T crank. It wasn't pleasant to push down and have it backfire—that was called "kicking". After the car started, the driver ran around, reached inside the car and pushed the spark all the way down.

I'll never forget the time I visited the garage where Dad bought his 1914 Model T Ford. They'd just received a new shipment of cars, and the workers were rolling one onto the floor to start it. Then the garage owner, an immigrant who spoke somewhat broken English, came in and suggested one of the workers sit behind the wheel and retard the spark halfway.

The owner himself did the cranking. Unfortunately, he pushed down instead of pulling up. As he continued to push, the man at the wheel pushed the spark all the way down.

The crank kicked mightily, throwing the owner to the floor. Getting to his feet, he walked angrily back to the car and pushed the crank down again. But the spark hadn't been retarded, so the car "kicked" once again.

After three such attempts, the owner ran into his office and called the Ford Motor Company to complain.

"When I wing at him," he reported, "he yump at me."
—*Harold Queck, Fontanelle, Iowa*

## Love Those Traveling Tune-Ups

THE MODEL T had a coil and points for each cylinder, and the box holding those four coils was just below the dashboard, within easy reach of the driver. So, whenever the car started

to "miss" on a cylinder, the driver could reach over and hold down each coil's vibrating points. When he pressed on one that didn't make another cylinder miss, he knew that he'd found the one that was missing.

He'd adjust the points this way and that until the car was running on all four cylinders again. This could be done without even slowing down.
—*Laurence Holdeman*
*Bonners Ferry, Idaho*

## T Featured "Adjustable" Night Vision

OUR 1917 Model T touring car had headlights powered by a weak electrical current from the magneto. The lights only functioned when the motor was running, of course, and even then, they were rather dim (the amount of light generated was directly proportionate to the speed of the engine).

When my father needed to have a clearer view of possible dangers in the road ahead, he'd ease up on the left of the three floor pedals to put the transmission in neutral, and then race the engine. That would increase how far into the darkness he could see.

Another thing I remember about the Model T is that its planetary transmission didn't always stay in neutral when the engine was being cranked. Sometimes the car would move forward a bit, nudging the person cranking it, much like a faithful old horse being harnessed.
—*Richard Pedrick*
*Winnebago, Illinois*

**LET'S GO FOR A RIDE.** While Grandma tends to her knitting on the porch, this New Jersey family sets out for a Sunday drive in 1913. While chances were good that any trip would involve a flat tire or other mechanical problem, a Model T could almost always be repaired.

## T Was a True Engineering Marvel

I WONDER if Henry Ford really knew what he had when he made the Model T. He had an automatic transmission from day one—and with its heavy oil, the car was never really out of gear.

The magneto was the best thing on the T. The car would not leave you stranded along the road. Even without a battery, it would still crank and bring you home—with headlights, too. There was no fuel pump to cause trouble. Gravity supplied the engine with gas (unless you tried a steep incline with a low gas level). Even then, you could still make the hill in reverse.

There was no fan belt because there was no fan or water pump. Hot water would rise to the top of the radiator and circulate just fine—better than a coffeepot perking. The generator was geared into the timing gear, so it never quit turning, and the car even had "cruise control": All you had to do was pull the rabbit ears down on the steering column, and your feet were free!

A neighbor of ours who had only one leg always preferred a Model T, because the driver could use any of the floor pedals to slow down. If you missed the brake, the reverse or low gear pedals would work just as well.

The only drawback was that if you cranked the car inside, it could pin you to the garage wall; crank it outside, and you sometimes had to run it down to catch it!

Despite that drawback, Henry Ford's Model T was probably the best thing that ever happened to rural America.
—*J. Ludwig Linnekohl*
*Dearing, Georgia*

## The Start Was an Art

OUR MODEL T was quite often difficult to start—especially in cold weather. At age 7, I was often privileged to assist my dad in this complex operation.

First, the right wheel was jacked up off the floor and two bricks were wedged on either side of the left wheel. I would stand by in the driver's seat while Dad prepared to hand-crank the engine. Two levers on the steering column needed to be adjusted. The left one retarded or advanced the spark, while the right one affected the gas (there was no accelerator on the floorboard).

My job was to be in charge of the battery/magneto switch on the dash. Dad would adjust the choke on the simple carburetor by pulling or pushing a length of baling wire threaded through the radiator core. He'd signal me to set the switch to "battery" as he started cranking.

With herculean effort, the crank would slowly move and the right rear wheel would begin to spin as the cranking effort speeded up (the rotating wheel acted as a flywheel to help turn over the engine).

Soon, after several backfires, first one cylinder and then the other three would bang and Dad would shout to me to switch the lever to "magneto".

When the motor was rocking pretty good, Dad would adjust the spark and gas levers and disengage the clutch while he lowered the jack and stopped the spinning wheel. When Lizzie was rocking more smoothly, she was then ready for our trip to town.

I doubt this procedure would be approved by OSHA today, since occasionally someone not too mechanically inclined would accidentally tip the car off the jack and be driven through the side of the barn—Model T and all!

Still, as a 7-year-old, I was mighty proud of my role in the father-and-son operation.
—*James Marks*
*Bradenton, Florida*

**THE FARMER'S FRIEND.** As you can see by all the Model T's lined up behind each other in the street below, a farmer and his Ford were not easily separated. Shown here bringing their grain to market in 1919 are a group of Iowa farmers.

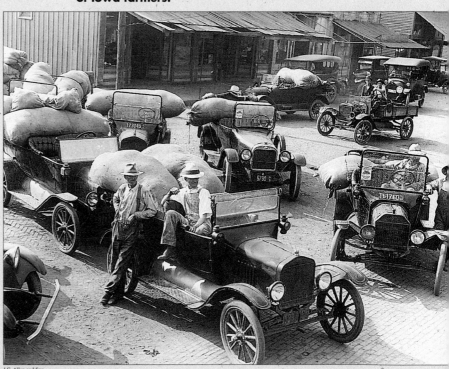

# Grandma Had Plenty of Get Up and Go

*By Robert Baldwin (as told to Dorothy Baldwin, Fredonia, New York)*

**A "CARRIAGE" WITH CLASS.** Purchasing the family's first car ever was always a proud and happy moment. This new 1915 Ford cost these Trenton, Missouri folks a hefty $815—a lot of money in those days. But from the looks on their faces, it must have been worth every penny. Lois Lenard of Moonachie, New Jersey notes those are her parents proudly riding in the backseat while an aunt and uncle are in the front.

Nearly everyone who was a youngster in the early decades of this century can recall a car that made a lasting impression. For me, it was Grandma Wright's new 1915 Model T touring car with the gleaming brass radiator.

Since Grandma was a 69-year-old widow when she bought the car and asked Dad to teach her how to drive, she was the talk of our Fredonia, New York neighborhood for quite some time.

One day Grandma suggested we take the car to Michigan to see relatives. "Michigan!" cried my father, aghast. "Why, that's 300 miles away!"

"Oh, Myrl, what's the difference whether you drive 300 miles to Michigan, or 300 miles around here?" Grandma said. "You and Georgina and I can

**GRANDMA'S GROUP.** After the family arrived in Michigan from New York, this group photo was taken. Robert Baldwin is fourth from left and his dad is second from left. Grandma—who else!—took the picture.

ride in front, and there'll be plenty of room for the three boys in the backseat."

My twin brother, Herbie, and I, then 4, ran outside dancing and clapping our hands. "Michigan! Michigan! Three hundred miles away!" we shouted. Even our 8-year-old brother, Aubrey, was excited. He knew we were as good as on our way (Grandma had great powers of persuasion).

It was drizzling the morning we left. Hours later, when the rain had stopped and the car was dry, we boys took turns riding on the back fenders, hanging onto the braces that held up the roof.

That sounds more dangerous than it was—our top speed was under 25 miles an hour. And, whenever the road got rough, Dad made us get back in the car.

Somewhere outside Cleveland, Dad stopped at a farmhouse to ask permission to set up camp. We boys helped unload the car, then raced around while the adults built a bonfire and set up the big tent.

After a meal cooked over the fire, we settled down for the night—adults in the tent, kids in the car. Next morning, after a breakfast of campfire-cooked bacon, eggs and bread, we resumed our trip.

It was raining when we reached Cleveland. Then, at 7 a.m., smack in the busiest part of the city, Grandma's Ford stalled on some trolley tracks. Jumping out into the rain, Dad told Mother to get behind the wheel and work the throttle while he cranked.

*Screech! Clang! Clang!*

Peering out the back windows, we saw a huge trolley car stopped just inches away. The motorman was giving us the gong, and Dad (who's temper had a short fuse anyway) shouted back at him as he turned the crank furiously.

## Time (and Trolley) Stood Still

It seemed like eons but was probably only minutes before the Ford sputtered to life and we were on our way again (with as much dignity as we could muster, considering the situation).

That evening, we arrived at Uncle Horace's place in Wyandotte. After a pleasant 3-day visit with aunts, uncles and cousins we kids had never seen before, we packed up the car and headed for home.

Stopping after dark one night, Dad somehow managed to set up the tent by the light of the moon. At daybreak, animal sounds woke me. I pulled myself up to the window and looked toward the tent. "Herbie! Aubrey! Look!"

The tent was surrounded by grunting pigs! "That's the first time I ever woke up to find the bacon staring *me* in the face!" Grandma laughed.

When we finally reached home, we were all asleep except Dad. He drove the car into the yard and turned off the engine. "We're home," he announced.

Grandma just giggled and said sleepily, "I told you that we could do it, Myrl." ✍

## Starting Ritual Provided Cheap Entertainment

IN HIS MEMOIRS, my late father-in-law, Ralston Hewitt, recalled a moment in the transition from horse and buggy to horseless carriage. Here's his story:

"Crank it again," they called. "It" was a Model T Ford in 1918 and "they" were a pair of seemingly permanent "sitters" on the front porch of a small country hotel in Greene County, Virginia.

I was a traveling salesman, and the Ford was about to take me on my rounds. Undaunted by their catcalls, I went to work on my machine.

I put the crank in place and tried one quick turn. Nothing happened. I cranked again. Still no action. I went to the steering wheel, leaned over and pulled on the accelerator, then went back to the front to crank again. Still nothing.

Returning to the driver's seat, I pulled out the choke, ran to the crank and gave it another hard turn. No reaction at all. Next I tried releasing the accelerator to half position and had another go at the crank.

There was a slight puff. Sensing success, I pushed the choke a little, then returned to the crank. Rewarded with another little puff, I cranked again…and again.

Two more puffs, and then the big one. She made contact and started…on-ly to stop almost immediately. After advancing the accelerator and pulling out the choke a little bit more, I cranked again.

One, two, three, four sharp pulls, and the trusty motor started in earnest. I quickly ran to the dashboard, pushed in the choke, released the accelerator and jumped in to feed the car a little gas to keep the motor running until it was warmed up. At last, victory was mine!

All this amused the sitters, whose choruses of "Crank it again" seemed, by now, to be slightly tinged with envy as I drove off, waving to whistles and applause.

*—Bill Riola*
*Lakewood, New Jersey*

## Granddad's Invention Was a Non-Starter

FASCINATED with the automobile, my grandfather decided to try inventing products to appeal to the growing number of car owners. His first attempt was a "car polish", a combination of several caustic cleaning products.

Fortunately, he tried the first batch

**NOW, THAT'S HORSEPOWER!** Henry Ford probably didn't have this particular use in mind when he designed the Model T. But these cowboys near Little Medicine Bow, Wyoming are enjoying a rare opportunity to get out of the saddle in 1919. Virginia Page of Mt. Prospect, Illinois says her father, Ray Burnett, took the picture.

on the fender of his own car—and thus became the owner of the first two-tone Model T in New Jersey!

Since it was clear that Grandpa's future didn't lie in the car cleaning field, he turned his efforts to creating a self-starter to eliminate the need for hand-cranking. The end result made the most outlandish Rube Goldberg invention look woefully simplistic.

The apparatus consisted of a 55-gallon oil drum with a handle protruding from one end. The drum was suspended in a steel frame and somehow connected to a huge coil spring and many feet of strong chain.

To operate this contraption, Grandpa wound the spring tight and attached the chain's loose end to the crank handle. At this point, a safety bolt was pulled, releasing the spring.

The barrel would spin as the chain wound into it, all the while turning the crank. For weeks, Grandpa tried to perfect his machine with little success.

The combination of the spinning barrel, flying chain and expanding spring created a cacophony of bangs and crashes. Grandpa had to abandon the project after neighbors complained about the horrendous noises coming from his garage.

That was probably just as well. Even if he could've made the "starter" work, it took more effort to *wind* the drum and spring than it did to simply crank the engine.

*—Russell Webster*
*Titusville, New Jersey*

**FLUNG BY THE FLIVVER.** Marie Perrine of Jackson, Michigan (with her mother above and at right) recalls a memorable ride in this Model T coupe when the door swung open going around a corner. Her dad reached over and caught her by the skirt just as she was about to go sailing out into the ditch!

**SNUG AS A BUG.** That's how James Oswald (the youngest child in the two photos above right) says he felt inside the family Model T (above) when it was raining hard and the isinglass windows were secured. The Oswalds dressed appropriately and took Sunday drives for summer picnics and fall outings... every time of the year except winter, James reports. (See his story below.)

## A Tent on Wheels?

MY DAD bought his first Model T in 1915 as a used car and was apparently quite enthralled with it, inasmuch as he purchased a new one the next year.

Those first T's didn't have storage batteries. What little electricity that was required to ignite the gasoline was derived from a magneto (which was itself energized by the cranking process).

The magneto also furnished electricity for the headlights and horn, such as they were. Without a battery, the speed of the car's engine determined the brightness of the headlights and the loudness of the horn.

An idling motor meant headlights the equivalent of candle flames and a virtually inaudible horn. The single taillight and the parking lights, of necessity, burned kerosene. What a pain to light and keep lit on a windy night!

I loved the scent of the shiny black leather upholstery. I also enjoyed riding in the rain, when Dad would snap on the leather side curtains with the small isinglass windows.

Hearing the pleasant "pitter-patter" of the rain was a sound I equated with the coziness of being in a tent. However, my poor old dad probably wasn't sharing my joy as he struggled to keep the windshield clean with the manually operated windshield wiper.
—*James Oswald, Chicago, Illinois*

## T Offended Uncle Earl Once Too Often

AS A YOUNGSTER, I spent a few weeks each summer at Aunt Emma and Uncle Earl's farm outside Indianapolis. They had no children of their own and loved to spoil me. I even got to "drive" their 1924 Model T Ford by sitting on Uncle Earl's lap and steering, something I could never do at home.

Uncle Earl was strong as a bull but gentle—unless he felt that he'd been wronged. Then he could cuss and rage for 10 minutes straight. Aunt Emma always said his cussing could turn the air blue, and one memorable day, I found out what she meant.

Uncle Earl was in the garage, getting the T ready for a trip to the feed store. He turned the ignition switch to "magneto", set the spark and throttle levers, pulled the choke button and set the emergency brake. But he failed to set the brake completely, and the high gear was still partially engaged.

So, when he gave the crank a spin, the engine fired and the Ford began bucking forward. Uncle Earl let out a roar, braced his legs against the garage wall and leaned into the front of the bucking car with all his might to keep from being pinned between it and the wall. His struggle was something to see.

Then he got mad. The Ford had wronged him, and his cussing was true to form. The air in the garage really *was* turning blue—I didn't realize 'til later it was actually smoke from the exhaust!

Slowly but surely, Uncle Earl backed up the Ford by sheer strength until the engine finally coughed and died. He spent the next 10 minutes sitting on the lawn, cussing the T, the entire Ford Motor Company and old Henry in particular for designing and building such a treacherous piece of machinery.

Never mind that he'd failed to set the brake properly; it was all the fault of that blankety-blank Ford. Once he'd recovered, Uncle Earl restarted the Ford and left.

When he returned 2 hours later, he was driving a brand-new Plymouth sedan. From that day until his death in 1948, he never owned anything but a Plymouth.
—*H.R. Keeler Indianapolis, Indiana*

# Gift of Wheels Delighted This 15-Year-Old

*By Cleora Homedew, Savanna, Illinois*

One lovely day in the spring of 1916, my father came home from work, handed me a booklet and told me to read it carefully. It was about the Ford cars everyone was buying.

I had seen several cars, but, at the age of 15, I'd never dreamed I would be able to sit in one or drive one myself.

When I finished reading, Father took me out to the shed and showed me *our Ford*. To my amazement, he said it was mine if I could remove a tire and put it back on.

### Unladylike Behavior

It was a determined struggle on my part, but with Father's direction, I did it. (I might mention that it was the only tire I ever changed—in those days, a lady sat on the running board and waited for a gentleman to come along.)

Father found someone to teach me to drive. On a Saturday, we drove from our home in Marion, Iowa to Cedar Rapids. It was quite an adventure, with horses, streetcars and other automobiles to avoid. I learned how to steer very quickly, and at least I didn't hit anything.

Two days later, Mother needed a spool of thread, and I volunteered to drive to town for it. But when I got out to the woodshed, I couldn't remember a single thing about driving that car.

Mother went back to the house and got the booklet. I read the instructions to

MOTORING COMPANIONS. Cleora Homedew (on left) posed with a group of friends in Savanna, Illinois about 1919.

her, then cranked the car while she sat in the driver's seat. Finally, it started …and flew backward out of the shed and into a neighbor's garden!

### "Whoa" Wouldn't Work

Rescuing Mother, I took over, put the car in gear and then drove it downtown. But now I couldn't remember how to stop the thing!

I drove around the block several times until I saw a man near the curb. "How do you stop a Ford?" I yelled to him.

"Turn off the key," he yelled back.

After that, I purchased Mother's thread, drove the car home safely and

parked it in the woodshed. From that day on, I had a car at my disposal, which was amazing for a 15-year-old in 1916.

### A Schoolmarm Special

When I graduated from high school in 1919, teachers were scarce because of the war. I applied for a job at a country school, and the Ford took me back and forth each day.

The roads weren't paved, and sometimes I had to leave the car at a farm and wade through the mud to the schoolhouse.

In very cold weather, I'd jack up the rear wheels once I got the car to the schoolhouse. To get it started again later, I'd pour a kettle of hot water on the manifold to make cranking easier.

The Ford and I were special friends for many years. I will soon be 97, but I'll never forget that day in 1916 when Father first turned me loose with my Ford.

---

### No Toolbox Needed

I BEGAN LEARNING my way around our 1917 Model T at age 14—after some of my older brothers had practically worn it out. The Fords came without batteries, just four coils and a magneto to run a combustion engine.

If something got on the magneto post, it could short out the whole motor. Then you had to take up the floorboards, remove a couple of screws and clean the magneto so you could go again.

Other times, the car's rear axle would twist off, and you had to know how to set the car on blocks so you could replace it. We also had to put in new bands for low gear, brakes and reverse.

Just about the only tools we needed for repairing a Model T were pliers, a monkey wrench, a screwdriver and some baling wire. If you had those, you were ready for a small trip of about 50 miles. —*Dale Emry Moses Lake, Washington*

THE ROAD TO FOREVER. The endless plains of Wyoming could be pretty intimidating to a little Model T, whether it was a touring car like Ruth Corbett's parents drove (see story next page) or, as in this case, a pickup loaded with mail headed for Little Medicine Bow, Wyoming. This 1923 photo from her father's collection was shared by Virginia Page of Mt. Prospect, Illinois.

"Howard, can that little auto take us clear to Oregon over those high mountains and so many miles?" Mother asked. He'd just parked his new Model T Ford touring car in front of our house in Ypsilanti, Michigan.

"She can do it—you bet!" he answered, wiping a speck of imaginary dust from the fender. "This one's the best Henry's made yet, Rhoda."

Driving from Ypsilanti to Salem, Oregon in 1920 was a huge undertaking. Most people thought we were foolhardy to even attempt it.

I was only 8, so my advice wasn't solicited. On the day we left, friends and family stood at the curb, waving good-bye and giving us warnings mixed with tears.

### Headed West at Last

"We're on our way!" Mother said with both sadness and relief. I blew a blast on the tin horn I'd snuck in while packing, but it was a little too close to Dad's ear.

"How'd that thing get in here?" he shouted. Thereafter, I tooted lightly to mark special accomplishments.

Illinois, Iowa and Nebraska were not unlike rural Michigan—except the miles seemed longer and the corn taller. But the empty vastness of Wyoming was awesome. When I saw

*By Ruth Corbett, Sun City, California*

those endless plains, I wanted to blow a fanfare on my horn but could only manage, "Gee whiz!"

Lizzie labored through a pass that opened to an immense stretch with mountains faintly visible in the distance. That's when the "road" became maybe a dozen sets of rutted tracks. It was as if every driver made his own way. A weathered board, unreadable, was the only "sign".

There wasn't a car in sight. "*What* are we going to do?" Mother wailed.

"Pick a track and hope it's the right one," replied Dad. But his tone told me he was worried, too. Lizzie settled into a set of ruts and we bounced along for mile after mile.

### Picked the Right Rut

We were lucky—those ruts eventually led to a pass through the mountains. Further on, we came to a river without a bridge. "How do we get across, Dad?" I asked.

Scratching his head, he walked along the bank, testing the riverbed with a stick. "See those tracks on the other side? We'll drive through like others have done."

Mother pursed her lips and hung on until her knuckles turned white. The water reached above Lizzie's running board at one point. When we finally came out, we all laughed hysterically from relief.

One day we were stopped along the side of the road while Mother answered a "call of nature" behind a sagebrush. Suddenly, a car came around the curve and stopped. Dad lifted the hood, pretended to tinker underneath and assured the man it was just a little spark plug trouble, nothing serious.

The Samaritan eventually left and Mother came out of hiding, but from then on, we all knew what it meant when one of us had "spark plug trouble"!

### Meeting of the Michiganders

In eastern Oregon, a garage mechanic stared at our license plates, then commented that he didn't see many from Michigan. "Are you from there?" Dad asked.

"Grew up in Saline," he replied. For a second, the men studied each other's faces intently.

Simultaneously, they shouted, "Howy Corbett!" "Carl Schmidt!" Then they threw out their arms and hugged while giggling like children.

When we finally reached the Columbia River Highway with its windowed tunnels blasted through the rock, the Vista House at Crown Point and Multnomah Falls, Mother was plainly awestruck.

"Howard, this is worth the endless plains, driving through rivers and all of my scares."

Dad looked proud of himself and our faithful Ford. "I always knew we'd make it to Oregon—or bust in the attempt."

I blew a terrific blast on my tin horn and this time, Dad didn't complain or even seem to notice. ❧

**DAUNTING DRIVE.** Traveling alone through rugged hills like these was scary business back in 1920. That's Ruth Corbett above, posing in front of some Wyoming boulders.

*A GIANT STEP FOR MANKIND.* **Thousands of motorists must have cheered heartily when they heard that the new Fords were going to come equipped with "demountable" wheels like those shown above. Finally, no more wrestling with tubes and tires every time you got a flat!**

*THE UNCOVERED WAGON.* **That's what Jefferson Farmer and his friends called this makeshift Model T with the top long gone that they bought for $7. Photo above was taken in 1928 while the group was on their way to a YMCA summer camp about 30 miles west of Boston. The picture below was taken while Jefferson worked as a bellhop at a hotel in Provincetown, Massachusetts that same year (which explains the sailor suit). He now lives in Mountain Home, Arkansas.**

### Tire-Changing Technique Was Truly Unique

IT AMUSED ME to see my husband, Buck, change a tire on the first car we ever owned, a used Model T. Everyone else put the jack under the car and pumped it until the car was high enough to remove the wheel.

But, after adjusting the jack to the height he wanted, Buck then handed it to me and said, "When I lift up the car, shove this jack under right here."

Then he'd get behind the car, look up and down the road to make sure no one was coming and quickly lift it onto the jack.
—*Ruth Hammer*
*Longview, Washington*

jack up the wheel with the flat, remove the tire from the rim, patch the tube, put a boot in the casing, put the tire back on the wheel and pump up the tire (about 200 licks with a hand pump), then let the jack down and start my journey again.

All this took 20 to 30 minutes, and changing a tire was a frequent occurrence (I don't think I ever drove 75 miles without changing at least one tire).

When planning a trip, you always had to allow time for a tire change—if not, you'd probably be late.
—*Charles McCarty (as told to Luanna McCarty, Wichita, Kansas)*

### T's Got "Tired Out" Fast

MODEL T TIRES weren't very sturdy since the material that held them in shape was cotton cloth. It broke easily whenever the tire hit a rock the size of a hen's egg. Within half a mile, the break in the fiber would chafe a hole in the inner tube, and the car would have a flat.

Changing a tire was a thorough process, as there was no mounted spare to put on. I'd unload the car, chock one wheel,

*HONEYMOON EXPRESS HALTED.* **Virginia Page of Mt. Prospect, Illinois says her mother and dad were on their honeymoon and headed for Lake Okoboji, Iowa in the summer of 1925 when this flat put a temporary stop to their journey.**

# A T at 10!

*By Jack Inman*
*Carrollton, Illinois*

I talked my uncle into giving me my first car, a 1918 Model T roadster, when I was 10 years old!

A gutsy, freckle-faced kid, I'd loved cars as far back as I could remember. We lived in a small steamboat town along the Illinois River, where the streets were dirt and there were no particular laws on vehicles (or at least little interest in enforcing them).

Once a year, a state police trooper might show up and drive around town —but I would just hide until he left. That first car ran on a magneto—no bat-

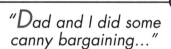

### "Dad and I did some canny bargaining..."

tery, starter or generator—so when it wouldn't run, pushing was the order of the day. Fortunately, there were always lots of friends on hand to push.

Soon afterward, I acquired a Model T touring car with no top for $5. This one had a starter, generator and battery. I'd come up in the world.

My buddy Vinton helped me paint it with pictures of Mutt and Jeff, Maggie and Jiggs, Popeye and even a bathing beauty. Vinton could fix anything mechanical, and with him as a best friend, my car was always running.

Finding parts for the car was never a problem either. We could fix almost everything with baling wire and pliers,

and if the radiator leaked, there was plenty of water in the river.

Our biggest problem was gas, which cost 18¢ a gallon. None of my friends had much money, but they'd chip in their nickels and pennies until we had enough to buy a gallon.

If that didn't work, my feet might be found sticking out from under Dad's car. Later, at suppertime, Dad would complain about how much gas his car seemed to be using.

My third Model T came a couple of years later. It was a bright yellow roadster with Shell Oil emblems and a wooden box on the back. The owner wanted $2 for it, but Dad and I did some canny bargaining and got him down to $1.75.

The last Model T of my childhood came into my life when I was 13. It was a coupe with an electric windshield wiper, heater, water pump, starter and generator plus an ammeter on the dash. Actually, Dad bought that one for me— possibly motivated by the fact I seemed to be getting interested in *his* car!

**RAPID TRANSIT.** Model T's were made into pickups, race cars, buses and even open-air jitneys like this one, which transported folks in a hurry from San Pedro Street to Slauson Avenue in Los Angeles.

---

## All the Way from Michigan ...In a Ford!

OUR Model T Ford, delivered in 1918, was the first on our block in Detroit. It was like a dream come true when Father cranked it and the engine sputtered to life.

Father loved working on his car and dreamed of driving it to Chicago to visit my grandmother. His brothers, both skilled mechanics, predicted we couldn't make such a trip in a Ford. They were sure the car would break down before we got far from home.

But my father was determined, joining the American Automobile Association and even ordering a "blue book" to map out the route. Then, after he'd prayed for God's help and protection, we set out from Detroit at 1 o'clock in the morning.

Despite some difficulties, we'd reached Michigan City, Indiana by 6 that evening. It'd taken us 17 hours to travel 200 miles.

We left the next morning at 7 and arrived at Grandmother's in Chicago at 11:15 a.m. There had been no trouble, no flat tires—just deep satisfaction and gratitude for a successful trip.

While the car was parked outside Grandmother's house, two teenage boys spotted it. Apparently, the Model T lacked respect in the Chicago area, because one of the boys remarked in amazement, "Gee! All the way from Michigan in a Ford!"

Our ride home was uneventful, but afterward, few could resist remarking on Father's courage for undertaking such an ambitious trip.

*—Esther Stahlke*
*Fort Wayne, Indiana*

## A Song for Lizzie Lovers

BACK WHEN I was a little girl, my dad had a Model T. Whenever he said, "Come on, let's go for a ride", he didn't have to ask twice. We were always ready to go.

As we rode along, we'd sing this little ditty to the tune of *Let Me Call You Sweetheart*:

"Let me call you Lizzie, I'm in debt for you. Let me hear you rattle, like all good Fords do. Keep your headlights burning, and your taillights, too. Let me call you Lizzie, I'm in debt for you."

—*Maxine Miller*
*Ashland, Ohio*

## Rocked in the Cradle of Ford

I'M TOLD that when I was born, my dad drove Mom and me home from the hospital in the Model T Ford coupe you see in this photo (below).

It must have been love at first sight for me because, for the next 6 months or so, whenever my parents couldn't get me to sleep at night, they'd drive the T up next to the front porch, where they slept.

Keeping the car running, they'd put me inside, and in no time at all, I'd be out like a light. By the way, that's my dad holding me when I was about 8 months old.

—*Ivan Pfalser*
*Caney, Kansas*

***BRIDE? WHAT BRIDE?*** These shots of a Model T were taken at the wedding of Helen Atkeson's parents in 1923. The funny thing about them, says Helen, of Mansfield, Ohio, is that they were taken by a cousin who got so carried away with her father's new car that he neglected to take any pictures of the bride and groom.

***FOUR-WHEELED SLEEP INDUCER.*** As you'll learn in the story above, Ivan Pfalser (shown with Dad) formed a special bond with the family flivver.

## Nothing Like a "Road Apple" Repair

RADIATOR LEAKS were always a challenge. Often I'd have to stop the car near a creek to get more water (wise travelers were never without something that could be used to dip water).

There were all sorts of products one could buy for radiator leaks back then, and many of them worked with some effectiveness. But the best product of all—a chunk of horse manure—could be found along the highway almost anywhere.

I often stopped to pick up one or two of these in an emergency, and they worked fine. They slowed down the circulation just enough so that the radiator boiled more evenly.

Of course, every now and then, the radiator had to be flushed out so that a new "stop-a-leak" compound could be put in. —*Charles McCarty (as told to Luanna McCarty, Wichita, Kansas)*

## If Only He'd Said "Flivver"

SOMETIMES the Model T's nickname could get folks into trouble.

A neighbor who lived several miles away had a wife named Lizzie, and one Sunday, my dad "rang him up" to ask them to come eat with us.

Without thinking, Dad asked, "Why don't you crank up old Lizzie and come over for dinner?"

Well, the neighbor was greatly offended and, while they did come over for dinner, it seemed to me after that, their friendship was never quite the same. —*Cecelia Frei Dober Pullman, Washington*

We were living near Charlotte, Michigan in 1918, when my father saw a real estate ad in the paper. Captivated by its descriptive language, he boarded a train for Farmville, Virginia, returning home a few days later the proud owner of a new farm.

Plans were made to sell our old farm and hold an auction. A railroad boxcar would take our work team, wagon and furniture on to Virginia.

Collin, an 18-year-old neighbor, volunteered to travel with the boxcar to care for the horses until we arrived. But the boxcar arrived a week early, and, because there was a war on, we were told we had to take it then or not at all.

Things were further complicated by the terrible influenza epidemic then sweeping the country. We'd planned on taking a train to our new home, but that influenza had to be avoided.

Crowded trains were too dangerous, so Papa bought a Model T Ford. Wisely, he didn't tell Mama why it was for sale—it'd rolled out a second-story barn window and landed on its top!

Papa made good use of the wide running boards. On the driver's side, he

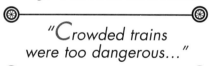

*"Crowded trains were too dangerous..."*

built a tall cupboard with a hinged door that swung down to form a table.

On the other running board, Papa bolted another homemade box, then topped it with a mattress for our dog. Other necessities were carried on top or tucked in the tent my parents slept in. I was 9 and slept in the car with my brothers.

Papa planned to stay out of the mountains as much as possible on our trip, but a chance meeting in southern Ohio changed that. A native of the area suggested Papa take a shortcut over the West Virginia mountains.

**It Was Do or Die**

A crowd overheard the conversation, and not one other person believed our Lizzie could make it. But Papa felt differently.

We started down the mountain on a steep narrow trail just wide enough for one vehicle. "Don't worry," the man had told us. "Nobody uses it except mule teams."

But I was worried—I couldn't see

# 'Worthless' Lizzie Proved Invaluable

*By Ruth Wright, Potterville, Michigan*

anywhere a mule team and a Model T could meet and pass. There was nothing to keep us from falling off the trail but Papa's steady nerves. We traveled safely down that impossible road to the valley below, then stopped for a well-earned stretch. We kids ran and yelled,

rejoicing that Lizzie hadn't let us down. Her brakes hadn't even overheated. We petted her and told her, "Good girl."

Further on, big cars passed us on the twisting, climbing trails, their occupants laughing and saying we'd never make it. But in due time, we passed them all as they sat along the narrow shoulder, their overheated radiators hissing steam. Meanwhile, Lizzie's radiator stayed cool.

As the mountains smoothed out into farmland, my parents worried how Collin was doing.

But when we at last came to the long driveway to our pretty new house, Collin burst from the kitchen door, whooping and laughing.

He'd had no trouble at all. The train engineers had even invited him to the engine's cab and shared lunches with him. At Farmville, when word got around that a young Yankee had arrived in a boxcar, Collin had more volunteers to help unload than he needed.

In the days that followed, many people came to look at our Lizzie. It was almost impossible to believe we'd come so far in that "worthless" little tin car. But we had. ❧

AT HOME WITH LIZZIE. When Gerald Gay of Oskaloosa, Iowa bought this Model T truck for $500 in 1918, it had solid rubber tires and a kerosene lantern hanging in front of the windshield. Gerald converted it into a camper and the family spent a summer traveling in Colorado. H. May Roberts, Gerald's daughter, of Mesa, Arizona, says this photograph was taken on that trip. Pictured with her parents are a sister and an aunt.

**LENDING A HAND.** Woody Hayward of Fruit Heights, Utah says that back around 1924, the nicest thing one brother could do for another was to help him overhaul the motor in the old car. Woody, his sister and his dog, "Pal", are at left with their father's brother, Dennis, who was visiting their home in Montpelier, Idaho when this photo was taken. Note how the door in this Model T makes entry into the backseat.

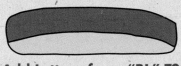

## Add Lettuce for a "BL" T?

ON A memorable trip to the Oregon coast, the front bearing in our 1920 Model T went out. We stopped on the road, tore it apart and found that the bearing was shot.

Since we didn't have a new bearing to install, one of the guys suggested we wrap a bacon rind around the crankshaft. We had to loosen and retighten it three times to get enough rind in to fit the shaft, but it worked.

And, when we installed a new bearing 3 days later, we found the bacon rind still in perfect shape!

—*T.M. Stevensen, Seattle, Washington*

## Sisters Drove in...Then Out!

ONE DAY, my two sisters were driving the family Model T to high school when they decided to stop at a service station for gas. Although they didn't have a whole lot of driving experience, they thought they'd mastered the three pedals on the floor—the clutch, the brake and reverse.

But the brakes weren't as good as they should've been, so the sister who was driving coasted slowly into the station. My other sister, fearing the car wasn't going to stop, lunged over and pushed on the brake—or so she thought!

Actually, she pushed the reverse pedal, and the car shot backward out into the street! The young attendant at the station was quite amused. Later, he told my brother that, next time, the girls should park out in the street and he'd *carry* their gas out to them!

—*Berniece Brown, Lenore, Iowa*

## Radiator Remedy Had One Major Drawback

ONE NIGHT, my boyfriend and I went to a dance with a friend whose Tin Lizzie had a leaky radiator. Every few miles, it would get low on water and become very hot. We frequently had to stop and fill it with water from roadside ditches.

After several such stops, we tried a

**ANGELES TO ANGELES.** Nelda Hoagland of Sun City West, Arizona (with her parents above) recalls that, 5 years after this photo was taken in 1922, their Model T made an 1,100-mile trip from Los Angeles, California to Port Angeles, Washington. In the steepest portion of the Cascades, the only way her dad had enough power to make it to the summit was to turn the T around and back it up the mountain. After that, the rest of the trip seemed easy!

then-common remedy for leaking radiators: horse manure. The manure did stop the leak. Unfortunately, it also "perfumed" the steam, which quickly encircled us in that open car.

By the time we arrived at the dance, I'm afraid we *all* smelled like horses!

—*Pearl Hetchler, Cornell, Wisconsin*

# If You Can't Stand the T, Get Out of the Kitchen

*By Rector Seal, Kingsport, Tennessee*

**M**y brother Grant and I were teenagers in the '20s when we decided we had to have a car of our own. We'd heard about a 1917 Ford that had been abandoned about 4 miles from our house in rural Hancock County, Tennessee.

It had been left along a creek bank after it stopped running and people had been taking parts off it ever since. The top, windshield and wheels were some of the parts that were missing.

Grant and I had no money, so we offered to saw eight cords of firewood for the owner in exchange for the car. That done, we took the car apart and hauled home everything but the body.

### Grandma's Grease Monkeys

We wanted to turn the car into a truck, so we returned later and cut off the body behind the front seat. Not wanting to bother the farmer again for his horse and sled, we each took an end and *carried* it home.

The next problem was finding a place to assemble everything. Grandma lived on our place, and her house had a large kitchen she didn't use. With help from some friends, we finally got all the components into the kitchen.

We put the frame on blocks and installed the springs, axles and engine, then mounted the gas tank. We found a steel dash from a later-model Ford and mounted the steering column with spark and gas levers.

Our car had no wheels, steering spindles or body, but we were ready to crank her up. It didn't work—the winding on the field coils was damaged. After some scouting around, we found a used field coil assembly and installed that, along

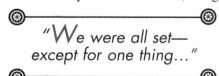

*"We were all set— except for one thing..."*

with new piston rings, and reinstalled the engine.

Grant set the gas and spark levers and pulled on the crank a few times. After two or three loud explosions, the engine was running smoothly.

We'd been so anxious to start the engine, however, that we'd forgotten to install the exhaust pipe—a huge blowtorch of flame streamed out of the manifold toward the gas tank! Fortunately, we got the engine shut off in time.

But Grandma didn't appreciate a hot-rod shop in her kitchen. She complained that the foul-smelling, fire-belching monstrosity was going to explode and blow the house to eternity. Small wonder her prediction never came true.

### Kitchen Crew Worked Hard

It took us a year to finish our project. We collected the remaining parts by hitchhiking 25 miles to a junkyard with burlap bags slung over our shoulders. Much of the work in the kitchen was done at night, by lantern light.

We were bound and determined to join the motoring world. When the truck was finally finished, we had to cut a large doorway to get it out of Grandma's kitchen.

Then we had to grade a 200-foot roadway around the side of the hill, and build a 20-foot bridge over a gully just to get the truck out to the road.

We were all set, except for one thing: We didn't know how to drive! That, however, proved to be a minor problem since we were so familiar with all the parts of the car.

That homemade vehicle could compete with any Ford of its day, so we were rewarded with lots of pleasure for those late-night sessions in the kitchen.

# When All Else Fails, Try a Cornhusk

*By Stanley Witzel Sr., Oceanside, California*

It was in late March of 1921, my junior year in high school, when I went to inquire about the forlorn remains of a 1915 Model T that I passed on my way to school every day. When the owner said I could have it for $15, I bought it on the spot.

A friend towed it home with his farm truck while I sat on the gas tank to steer. When Father saw what my $15 had bought, he was disgusted. "We don't need an old pile of junk littering up the farmyard," he said.

"We can make a spring wagon from it," I offered. "The tires are good. If I can get the motor to run, we could saw wood with it."

"Humph," Father said. "We already have a belt pulley we could use for sawing." I hadn't convinced him.

"All right, I'll get rid of it," I said reluctantly. "But please let me do it my way."

"You'll be wasting your time," Father retorted.

## Son Had Something to Prove

What a challenge! I decided I'd have to keep any further expenses under $25 or my father would say, "I told you so."

I bought a new cylinder head gasket, radiator hoses and spark plugs. But after grinding the valves, I was unable to tighten three of the dozen or so cylinder head bolts.

I tried wrapping them with different kinds of cloth, but nothing worked. In desperation, I rolled up a dry cornhusk, shoved it all the way to the bottom of one hole and screwed the cap screw through the center. It held.

It also worked for the other two failed screws. The radiator didn't leak and neither did the cylinder head gasket. With new oil and a gallon or two of gas, the motor started after a couple quick turns of the crank.

I sat on the gas tank and tried all three pedals. They worked, so I took off excitedly and drove down the road. When I saw the neighbor come out of his barn, I drove up to him to pass the time of day.

As we talked, he walked around the car, kicked the tires and listened to the motor. Gradually I realized that he was interested in it. Before I knew it, he was asking whether it was for sale.

"Yes, it's for sale," I said.

When he offered me $50 for it. I couldn't believe my ears! He paid me then and there and offered to take me home.

No, I told him, he had chores to do and I needed a brisk walk—no way did I want to risk him not being able to get back home in his new purchase!

I was excited about telling Father how I'd doubled my money. Nevertheless, I secretly laid the $50 aside for a refund, just in case it would be needed.

Apparently, the neighbor had no complaints about his purchase because, some weeks later, as we worked in adjoining fields, he gave me a very friendly wave.

Had he ever noticed those cornhusks? If he ever did, I never heard about it. But I have to admit I've had an occasional guilty thought about it over the years. 🐚

***"T" IS FOR TROUBLE.*** That's Betty Brooks Vinson, now of Atlanta, Georgia, sitting disgustedly on the running board above as her brother and a friend probe the mysteries of the Ford engine. This photo was taken in a park in Nashville, Tennessee in March of 1936. To be fair, Betty says she has many, many fond memories of good times in this 1917 Model T.

***LIZZIE GOES TO SCHOOL.*** This 1924 Model T pickup was still at work in Rockville, Nebraska in 1932 as a modified "school bus". Victor Stein of Fort Wayne, Indiana was the driver back then. He says the canopy was the sunshade off a farm tractor, and the side curtains were old grain-binder canvases used to protect students from those cold Nebraska winters.

***SOUTHBOUND.*** These three gentlemen were on the way to Florida from Long Island, New York in their 1924 Model T when this photograph was taken. Only 18 then, Austin Wetherell (right) of Leesburg, Florida is 89 now. He recalls their top speed was 30 miles per hour. It took 10 days to reach Miami—and they arrived the same time a hurricane did!

# 14-Year-Old 'Chauffeur' Faced Major Road Test

*By Francis Stephens*
*Lincoln, Nebraska*

I arrived at the bus depot in York, Nebraska at 8 a.m. on an April morning in 1923, ready to return home to Lincoln after visiting my grandparents. I was 14.

I was about to enter the station when two young fellows in their 20s came out. One of them asked me, "Hey, kid, can you drive?" I said sure. Did I know the way to Lincoln? Of course I did, I lived there.

"We've gotta get to Lincoln and we've had a little too much to drink," one of the young men said. "Will you drive us there?"

Now, I'd stretched the truth to the limit when I said I could drive. But I *had* sat beside many a Model T driver, and none of the mechanics had escaped my attention. I was a kid with just enough money to get home, and here was a chariot to carry me there—for free. You bet I could drive!

### He Was Their Last Option

Later, I realized these fellows had hoped to find a more likely prospect for a chauffeur, but business was slow. It was me or nothing.

While their Model T touring car sat idling at the curb, they climbed into the backseat, reclined against the black leather cushions and immediately closed their eyes. I climbed behind the wheel. I was in command. In *command*? What had I gotten myself into?

For a few minutes, I studied the controls. The spark was under my left hand, behind the wheel; the throttle was to the right. I knew how all three floor pedals worked and that the lever under my left hand was the emergency brake.

I eased the clutch all the way down, widening out the throttle a bit, then let out the clutch as I released the emergency brake. We were in high gear. And by golly, there we went, headed out on the Seward York Aurora Highway for Lincoln, 50 miles east. Hot dog!

The SYA was just a two-lane gravel roadway, laid out on the contours nature had provided. Few roads then were planed for easier climbing, and if too much gravel had been applied, a car could easily flip over.

As I drove along—at the subsonic speed of 25 to 30 miles an hour—I kept one eye on the clouds. With no top, we were going to get soaked if it rained.

I shook a little as we approached Seward. The road went through the center of Seward, right past the courthouse square. There was no way to avoid it.

I was afraid that if I braked too hard, I'd kill the engine, which would mean cranking it. There was no way I was going to expose my ignorance of starting procedures to those two backseaters.

### Luck Was with Him

As we came into town, I controlled the speed with cautious use of throttle and clutch, bringing us to a near standstill at the first main intersection. But someone was looking after me—there were no pedestrians crossing the street at the moment, and the only driver I saw waved me on ahead of him.

After Seward, there were no more towns to pass through. The rain didn't materialize, the road was good and the cool breeze felt nice. My passengers even came to life a little bit (although they didn't offer a single comment on the entire trip).

When we reached Lincoln, I parked at 10th and O Streets, climbed out and wished my passengers well. They chugged east on O Street as I trudged the eight blocks home with a great sigh of relief.

But there was elation, too. After all, I'd "soloed" on my first attempt to ever drive a car! ❧

> *"I wondered just what I had gotten myself into..."*

**NO MORE RAINDROP DODGING.** It was a proud moment for R. Donald Moore's father and grandfather when this picture was taken in Kent, Ohio back in 1921. R. Donald, of Cuyahoga Falls, Ohio, says they'd just picked up the family's first "closed" car—a brand-new Model T Ford.

## Cedar "Band-Aid" Saved the Day

ONE TIME, a friend of mine was out for a drive in the country with his girlfriend and another couple. When they came to a sandy hill, the Model T's low gear band wore out.

Old Lizzie wouldn't move, and the reverse band wasn't any better in the sand, so they couldn't back up either. His passengers were ready to start walking home—but my friend had an idea and told everyone to wait just a bit.

While his buddy pried loose the floor and unscrewed the transmission cover, he walked to a roadside fence post and peeled off a strip of cedar bark about the width and length of the transmission band.

Pushing the bark between the worn-out band and the transmission drum, he put the transmission cover back on, screwed the floor back in place and away they went to their destination.

—Richard Garnell
Hancock, Michigan

## When Carburetors Grew on Trees

WHEN I was about 13, my grandfather bought a 1925 Model T touring car. I was the only person in our family who could drive, so I painted the bumper and wood spokes bright yellow. That car attracted more attention—and girls!—than a Cadillac.

One summer, my uncle's family wanted to visit a lake that was 40 miles away. We were about halfway there when the old Ford stopped in its tracks. There was a strong odor of gasoline, and my grandfather and uncle began looking for its source.

They soon discovered that the drain plug on the bottom of the Model T's carburetor had fallen out somewhere. Cutting off a small limb from a nearby tree, my industrious uncle began whittling a makeshift plug.

When he'd finished, he inserted it into the hole and the gas stopped leaking. Continuing on our way, we had a great time at the lake, then returned home with the plug still in place.

It's been said that anyone could fix a Model T with baling wire—but I can attest that wooden plugs worked, too!
—James Brock, Memphis, Tennessee

## Pump and Pork Kept Us Going

GETTING to our home in Pennsylvania meant driving up a hill that was 1-1/2 miles long.

Because the engine in a Model T was gravity-fed, my uncle's Model T had trouble making it up that grade—until my dad came up with a novel solution.

He brazed a tire valve on top of the gas cap. Then, as we drove uphill, I pumped air into the tank, forcing the gas into the carburetor and keeping the engine running.

Another example of Dad's ingenuity came on the day we were driving out in the country and the T threw a rod. Dad took the pan off, put pork rind on the rod, added some oil and off we went. The rind stayed there for several weeks …and the car ran fine the whole time!
—George Furch
Canon City, Colorado

THE "BUS" TO GRANDMA'S. Without this trusty old Model T, June Martinko (standing on the running board) and her brothers and mother would not have been able to visit their grandmother as often. June, now of Estero, Florida, says it was a 300-mile trip from their home in Strathcona, Minnesota to Grandma Laura's in the southern part of the state.

THE HEIGHT OF SUCCESS. Olen Wray was mighty proud of this 3-year-old Model T. He bought it for $75 after his graduation from high school in 1929, recalls his brother Dewitt of Phoenix, Arizona.

## Crowds Flipped for "Leaping Lena"

FOLLOWING PLANS provided by a World War I buddy (and much to the consternation of my mother!), my dad converted a Ford into "Leaping Lena" in the early '20s. He altered the car so he could raise its front wheels into the air or spin it around like a top.

From then on, Dad and his car were regulars at state and national American Legion conventions. Crowds particularly enjoyed when one or two clowns in the rear seat would do back flips out of the car as Dad raised the front wheels into the air.

Dad kept the car in good shape until 1942, when he enlisted in the Seabees and put it in storage.

Upon his return from the war, he found Lena rusted out from a leak in the roof. He patched her together for one last appearance in a local parade...and then she fell apart for good.

—*Earl Shostrom*
*Des Moines, Iowa*

### Mom's Bail-Out Left The Driving to Dad

THE secondhand Model T we bought about 1916 was the first car we'd ever owned. What luxury! No more sitting on the floor of the buggy and having the reins occasionally clip my ears.

Soon after the purchase, Daddy took Mama out for a driving lesson, and she left it in low gear a little too long for his taste.

When he asked her if she was ever going to put it in high, Mama got so irked that, while the car was moving, she climbed over the backseat and told him to drive the car himself!

Luckily, there was no harm done. We were traveling on a prairie road in Saskatchewan with no other traffic—and were going all of 15 miles an hour at the time.

—*Nina Miner*
*Cashmere, Washington*

### Time to Flop the Flivver

AROUND 1920, I took our family on a trip to the Yosemite Valley in our 1918 Model T. My parents didn't drive, so I was behind the wheel.

The planetary transmission on that model had only two speeds, high and low. For low, you had to push in the left pedal and hold it down with your foot.

During the trip up into the mountains, I wore out one of the bands and, while replacing it, accidentally dropped a nut down into the transmission.

So, we laid the Ford on its side and got the nut out!

—*Walter Hamilton*
*Magalia, California*

**SUMMIT BUSTERS.** From San Francisco to the summit of the Sierra Nevada near Lake Tahoe was a tough, adventurous trip in 1921. Walter Hamilton (at right below, beside his mother) was the driver of the Model T below left. He recalls many occasions when everyone had to get out and push on the steep grades.

# $15 Investment Took Them Across the Country

*By Donald Eldridge*
*Amherst, Massachusetts*

**B**ack in 1929, I was reckless enough to join my college roommate in buying a Model T Ford we'd found jacked up in a farmer's barn near Granby, Connecticut. After a superficial inspection (during which Lou and I pretended to know what we were looking for), we bought it "as is" for $15.

The price seems incredible now, but at the time, we wondered whether we'd been "stuck" when one of the tires went flat as we drove out of the farmer's driveway. It was the first of many, many such flats.

### Dad's Training Came in Handy

There were no demountable rims on this antique either, so I made good use of the techniques I'd learned from my father—and had a great many whiffs of rubber-patching glue in the process!

Still, that amazing old T transported Lou, me, my collie, "Tiff", and all our camping equipment across the USA to Yellowstone Park and back to Connecticut (though not without problems).

Our T used lots of oil, so we carried a 5-gallon oil can, which we filled up free each day with oil drained off cars we saw up on racks at service stations along the way. (We preferred "tapping" quality cars like Packards and Pierce Arrows and were always treated cor-

**TRUSTY T's COULD HAUL JUST ABOUT ANYTHING.** This family appears to be on their way to pick up a load to tow behind their Model T. While early Fords had their flaws (see Donald Eldridge's story on this page), they were also resilient machines that usually got the job done.

dially by the service station operators.)

With no turnpikes or center-of-town bypasses, we had many opportunities for free oil as we chugged through Albany, Buffalo, Detroit, Chicago, Des Moines and Cheyenne, to name a few. While traveling paved roads, we averaged one flat tire a day.

West of Chicago, there were no paved roads, just dirt, gravel—or mud. One day, driving over hot, rough gravel

in Montana, we had nine flats! Each flat necessitated jacking up the car, prying off the tire, patching the tube, inflating and remounting. Had the railroad run closer to the highway when number nine went "pop", we would've gladly hopped a freight and "hoboed" it home!

The radiator leaked, and we couldn't find a replacement, so we carried a large can of water and regularly emptied it into the open radiator—often while moving at 25 miles per hour.

### Prune Juice for Lizzie

Wen we camped at Old Faithful, the temperature dropped below 32° and we awoke to find icicles hanging from the bottom of the radiator. So, of course, we thawed the ice and poured the water back in through the spout. We'd been soaking prunes overnight, so we thawed the prune water and poured *that* in, too.

On the positive side, we learned to tune up the Model T motor—which we did regularly under a shady tree or other shelter. This included taking off the head, cleaning out the carbon, adjusting the spark plugs and attending to a few other details, all in about 30 minutes, including reassembly.

A truly remarkable machine, the Model T—there's nothing like it on the road today, that's for sure! ✍

### When Ford Phased Out, He Stocked Up

IT WAS 1927, and my neighbor Mack was disgusted and indignant. How dare the Ford Company pull a dirty trick like this?

Mack had been driving Model T coupes, one after another, for years.

He'd told all his neighbors that he was Ford's best customer. And now they were going to stop making Model T's?

Mack wasn't going to learn to drive a Model A with a stupid gearshift! He went to the Ford garage, put down a cigar box full of money, and said, "I want to buy three Model T Ford coupes. That'll last me the rest of my life."

And that is exactly what happened. Mack had the cars delivered to his barn, where he stored them tenderly. He continued driving 1927 Model T coupes until he was no longer able to drive.
—*Wesley Peterson, New London, Iowa*

# CHAPTER 3

Brown Brothers (hand-tinted by Melissa Burghart)

*MUD BUGGY.* This Model T found itself stuck in a real nasty mud hole. Unless these folks could talk a farmer into pulling them out with a team of horses, they probably had to wait until the road dried before they could move on. In the early days of motoring, cars capable of going on surprisingly long trips did exist, but road conditions were totally dependent on the weather.

# When Highways Were Horseways

Travel was not for the faint of heart during the first quarter of the 20th century. Not only were autos capricious critters, but highways were just about nonexistent. What we had was a helter-skelter collection of old cattle trails, former migration routes (the Oregon Trail, the Platte River Road, etc.), country lanes, widened paths, and a spiderweb of dirt or gravel or log roads that connected towns and settlements but were linked by no master plan.

There were few signposts when you came to a crossroads. Nor were there official road maps. When you reached a creek or river, there were no bridges. You just drew a deep breath, told the family to hang on and plunged into waters of uncertain depth.

When winter snows covered the road, your best bet was to steer a middle course between farm fences. Snowplows were still waiting to be invented.

And when the spring thaws and rains came, country roads became bottomless quagmires, Out where my family farmed, you would pick out a pair of deep ruts and hope you didn't meet someone coming toward you.

### Prepared for Anything

A trip of any distance took considerable planning. Things you "couldn't leave home without" included several extra tires and rims, tire irons, a jack, patching material and a "boot" for blowouts, and a good tire pump.

Wait, there was more! The prudent driver also tossed in a shovel, a length of sturdy rope, some wrenches for engine repairs, a hatchet, a selection of fan belts, a can of gasoline and another of water, some motor oil and a little grease, plus a couple of heavy lap robes (if this was a winter trip).

For really long trips, you also had to make room for luggage, food, a tent and, if you wanted to go first-class, a few of those wood-and-canvas fold-up army cots for the adults.

That's why those old pictures of cross-country motorists show cars with tires strapped atop the hood, luggage tied to the fenders and crates perched atop the roof. They weren't all of them

Okies. Some were bankers and their families, headed for Yellowstone. Remember, the popular Model T Ford was just 7 feet long!

Travelers set out from home knowing where they were headed, but little else. They were likely to have only the vaguest notion of how to get there and where they would eat, sleep or get repairs along the way.

I believe it was Blanche DuBois in Tennessee Williams' *A Streetcar Named Desire* who said during her life she had "depended upon the kindness of strangers". That was pretty much how you traveled in the early days of motoring, too.

### Opportunity for an Inspection

Cars were still a curiosity and people were eager to see one up close and hear about your experiences. If the trade-off was to hitch up the horses to pull you out of the mud or even put you up for the night, so be it.

Besides, life was geared to a slower pace. It was generally accepted that you had an obligation to help strangers in trouble.

My wife once navigated us across France without a road map or hotel reservation, even though no one in our family spoke or read a word of French. At the time, it seemed like a remarkably foolhardy adventure. But it was indeed a modest feat compared to the travel memories you'll read in the pages that follow.

—*Clancy Strock*

**QUAGMIRE. Soft spots in an unimproved road like this could very nearly swallow up a big car.**

# Unmarked Roads Were a Traveler's Nightmare

*By William Webb, Mesa, Arizona*

Though just a child in 1912, my mother well remembers a trip her family took that year from their home in Snover, Michigan. Grandfather had just bought a new Buick touring car and wanted to visit his parents in Hillman, about 150 miles away.

That's not far by today's standards, but in the early 1900s, roads were often only trails and the average driving speed was probably 10 miles an hour.

For the trip, Grandma and Grandpa both donned "duster" coats and hats. Mother recalls that Grandma's hat was very large and held on with a white flowing scarf.

Grandma and Grandpa and the baby rode up front and the three girls in back. They drove with the top down to make better speed.

The first day went relatively well and they reached Saginaw (about 70 miles), where they spent the night in a hotel. When they set out the next morning, the first 20 miles or so were fine, but then the roads became narrow, rutted and unmarked.

Grandpa had to stop at many "water crossings" to gauge the water's depth before driving through it. The woods were thick with branches often hanging low over the trails. Road signs were

> "She insisted that these complete strangers stop in for tea!"

rare, and those that did exist often bore only the names of families living in that direction.

Forks in the road were particularly risky. Grandpa would stop, check his compass, look at the sun and hazard an educated guess as to which trail to take. Oftentimes he was wrong and they would have to backtrack a ways.

About midday, the trail they were following dead-ended at a farmhouse. A woman came running out, very excited and happy to have visitors, the first she'd seen in months.

She insisted that these complete strangers stop in for tea!

As they drove away later, Mother remembers the sight of their lonesome hostess waving and waving until the car was out of sight.

That day, they kept driving until it got too dark to see and they had to stop. They spent the night sleeping on the hard wood floors of a schoolhouse.

Setting out again early next morning, they finally arrived at the family homestead late that afternoon. It had taken them almost 3 days to go 150 miles.

The return trip was much easier since Grandpa had the foresight to record his many turns. This time they made it home in 2 days—and only had to backtrack once! ❧

## Stopping Was the Scary Part

WHEN I was a young fellow, I heard an old man telling about the early days of automobiles when a friend of his had come into some money and bought a new car.

Soon after, the two of them took a long trip together. They'd just started out when the man made the mistake of starting a conversation with the driver.

"You must be quiet!" cautioned the driver. "I need to keep my mind concentrated on what I'm doing." At the time, they were headed down the road at maximum speed ...about 15 miles per hour!

People nowadays sometimes try to make out how silly it was that those old folks were so scared of speed. Not so—it wasn't so much the speed as the cumbersome and ungainly way those rigs handled on extremely rough and unimproved roads.

After all, horses could go much faster than 15 miles per hour. When our horses got away from me and were running as fast as they could, it wasn't the speed that scared me—it was not knowing what was going to happen before I got them stopped!

It was the same with driving a car: On those treacherous roads, a person never knew what was going to happen next—but the faster you were going, the more likely it would happen *before* you could do anything about it.

—*Laurence Holdeman*
*Bonners Ferry, Idaho*

**HITCH UP A TEAM!** As Laurence Holdeman points out in his story, roads like this one severely limited the speed of early autos.

## These Highways Were Anything But Super

THE ROADS were snow-covered and slippery in 1913 when Oliver and Howard Pease (and Howard's wife, Lena) left Springfield, Massachusetts (1) on their way to Daytona Beach, Florida. But as they worked their way south, things got worse—much worse!

What passed for highways in those days could, with a little rain, turn into impassable quagmires (2). Sometimes a push (3) could help get a stalled automobile moving. But there were other times (4) when vehicles got so hopelessly bogged down that the only thing motorists could do was wait for hours—or even days—until the roads dried up.

Apparently, the Peases tired of such situations because, upon reaching Georgia, they decided to put their Cadillac on a railroad car (5) and finish their journey by rail. They finally did make it to Florida and, after the ordeal of getting there, driving on Daytona Beach (6) must have been sheer pleasure.

Oliver's nephew, Horace Pease of Somers, Connecticut, provided these photographs of what had to have been a memorable trip.

**ROLLIN' IN THE ROCKIES.** Unlike the Hagelin family (see memory below) these motorists all rode *inside* the car while traveling in the Rockies in 1915. Paul Wilcoxson of Arvada, Colorado says the woman in the front seat is his grandmother, Anna Belle Wilcoxson, and the couple in the back is his great-grandparents.

## Mountain Climbers Set Blistering Pace

SOMETIME between 1913 and 1915, my family (we lived in eastern Nebraska) was on vacation, visiting my Aunt Ame and Uncle Wes in Loveland, Colorado. The families decided they'd take a trip up through the scenic Big Thompson Canyon to Estes Park.

I was only 3 or so at the time, so I have no memory of that 30-mile journey, but I've heard the story told numerous times by my parents. The day before we left, a big planning session was held and each person was assigned their seat for the trip.

Since it was likely to be an all-day drive, the time of departure was set early, about 6:30 a.m., and even though Uncle Wes had driven the road before, Dad was a better driver, so it was decided he'd be behind the wheel.

Meanwhile, Uncle Wes' job was to stand on the running board and honk the Klaxon horn whenever we came to one of those sharp, blind curves. That way, Dad never needed to take his hands off the wheel on a narrow mountain road.

The plan worked well and we made great time, congratulating ourselves at reaching Estes Park by 4:30 in the afternoon.

The only negative note was that Uncle Wes had sounded the horn so often that he ended up sporting a big blister on his hand.

—*Carl Hagelin*
*Citrus Heights, California*

## He Was a "Left-Brain" Thinker

MY FAVORITE early-day car story from my husband's side of the family concerns his maternal grandfather, Arthur Reynolds.

I've been told that, in those days of rough roads, if no one was coming in the opposite direction, he'd steer the car over to the left side of the road, claiming it was "smoother over there".

The funny thing was that, on the way back home on the same road, he'd still drive on the left side, claiming once again that it was "smoother" on *that* side.

—*Patricia Biery*
*Frankfort, Indiana*

## They Played in Traffic

WHEN I was 3 or 4, I can recall three of my cousins digging a hole in the beautiful white sand on the road in front of our Texas home and burying me completely—except for my head.

No need to worry about a car coming since they were so few and far between. But then we heard my mother's shrill voice yelling, "There's a car coming!"

You can bet that my cousins dug me out pretty quick and we all ran into the house as an old Model T chugged by at about 15 or 20 miles per hour.

—*Verna Ray Humphrey*
*Palestine, Texas*

**STOPPED IN ITS TRACKS.** In July of 1916, an auto dealer decided to see just how far up Mt. Hood this new Paige could get under its own power. A summer snowstorm on July 1 left the Paige stranded right where you see it, says Howard Davis of Shedd, Oregon.

# 'Cotten's Caravan' Was Bumper-to-Bumper Buicks

*By Anna Menke, Greenville, Ohio*

Around 1912, my great-grandfather, Thaddeus Cotten, became a partner in a Buick agency in Petersburg, Virginia. The Buicks were made in Flint, Michigan and, with such poor roads in between, Great-Grandpa had to be extremely resourceful to get those cars home.

Sometimes he'd go to a nearby Army camp (Camp Lee) and ask the fellow in charge of the motor pool if he could "borrow" some soldiers to go to Michigan with him and bring the cars back (there were 10 to 20 cars on each trip).

The motor pool fellow pointed out that most of the soldiers came from "way, way back in the woods", and many had never even seen a car. Great-Grandpa assured him they'd be proficient drivers by the time they returned —and that would be a big plus for the military.

## Maneuvers in Michigan

With the Army's consent, Great-Grandpa put the soldiers on the train to Flint. After picking up the cars at the factory, he'd drive to a hardware store and purchase a big roll of rope. Then he'd buy at least five extra tires, two extra tailpipes and two extra mufflers for each car and throw them in the backseats.

Now the caravan was ready to leave. When Great-Grandpa came to a steep hill or a rough stretch of road, he'd pull over and park. All the drivers would pull up right behind him until their bumpers touched. Then the men tied the bumpers together with rope.

Great-Grandpa would tell the soldiers, "I'm going to aim for the top of that hill over there. When I take off, everybody just put your foot all the way down, and we'll go. There will always be enough cars that have traction to push and pull those that don't, so we'll end up at the top of that hill."

## Took Stock on Top

At the top of the hill, they'd stop and take off the ropes. By then, some of the cars might be missing tailpipes or mufflers, so they'd replace them before reaching the next town. By the time the soldiers got back to Camp Lee, they were proficient drivers—and pretty good at repairing cars, too!

Sometimes Great-Grandfather's Buick caravan was lucky enough to

**MAN ON THE MOVE.** Thaddeus Cotten was a car dealer in an era when dealers literally had to be "go-getters". For Thaddeus, the challenge was finding a way to transport new Buicks from Michigan back to Virginia to sell them. Some of his "caravans" must have looked a lot like the one below.

catch a ferry across Lake Erie to Cleveland, Ohio. This shaved 100 miles off the drive and left the drivers rested and ready to go.

On a few occasions, Great-Grandpa had to pick up the cars alone. He'd park them on the street outside the factory, get in the last car and drive it to the front of the line. He did this over and over, moving the line of cars forward one car length at a time.

## He Always Thought Ahead

The fellows at the factory liked to kid him. "Are you going to drive those cars like that all the way back to Virginia?" they'd ask.

He'd reply with a smile, "Not unless I can't think of something else on the way!" Being the dry wit that he was, he wanted them to think that might be what he was doing. Actually he had a plan: A friend at the railroad company would see about getting him some railcars.

On one trip, he got the cars down to the rail yard when the yard master said, "I'm sorry, I just don't have anything here now that could take those Buicks to Virginia. But if you can find a railway car out there, it's yours."

Great-Grandpa found some coal cars and asked if he could use those. "Well, I've got a crane," the yard master said. "I suppose I could lift your cars up and put them in. But will you be able to get them out back in Virginia?"

Great-Grandpa replied, "Not unless I can think of something on the way!" With all the stories I've heard over the years about Great-Grandpa's ingenuity, I've no doubt he did think of a way.

# The Empire Strikes Back

*By Marie Freesmeyer, Jerseyville, Illinois*

My parents bought an Empire automobile in 1913 and a year later, they planned an adventurous 200-mile trip from Alton, Illinois to the northern part of the state.

My 16-year-old brother would be the chauffeur—Papa considered himself "too old" to drive. Meanwhile, my younger brother won the dubious honor of riding in the front and serving as "lackey boy".

He would change flat tires and crank the engine when necessary. My 3-year-old sister and I, age 8, were probably the most excited passengers of all.

The day finally arrived and Papa got us up early so we could do most of our traveling "during the morning hours before it gets too hot". Soon we were chugging our way over the rutted dusty trail that led to the main road along the Mississippi River and our little village of Alton.

After filling the gas tank there, we settled in for a long ride. The first 20 miles or so, we followed a familiar road that hugged the bluffs along the Mississippi.

Suddenly, without warning, we came to a halt. Like most dirt roads, this one had two main ruts worn by wagon wheels with a high ridge in between. The Empire's undercarriage had dug into this ridge and so firmly wedged there that we couldn't move forward or backward!

Papa knew what to do. "I'll go back to the house we just passed and get a spade," he said. Returning, he dug out enough of the high spot that we were able to back out and go around.

As we neared the Illinois River, the dirt roads became quite muddy. All the

⚙——————————————————⚙

## "Suddenly, without warning, we came to a halt..."

⚙——————————————————⚙

creeks we forded were swollen from recent rains and in the middle of one of them, the motor died.

Now it was time for the lackey boy to earn his keep. My younger brother pulled off his shoes and stockings, then climbed around the windshield out on-

to the hood and out toward the front of the car.

By standing there spraddled out like a giraffe drinking, he was able to give the crank enough of a spin to get the motor started. Another crisis averted!

That night, we stayed at a hotel in a little town called Table Grove. The roads were better on the second day, a few even had a hard black surface, different from any we'd ever seen. But there were still those nasty right-angle turns to slow us down. Hedge fences and cornfields prevented us from seeing around those corners, so we had to take them very slowly.

### A Honk and a Hope

Those blind corners were why the Empire was equipped with a bugle-and-bulb contraption on the driver's side. When my brother squeezed our horn, the "hon-n-n-k" could be heard half a mile away.

Hearing it delighted my sister and me, but we soon learned not to use it when approaching a horse-drawn vehicle. Horses weren't yet accustomed to automobiles and were apt to give their owners a difficult time as we passed.

Around dark on the second day, we finally arrived at our relatives' home, weary and dirty. Shortly after, Papa decided the 200-mile trip had been just too tiring for Mama.

So she and us girls made part of trip back home on a steamboat down the Illinois River. We enjoyed that very much and—unlike the Empire—our steamboat made no unscheduled stops.

**JOHNNY POTATO SEED?** Donna Weigel of Oxnard, California isn't sure what kind of car her grandfather and father are posing with. But she does know that, on a trip from Michigan to California in about 1918, a large sack of potatoes on the running board developed a tear, which caused them to "plant" potatoes all along their route.

*A MAJOR "HIGHWAY".* Ruts and all, this was the best road between Yellowstone National Park and Livingston, Montana in 1916, says Bob Burrowes of Yerington, Nevada. Bob's dad took this picture of what appears to be an Overland.

*FOUR WHEELS—OR TWO?* The cart or the carriage (horseless, that is) was a choice new car owners often faced in the early days of automobiles. John Kautz of Fairfield Bay, Arkansas sent these two pictures of his Aunt Bess (standing in front of the pony cart and sitting beside the driver of the shiny new auto) taken about 1916.

*MAKE WAY FOR THE WILLYS.* For a while, this Willys Overland shared a shed with a more old-fashioned kind of carriage on an Emerson, Nebraska farm. Weather conditions determined which type of vehicle was taken out. Two uncles of Robert Hansen, Sioux City, Iowa, are shown working on their Willys.

**CADILLAC COUNTRY?** Harold Conright (above right) was all set to make a big delivery to Jordan, Montana in 1915. He thinks the truck had been a Cadillac touring car before its conversion. It certainly was a reliable machine for its day since it helped set a record (see story below).

### Dad's "Prairie Freighter" Was a Cadillac

MY DAD'S Uncle Howard had a dray line that ran from Jordan, Montana to Miles City and on to Broadus, Montana. When he was 13 years old, Dad was sent to work for Uncle Howard. He drove for several years, hauling all types of freight across the prairie.

This was at a time when there were no roads as we know them now—just wagon and cattle paths. Dad, who's still with us at the age of 97, can tell tales of hauling beer to Jordan and corpses to Miles City.

He says this photograph (above) was taken in Miles City in 1915, just before he hauled a 4,650-pound linotype machine to Jordan. He believes the truck shown was a 1915 Cadillac, which had one of the first V-8 engines. Dad made that 90-mile trip in about 10 hours, which set a speed record of sorts at the time.
—*Gordon Conright*
*Duluth, Minnesota*

### As Overland Salesman, Dad Was a Great Dane

MY FATHER, Nels Wind, came to this country from Denmark just before the turn of the century. After a bout with tuberculosis, he was advised to live in the country but found that farm life wasn't for him.

In 1913, when I was 6, we moved to New London, Iowa and he started an automobile dealership with my four brothers. Known for his honesty and integrity, my father's business flourished, winning many national awards for Overland sales.

People would come from as far as 60 miles away just to buy from Nels Wind. When selling a used car, he would say in his broken English, "Dis car is yust as good as new and runs tirty miles to the gallon and is so inconwenient."

Buyers would smile at his mispronunciations—but they'd still buy because of his honesty. According to newspaper articles from that time, it was also in New London that Overlands were first called "puddle jumpers"—a nickname that became known all over the country.

By the looks of the 1913 photo (below), it would have taken very little rain for "puddle jumping" to commence right in front of Dad's dealership!
—*Mamie Alvine, Pittsburg, Kansas*

**WINDS AND OVERLANDS.** Nels Wind (center) and his sons, Harry and Horace, lined up their Overlands on the street in front of their dealership in New London, Iowa.

# Reo Riders Shared Camaraderie of The Open Road

*By William Bowles Sr., Baltimore, Maryland*

For many years, my Canadian-born parents returned to Dad's parents' farm about 100 miles north of Toronto every summer. In 1916, we made the trip from Washington, D.C. in Dad's 1915 Reo Speedwagon.

It took us about 5 days because of all the delays due to tire repair, engine trouble and hub-high mud on the roads. For two small boys (I was 7-1/2, my brother 5), all that driving was exciting…for a while.

When we got bored, Mother started us playing a game. She assigned point values to various animals, and the first one to score 50 points won. A cow counted as one point, a horse two, a dog five and a cat 10.

At lunchtime, we searched for places to stop and eat. Schoolyards were ideal, since they always had wells and outdoor toilets. Those same features made them attractive places to camp at night.

I vividly recall driving past a school late one afternoon and seeing several tents already set up. As we drove by, some men leaning against the fence called out, "Time to camp!"

After we'd passed by, Mother and Father debated whether we should continue a few more miles or go back. They decided to turn back and, as soon as we approached the schoolyard, the men by the fence knocked out their pipes and came over to offer their help in setting up our tent.

There was companionship out on the road back then. And, if we were lucky, there'd be other children to play with.

At bedtime, the car seats were moved into the tent and our parents slept on a double-wide folding cot. If mosquitoes got inside the tent, Dad would light sticks of punk. Mother didn't like the odor, but we boys did because it just added to the excitement of sleeping outdoors.

### Dad Pumped and Patched

The worst and most common problem on that trip was the tires. Poorly made, they operated with an air pressure of 60 to 70 pounds, so sudden failures were usually accompanied by a loud bang.

After changing and/or patching the tire and putting it back on the rim, Father had to hand-pump the tire back to its original 60 to 70 pounds of pressure. What a job that was—especially after all the other physical labor involved!

One day, the Reo stalled on a lonely stretch of road. Another motorist happened by, but he and Father had no luck getting it started. Finally, the other driver offered to tow us in to the next town. My brother and I were so embarrassed—our big car had to be towed by a Tin Lizzie!

Fortunately, the problem turned out to be a piece of rust in the distributor and we were soon on our way again toward the most exciting part of the trip. That occurred near Buffalo, when we reached a section of the road that was paved with bricks.

After days of seeing only mud, we urged Father to see how fast the car would go. With the engine roaring, the speedometer surged past 20 miles an hour to 30, then 35.

Father's foot was to the floor and the wind whistled as we urged him on. Our speed crept up to 39 miles per hour and we all thought we were going to reach the unheard-of (for us) speed of 40!

Alas, it was not to be—39 miles an hour was as fast as the Reo could go. But consider this: A few days earlier, it had taken us 3 hours to travel 39 miles! ❧

**THE ROAD TO RAINIER.** Back when Edwin Nelson's mother picked up this postcard in 1915, folks often arrived at Mt. Rainier in chauffeur-driven vehicles. Edwin, of Spokane, Washington, says his mother was once part of a tour group like this.

**REO IN CHAINS.** Unlike the Reo in the story above, this 1909 model probably never challenged the 40-mph barrier. Besides, those chains on the back tires suggest that even summer roads were apt to be too treacherous for such a feat. This photo was probably taken near Chelsea, Iowa, says Helen Standley of Salem, Oregon.

# Dad and Mom Drove Cross-Country the 'Hard Way'

*By Loring Bigelow, Laguna Hills, California*

Foreman of a ranch in Torrance, California in 1916, my dad modified his 1913 Model T Ford convertible into a homemade camper. He'd been inspired by a notice in *American Motorist* magazine offering a medal and certificate to anyone crossing the continent in an automobile.

Dad had other reasons for wanting to head east. A Yankee from Massachusetts, he'd come to California by train in 1906. Not only did he want to visit relatives, he wanted to see some of the country that had passed by his train window 10 years earlier.

For such a long trip, the T needed modifications. Dad built a wooden trunk to fit onto the T's trunk rack, fixed the front seats so they'd recline into beds and built a reserve gas tank. The passenger-side running board was essentially a rolling kitchen with a one-burner stove.

"I usually tried to park alongside a fence when I stopped for the night," my dad wrote in his diary. "We had a canvas tarp that fastened to the running board on the driver side, went up over the car roof and extended out to the fence…to give us shelter for our cooking area."

One of the last things Dad did before departure was to paint a splashy red stripe across the Model T's upper chassis. Then he and my mother put on dusters and goggles and hit the road.

## Cheating Was Not an Option

Lewis and Maude Bigelow endured lots of hardships in the next 3,684 miles. Rumor had it that wealthy car owners entering the contest were shipping their cars to Chicago by rail, then driving the rest of the way on good Eastern roads.

My father was determined to do things the "right" way. Roads back then were rough—in his diary, my dad mentioned that, with the exception of cities, they encountered no paved roads between San Bernardino, California and Pittsburgh!

What roads there were tended to parallel railroad tracks. As it turned out, August of 1916 was an unusually wet month—it rained 21 of the 28 days my parents were on the road!

East of Williams, Arizona, the old Ford edged up to what seemed to be a huge lake. It was probably just an overgrown puddle, but there was no way to know whether a drop-off was hidden under all that water.

So, they drove the car up onto some nearby train tracks and my mother walked ahead to flag down any approaching trains. For 3 tense and bone-rattling miles, they proceeded until they found a way off that elevated roadbed.

## Mechanical Problems Mounted

The damage was done, though. By the time they reached the Grand Canyon, an axle had broken. A replacement was shipped by train and Dad installed it himself. The ride along the tracks probably cracked a spring, which eventually failed, too.

Dad kicked himself for not watching the mechanic replace it because, a few miles later, the car's chassis nearly slid off the frame because a crucial bolt hadn't been replaced.

Using a fence post, Dad levered the frame back on the chassis, then whittled a wooden spike from the same post to use as a replacement bolt.

My mother used to tell of a bad thunderstorm they encountered, during which electricity skimmed around in her frying pan! At any rate, a bolt of lightning did hit a nearby tree and scare her so badly they went without dinner that night.

Animals were a problem, too. Wandering cattle would spot the white tarp in the moonlight and crowd around—they often woke Mom and Dad in the middle of the night.

After they crossed the Great Plains, my parents received a write-up in the *Kansas City Star* and an affidavit proving they'd driven through the area.

Once they reached the nice firm roads of the East, they made good time. In Massachusetts, they received their medal and certificate and enjoyed the notoriety of local newspaper coverage. They spent the winter there and returned to California in 1917.

My dad talked about that trip the rest of his life, and the medal and certificate were centerpieces of family lore for years to come.

**TRIP OF A LIFETIME.** Lewis and Maude Bigelow accomplished something few couples in 1916 even attempted—a cross-country auto trip. Below, relatives in Massachusetts wished the couple well before they headed back home to California.

## Roustabouts to the Rescue

WE WERE as poor as church mice in 1922, so I knew my dad must have saved up a long time to pay $450 for the new Ford touring car we got that year.

All of us were so proud of our shiny new black vehicle. I can recall Mother and I wiping the dust off the fenders with our hankies while Dad cranked to get it started.

Almost every Sunday, we'd take the hour-long trip to Grandma's house, packing a lunch to eat under a big tree beside the road.

One Sunday, we were driving in deep ruts when we came upon a carnival troupe heading in the opposite direction. We all stopped because there was no way to pass each other. Finally, the head man of the carnival came over and asked us to get out of our Ford.

Then he called all the roustabouts with the carnival to come and lift our vehicle out of the ruts and set it on the side of the road.

After the entire carnival drove past, the roustabouts returned, lifted our car back into the road and we were on our way again!
—*Mildred Herman*
*Dover, Ohio*

*A SHINY MECHANICAL MARVEL.* **This gleaming new 1919 Dodge was 20-year-old John Holhubner's very first car, says his son George of Olmstead, Illinois. Riding next to John is his father, Johann, who immigrated to the United States from Austria in 1884.**

## Dad Was a "Rock 'n' Roll" Preacher

MY DADDY was a Texas preacher and needed a car to drive the many miles to his different churches. The car also had to be one he could afford on his small salary.

One day when I was 7, he was thrilled to find a used Studebaker he could afford and proudly drove it home. The next day, he took it to his church in County Line, which was about 80 miles from where we lived in Abilene.

Usually my brother accompanied him, but on this day, he was sick and couldn't come. The route to County Line wasn't on a highway or even a county road—Daddy just drove across the rangeland. Since he had to cross several ranches, it was necessary for him to go through a series of gates. At the first one, Daddy discovered his brakes wouldn't hold after he'd brought the car to a halt.

So, at this gate (and every one thereafter) he had to stop the car, get out quickly, jam a rock in front of the wheel, open the gate, drive through, stop, put the rock in front of the wheel again, go back, shut the gate, remove the rock, get back in the car and drive on.

After doing this 13 times, Daddy decided his "new" car wasn't all that great after all.
—*Bettye Sue Drury*
*Fort Worth, Texas*

*LET HEZZA DO IT.* **Even when roads were relatively dry, tire problems caused frequent headaches. Mary Barber of Orland Park, Illinois supplied this photo of her parents, F.R. and Adele Barber, watching as a friend, Hezza Morse, changes a tire on their Stevens-Duryea on a road somewhere near Warrens, Wisconsin. Given the size of those tires, Hezza had to do lots of pumping.**

## Dad's Little Helper Kept Mom Calm

IN THE summertimes of my youth, my father would gather the family outside our home in Wauwatosa, Wisconsin, pack us in his seven-passenger Studebaker and off we'd go to visit Uncle Fred's farm near Monroe, Wisconsin. I was born 2 years after this photo (above) was taken.

If I was lucky, I got to sit in the front seat between my parents, where I could see the dials and gauges and watch my father manipulate the car's controls. Master of the machine, he was my hero as his gloved hands grasped the polished wooden steering wheel or moved the gearshift lever.

As our speed approached 30 miles per hour, I could see the tops of trees and telephone poles flash past.

"Henry, please," my mother would plead. "Slow down!"

"Sorry, sweetheart," my father would reply. "This new car is so smooth I didn't even notice."

Then he'd give me a wry smile and a wink and say, "Butch, why don't *you* watch the speed and tell me when we're going too fast."

"Sure, Dad," I'd reply. Then, together, the two of us would safely transport my mother and the rest of the family through the shimmering fields, cool woodlands and quaint towns of southern Wisconsin. —*Henry Digman Anacortes, Washington*

## Map or Not, Early Motorists Were on Their Own

IN 1918, my mom and dad and sister and I drove from Twin Falls, Idaho to Hampton, Nebraska in a new seven-passenger Studebaker.

I was 17, so Dad let me drive the first few miles with the understanding that he'd drive when we got to the mountains. But he was so satisfied with my driving that he let me drive the whole way.

Dad had bought a "blue book" that was supposed to give us directions on which route to take.

Unfortunately, it was virtually useless because the "red barn" where we were supposed to turn would be torn down. Or the road had been changed since the book was written to avoid mud holes, etc.

We'd come to a place where the road divided and have no idea which way to go. Dad would get out and try to determine which fork had the most travel. Sometimes, after much deliberation, we'd choose one—only to see the two forks join again within a half mile!

Although it was June, the roads had deep ruts. When we saw another car approaching, we'd look for a place to turn out and let them by. If neither car found one, we'd each get two wheels out of the rut, pass each other, then help lift each other's car back onto the road.

We rarely saw more than three or four cars in a day so, fortunately, this didn't happen often. —*Erle Jones Kent, Washington*

J.C. Allen and Son

BUMPING ALONG. Not only were early roads often obstacle courses like this rough stretch in Indiana, but, as mentioned in Erle Jones' memory of a trip to Nebraska above, at least half the time, motorists couldn't be sure they were even traveling in the right direction!

A month before my 17th birthday, in mid-November 1918, World War I had just ended and people were celebrating all over Denver, Colorado.

The great flu epidemic wasn't over yet, but Thanksgiving was right around the corner. My employer, a truck dealer, called me into his office to tell me he'd selected me to drive a new Federal truck to a buyer in Monte Vista and collect the final payment.

It was a 200-mile trip—about 12 hours driving time if I could average 16 miles per hour. I left early Wednesday and soon began climbing into the Rockies. The road was fairly well traveled, but I had to put chains on the tires because of the snow.

### Situation Would Get Worse

At last, I made it over Kenosha Pass and could see down into a small valley, where the road wound into the town of Fairplay. After having a meal there, I pressed on.

From Buena Vista to Salida, I had some 20 miles to go with night coming on. Reaching Salida, I checked into a hotel, where I intended to stay for 2 nights before pushing on.

The next day was Thanksgiving, and I had a lot to be thankful for: My inquiries about road conditions gave me some assurance that Friday's 56-mile drive to Monte Vista would be easy. Little did I know!

I left Salida later than usual Friday morning. With a good rest and a sack lunch beside me, my confidence was fairly high. But when I reached the base of Poncha Pass, the road became a mass of slick mud and I was forced to resort to chains.

But there were no chains! They'd either fallen out of the truck or been stolen. My one hope was that a passing motorist would come by and send help. I waited hopefully, but no one came.

Night was coming on and I noticed the mud beginning to firm up as it froze. But that also meant the truck was in danger of freezing, too. I dragged several railroad ties from a nearby hillside and lit them.

They were soon fur-

# 16-Year-Old Trucker Endured One Torturous Trip

*By A.B. Blake, Logan, Utah*

**TROUBLESHOOTER.** By 1922, 4 years after his truck delivery ordeal, A.B. Blake (still only 21) was wearing a suit and tie and working for the Chevrolet Company in Denver. His job was to respond to customer complaints and resolve the tough problems.

nishing enough heat to keep the frost away. Next morning, the mud had frozen hard, and if the engine could be started, I could be on my way. I hand-cranked for a long time before that engine finally caught.

From the summit of Poncha Pass, the road dropped toward Saguache with many curves and horseshoe bends. Without chains, it was very slow going and it took me most of the day to make the 40 miles to Saguache.

Approaching town, I was stopped by a group of armed men. They asked me what I was doing, then strongly suggested I turn back. After hearing my story, they relented and let me proceed— but with no stop in town.

"Saguache has had no flu cases and we're only protecting our own," they told me. With a garment from my suitcase as a mask, I was escorted through town with armed men riding beside me.

By then, daylight was nearly gone. But it was now a straight shot into Monte Vista and I was able to get the truck up to 16 miles per hour for the first time since leaving Denver.

When I found a place to stay for the night, I thought my troubles were over. They weren't.

### Would the Bridge Hold?

Next morning, when I delivered the truck to the purchaser, he told me he would need a demonstration before I could receive the final payment. So, the truck was fitted with chains and I then drove it to a logging camp along a narrow winding road that crossed a rickety bridge.

After the truck was loaded with logs, I turned it around and went back out the way we'd came. There was enough power in lower gears to handle the load, but whether that bridge would hold was my worst fear.

Not until the trailer wheels cleared did my breath return to normal! Back in town, I received payment for the truck and caught the next train for Denver.

Monday morning, I checked in for work as usual. In return for my services, I received a week's pay and $20 in gold coins—it was quite possibly the toughest $20 I have ever earned! ✺

# Grandfather's Buses 'Stretched' All the Way to Florida

*By Kenneth Ross, Penn Yan, New York*

My grandfather was a fascinating man. Handsome, powerful and about 6-foot-6, he called me "Boy", never Ken or Kenneth (but never unkindly, either).

I can remember visiting him in the '20s when he and my grandmother lived in Milford, Connecticut. My mother, a fine kindergarten teacher, had tried to teach me how to tell time but without much success.

My grandfather, however, had a special knack for explaining things. He sat me on his knee, pointed to the large oak kitchen clock and proceeded to show me how to read it. I caught on quickly and proudly—and I still have that clock today.

Born the year the Civil War ended, Ward Beecher Brown moved to Derby, Connecticut around the turn of the century. From the years of 1902 to 1928, the city directories of Derby and Milford (a town he moved to later) list his occupations as "blacksmith", "chauffeur" or simply "buses".

It was after he came to Derby that Grandfather Brown combined blacksmithing and auto repairing. It was also there that he built the first of about six

**GRANDPA'S BOY.** Sitting on the front porch with his grandparents was a mighty comfortable spot for Ken Ross when he visited in the '20s.

"stretch limousines" in his garage. Grandfather converted Cadillacs, Pierce-Arrows, Whites and others, making four-passenger cars into homemade 10- or 12-passenger "buses". I don't know the details of these conversions, but he probably cut and extended the main frame, drive shaft, rear brake rods and running boards.

This was all the more amazing when you realize that he was self-taught and did not have any motor-driven tools that I am aware of. I can remember his large workbench made from an old grand piano, a hand-operated drill press, other hand tools and a forge with a hand-operated blower.

After he had lengthened those Pierce-Arrows and Cadillacs, my grandfather began using them to drive people around locally, including trips to the exclusive Poland Springs Hotel in Maine.

But by the late teens, he'd extended the service all the way to Daytona Beach, Florida, driving one bus himself while my Uncle Royal drove the other. What pioneers those two men were!

They drove Route 1 (also called the Dixie Highway then) all the way to Florida. The roads they traveled

**PLANKS NOT ALWAYS THE ANSWER.** Grandpa Brown would try his best to make mud holes like these more navigable with boards.

**ROCKY MOUNTAIN "BRAKEDOWN".** Every year, Harry Taylor (right), his wife, Gertrude, and a cousin drove to Yellowstone from their home in Farnam, Nebraska to go fishing. Logs like these were fastened to the rear of the car to prevent it from gaining too much speed traveling down steep mountain roads. Harry's niece, Georgia Lemire of Seattle, Washington, shared the photo from the '20s.

**THE BLACKSMITH'S "BUS".** Ward Beecher Brown (on right in photo at left) was a blacksmith who turned autos into "buses", then drove them between New England and Florida.

on were dirt that quickly became impassable mud when it rained.

Often the "highway" was only two deep ruts—with even deeper potholes. Where bridges were washed out, they crossed rivers on hand-poled ferries.

Grandfather Brown retired in 1929 and died in 1932, when I was only 11 years old. I'll bet that blacksmith-turned-bus maker-turned-bus driver must have had some tales to tell about the incredible trips he'd taken.

How I wish now that I'd known him better! ✆

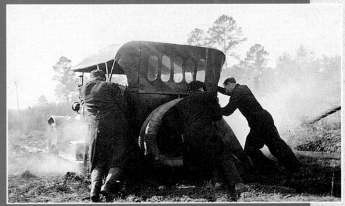

**AUTOMOTIVE ORDEAL.** A river crossing by ferry gave these "New Englanders" a respite, but it was likely they'd soon be stuck again.

**ANOTHER SUNDAY DELAY.** After attending church in Bourbon, Indiana and eating dinner, the Kester family loved going for Sunday drives. John Kester (the small boy at left) now resides in Elkhart, Indiana and can still recall how quickly a "flat" could put a crimp in their Sunday fun.

**POWDER RIVER PULL.** When Heidi Schleiss Ellis' great-grandfather's car stalled crossing the Powder River in Wyoming in 1926 (right), it took a lot of elbow grease—and a big white horse—to get it out on dry land again. Heidi, who lives in Astoria, Oregon, says her great-grandfather is at the wheel, her grandfather is second from left on the rope and her Uncle Caleb is riding the horse.

**TENSE IN TEXAS.** Crossing the Trinity River on a ferry was nerve-racking for Verna Humphrey's relatives.

## T Served Up a
## Double Dose of Terror

ABOUT 1925, my father took a job in Mexia, Texas. That meant we had to cross the Trinity River near Palestine. My father drove an old pickup truck with most of our belongings inside and I rode with my mother, who drove our Model T touring car.

The first hurdle was crossing the railroad tracks in Palestine. Sure enough, just as we got to the middle of the railroad track, the car died. I was terrified because there was a train coming around the bend.

And Mother was so nervous that her foot was dancing all over that little starter knob on the floor. Finally, the car started, jumping and sputtering as it rolled off the track, just as the train went by with a "swish"!

Next came the agony of crossing the Trinity. Again, my father went first, rolling his pickup onto the one-vehicle

ferry. His pickup was pulled by a cable across the river, then he rode the ferry back across the river to help us.

Since it had been raining, the side of the riverbank was very slick clay. That old Model T spit and sputtered as it literally *slid* onto the ferry.

The ferry bobbed up and down as the T came on board, and waves splashed against its sides. I was so frightened that the car would keep on rolling and drop right into the river. But somehow it didn't, and we made it safely across to the other side. —*Verna Ray Humphrey*
*Palestine, Texas*

## Sunday Drive
## Saved Four Lives

ONE NICE DAY in about 1919, my dad decided to take my mother and me on a picnic down along the Yellowstone River near Fairview in eastern Montana. The road was just a wagon track weaving through the trees and brush.

We'd just decided to go on a little farther before turning back when we rounded a bend and saw something I have never forgotten.

In the clearing ahead, four people stood next to a stalled car. A father, mother and two little girls had somehow caught their hands between the car's fender and wheel. They'd been trying to fix a broken spring by putting a block of wood between the axle and frame when something had gone terribly wrong.

Stopping immediately, my father

quickly got a jack under the frame and freed them. Next he rubbed the man's fingers to get the circulation going again. Meanwhile, my mother worked on the woman and older girl while I rubbed the fingers of the younger girl. Then we bandaged the girls' hands with carbolic salve and strips of pillowcases we always carried.

The family told us that they had given up all hope. If we hadn't come along when we did, they could have easily starved since there were times no one used that road for days.

After they'd been caught between the wheel and fenders, the mother had said, "Everyone stand still and we will pray for God to send someone to help us." So, when we came along, they considered us the answer to their prayers.

It *is* true that my parents had an urge to go down along the Yellowstone that morning and that it was the first and only time we ever went below Fairview for a picnic. —*Wesley Westerman*
*Valleyford, Washington*

**PINT-SIZE RESCUER.** Wesley Westerman helped his parents save a family in distress.

# Their Red Nash Was Really a Rambler

*By Christine Byrne, Fort Myers, Florida*

For 3 weeks every summer in the 1920s, my sister and I took trips with our parents and grandparents in our bright red Nash touring automobile. In that era of black cars, a red car was quite a conversation-starter.

We would drive from our home in Scottdale, Pennsylvania to pick up Grandma and Grandpa in Louisville, Kentucky, then head off on our excursion.

Grandmother thought we should have touring outfits, so she made something different for Charlotte and me each year. For our first trip, we had checked black and white knickers with matching sailor tops.

Roads were either dirt or gravel, and the dust was terrible if you were behind another car. You had your choice of laying back and letting the other car get far ahead or trying to pass it.

There were very few maps, so Dad bought the 1924 *Official Automobile Blue Book*, which covered the mid-Atlantic and Southeastern states. The 770-page bound volume cost $8. Here's an excerpt from page 609:

"Route 526R—Arcadia to Fort Pierce, Fla.—113.2 miles. Via Cabbage Bluff Ferry and Okeechobee. First 12 miles paved; 15 miles rather rough prairie road; 37 miles winding prairie road thru hummocks and pine woods; 3 miles graded sand to Okeechobee; then 12 miles pavement; 12 miles sand-clay; balance pavement.

"This route is to be used in dry weather only and is not recommended…at Cabbage Bluff ferry, the Kissimmee River is crossed on a frail scow hauled by a small motor rowboat. Raise flag on pole to attract attention of ferryman, who lives on the opposite side of the river. At 66.4 miles from Arcadia, fork at ferry house; right. At 73.6—end of road; right, avoiding left beyond. Avoid left at 74.3. At 75.9 fork, beyond small settlement; left. Thru 4 corners to 76.1…"

With instructions like that, how could you go wrong?

Luckily, the farmers along the way were very helpful with directions and often invited us in for a cool drink and cookies. Grandmother always left her address with them and invited them to visit her and Grandpa in Louisville.

Only a few towns had hotels, so if we couldn't find one, we'd stop at the country store and ask about a place to spend the night and have supper. Sometimes a boardinghouse could take us for a dollar a room and provide meals for another 25¢ each. Other times, the store owner would send us to neighbors up the street. We met a lot of great people this way.

The local residents were really wonderful. On one trip, our car broke down on a muddy road, and we sat there for a couple of hours. Finally, a farmer came along with a mule team and pulled us to the nearest village, with the mules' hooves throwing thick mud on us the whole way.

We found a man who was able to get the Nash running again, and, of course, Grandmother invited him and the farmer to visit her. As we parted, the farmer told us cars would never replace mules. We all had a good laugh and agreed with him that he might just be right. ❧

# 'Tin Can Tour' Featured Chiggers, Possums and Woodpeckers

*By Francis Brown*
*Woodbine, Maryland*

ith 3 weeks before school resumed at George Washington University in 1923, a classmate and I decided to drive from Washington, D.C. to Miami. We called it "the tin can tour".

Mac and I set off in a borrowed 1920 Model T. The pavement ended in Accotink, Virginia and, except for cities, it was dirt roads from then on. That night, we pitched our tent in a pine grove just outside Petersburg, Virginia.

Before we'd finished preparing dinner, a barefoot farmer and his sons showed up and offered us just-from-the-cow milk. It tasted awful!

We slept well on the pine needles, but woke to find we'd been adopted by chiggers. The itch was terrible, and none of our remedies seemed to help.

### Drove into a "Trap"

As we cruised along a dusty North Carolina road we were shocked to see a man jump into the road and wave us to a stop. A local sheriff, he told us we'd been speeding through the town of Wake Forest.

We could see no evidence of a town and asked where it began. "Back at that big tree," the sheriff said.

He asked why our car had two license tags (at the time, District of Columbia residents needed separate tags to drive in Maryland). I tried explaining there was no reciprocity between Maryland and D.C. but don't think he understood the word.

Then he asked what "D.C." was. After I told him, he asked if we worked for the government. Tongue in cheek, we assured him we did. At that point, he gave up and sent us on our way.

In Vass, North Carolina, we checked into a hotel and enjoyed a hot bath. But since it was Sunday, all the restaurants were closed—so "dinner" that night

was peanuts and candy we got from a vendor at the train station.

As we drove into Georgia, the roads got worse. We were directed onto "The Woodpeckers Highway", which was really a series of narrow wooden bridges through a swamp. We were horrified

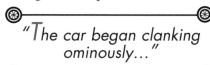

*"The car began clanking ominously..."*

this was called a "highway". Adding insult to injury, we had to pay tolls!

In Jacksonville, Florida, we found a lovely palm-lined park fronting a nice hotel. After enjoying one of the finest dinners we'd ever tasted, we took the car in for "routine maintenance".

Next morning, about 10 miles out of town, we smelled something strange. The right rear brake drum was white-

hot, so we limped to a country garage, where we learned the Jacksonville mechanic had left out the main bearing.

Route 1 took us over a brick-paved road to Daytona Beach. It was thrilling to drive on the hard-packed sand. Since it was dark and no one else was around, we took a swim in the raw. It was wonderful—and, incidentally, spelled the end of our chiggers!

### Meal for Mosquitoes

The next day, we drove to Palm Beach, admiring the homes and estates. Parking near the water's edge that night, we tried sleeping in the back of the car, but the mosquitoes were voracious.

Around dawn, we gave up and headed to Miami, where we found a campsite for auto tourists. Our accommodations consisted of a wooden platform with canvas sides and top for $1 a night.

Next day, the car began clanking ominously, then abruptly stopped. The universal joint had dropped off. This was a near-disaster financially and took 3 days to repair.

When the car was fixed, we started back along a different route, through the Blue Ridge Mountains and Shenandoah Valley. One memorable night in the hills of North Carolina, a group of local boys visited our camp and invited us to go possum hunting with them.

By the time we reached home, the Model T was limping badly, the tires were in poor shape and the brake and reverse bands were almost gone. We returned 20 days after we'd left, weary, happy and none the worse for wear.

Unfortunately, the same couldn't be said of our car. ❧

## Leather-Clad Newlyweds Dressed for the Road

MY PARENTS, Lawrence and Hope Klotz, left Seattle on their wedding day, October 12, 1919, and drove to San Jose, California—a trip that took them 2 months.

As you can see in the photo (below), they left town in their wedding clothes, which were all leather. Note where the bridal bouquet is!

It was probably just as well they weren't wearing regular clothes, because the roads were horrible—in some places, no more than a narrow path. And, of course, there was lots of mud and flat tires.

At one point, they got stuck in a mud hole. My father had to cut down a *tree*, put it under the rear axle and pry while Mother operated the throttle till they were out of their predicament!
—*Pat Wells, Oak Harbor, Washington*

*DO YOU KNOW THE WAY TO SAN JOSE?* It took honeymooners Lawrence and Hope Klotz 2 months to make it to San Jose from Seattle in 1919. The route they took would later become Highway 99.

## These Kansans Rode High on the Hog

IN THE EARLY '20s, my family and my aunt's family visited another aunt who lived in Poplar Bluff, Missouri (all the families involved in the trip lived in central Kansas).

My folks had a Star touring car to transport us five children. Mother's sister and her husband had a Model T for their two kids and a brother.

The first day, we got as far as Springfield, Missouri and spent the night camping in a park. On our second day of travel, we noticed that livestock seemed to have free range of the countryside.

At one point, a big razorback hog ran across the road and went right under my uncle's Model T. Then the car began moving sideways—that hog was so tall it was *carrying* the car on its back!

We kids thought this was all great fun, but the adults were afraid the car would end up in the ditch. Somehow, the hog freed itself and we journeyed on…until we came to muddy roads that slowed us down considerably. Finally, my father stopped the car to ask a woman beside the road how much farther we could expect to drive in mud. She answered, "A real smart piece!"

Well, it was nightfall when we finally arrived at my aunt and uncle's farm home, 500 miles from where we started. And, just like the lady had said, it had been "a real smart piece".
—*Bessie Suffield Florence, Kansas*

## "Whistle Stop" Nearly Did Dad in

AFTER my Grandpa and Grandma Marshall moved from Illinois to a farm near Klemme, Iowa, we didn't get to see them as often as we had when they lived in the next county. So, when Papa bought our first car, a 1917 Model T, we made plans to drive out to visit them.

All of Mother's family (including her three brothers) now lived in Iowa, so she was quite eager to see them. But first, she thought it might be a good idea to buy some little things at the dime store for us kids to play with during our 2-day trip.

However, her choice for my little brother, John, was not one of her better ideas. Being a new driver, Papa was concentrating mightily on his driving and was far from relaxed. Just as we came to a railroad crossing, Johnny decided to try out his new whistle.

Poor Papa! Thinking for sure that a train was bearing down on us, he slammed on the brakes, then made a right-hand sweep up along the side of the tracks. Needless to say, that was the end of that whistle.

Although it about scared Papa to death, it sure made for a great family story in the years to come.
—*Mildred Blaum New Holland, Illinois*

*ILLINOIS-TO-IOWA "EXPRESS".* Mildred Blaum (above right) and her sister were along for the ride to their grandparents' house when a little brother's toy nearly gave their dad a heart attack! The car shown in this photo belonged to Mildred's grandparents.

## Florida-Bound Flint Faced Many an Obstacle

MY FAMILY took a trip from rural Edina, Minnesota to St. Petersburg, Florida in our Flint in 1928. Motels were scarce and expensive—as much as $3 a night—so we camped along the way instead.

Half the roads were dirt then, and a deluge the first day found us stuck in the mud in Iowa. We waited an hour for another car to come along—and then that car got stuck, too!

A few days later, while driving in the mountains of Tennessee, Dad took a shortcut and got lost. He stopped to ask a fellow for directions, which went something like this:

"Go to the cherry tree in the middle of the road, then look yonder a distance. You'll see a narrow wood bridge. Cross it slowly, as the boards fly up behind you. Then keep going a piece and you'll come to your highway."

That "piece" was 20 miles! Next day, a detour took us over a logging road through the woods and across a couple of streams. Midway through the second stream, Dad stopped the car. Water was seeping through the floorboards, and he couldn't see a trail on the opposite bank.

We managed to climb the bank anyway, then drove through a wooded area. To get back to our highway, we all had to get out so Dad could get a running start up a steep embankment.

Our closest call came when Dad got tired of following in another car's dust and sped up to pass him at 55 miles an hour. But there was so much dust that he couldn't see.

He missed a curve in the road, and, with camp gear flying everywhere, we plunged down an embankment!

Miraculously, the car didn't tip over. When it stopped, we got out, retrieved everything and then waited while Dad made a run back up the embankment. From then on, he held his speed at a steady 35 miles an hour.

We had almost reached our destination when we camped for the night on the hard white sand of Daytona Beach. Much to our surprise, we woke up in the water—the tide had come in overnight!

You can bet we were very glad to reach St. Petersburg the next day.

—*Natalie Gammey*
*Calimesa, California*

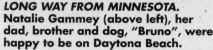

***LONG WAY FROM MINNESOTA.*** **Natalie Gammey (above left), her dad, brother and dog, "Bruno", were happy to be on Daytona Beach.**

## "Spring Fling" Soured Dad's Outlook

WE LIVED on a homestead near Vermilion, Alberta in 1927. On Sundays, my parents, my sister, Eunice, and I dutifully attended church.

We drove across the prairie in our Model T to get there. One spring Sunday on our way home, the day was warming nicely, but we still had a coulee to cross and a hill to climb.

That's about when the Model T got stuck in the softening soil. Mother took the wheel while Dad got behind to push. She pulled down the gas lever on the steering wheel and the engine roared.

Then she stepped on the low-gear pedal and, with wheels spinning and mud flying, we slowly emerged from that soft spot. But when Dad came around from the back of the car, we saw that he was completely covered with mud!

And he was *not* happy about it. The rest of the trip was made in complete silence (although, in the backseat, my sister and I had a hard time holding back the giggles).

—*Harvey Rankin*
*Stony Plain, Alberta*

***SPRING ON THE PRAIRIE.*** **Spirits were high when Harvey Rankin's mom took this photo of him, his sister and his dad (see story above).**

**IT COULD'VE BEEN WORSE.** Actually, this Iowa road in 1919 looks fairly dry. Imagine what it would be like trying to drive on it after a heavy rain!

# Puncture Parade Didn't Stop Determined Pair

*By Fred Culp, Nappanee, Indiana*

After graduating from high school in Nappanee, Indiana in 1928, I decided it was time for an adventure in the West. With money I'd earned over the summer, I bought a 1924 Model T touring car for $55.

My friend Dale Watts and I loaded the car with camping gear, tools, extra tires and rims, plus a can of white enamel paint and a brush. We were so proud of our packed Model T—it was "real sporty", as they said in those days.

Before pulling out of Nappanee on September 26, we painted an outline of Indiana on the left side of the hood. As we traveled, we added to our "map" to show the route we'd followed.

On the second day, we arrived in St. Louis—the first big city we'd ever seen. A parking garage became our sleeping quarters that evening.

Next morning, the Mississippi River stretched out beside us as we sped along toward Cape Girardeau, Missouri. We made good time, but in Arkansas, we said farewell to paved roads as we crossed plank roads over the swamps. We took a ferry across the Mississippi over to Memphis—another big city for two awed Hoosiers to explore.

### Perfected Patching

Then the roads turned to gravel, and flat tires became a way of life. The rubber tires punctured easily, with shredded rubber flying in all directions. With all the practice we got, Dale and I became a well-orchestrated patching crew.

In Batesville, Mississippi, we slept on bales of cotton at a cotton gin, but were awakened early by the night watchman, who told us to move along. The next 75 miles were bumpy, and by the time we reached Winona, Mississippi, the old Model T needed a new spring.

Upon our arrival in Jackson, we were glad to walk about and stabilize our bouncing bodies. Next stop was New Orleans, truly an exciting place for two boys from the Midwest.

We spent 2 days in New Orleans, then headed for Texas. It took 4 days to cross that state, and the gravel and graded dirt roads were challenging. Even with eight tires and rims, we were forced to buy a new tire!

**HOOSIER HOTSHOTS.** Fred Culp (right) and his friend Dale Watts can be forgiven for looking pleased with themselves. Their car took them 3,000 miles.

We entered the deserts of New Mexico on October 9 and were greatly amused by the way the roadrunners there would race our Model T down the road!

By the time we drove into Arizona, the hand-painted map of our journey stretched around the back of the Ford and up the right side.

During our first sandstorm in the California desert, the Model T filled up with about 2 inches of sand. After following intermittent plank roads through the desert, we welcomed the paved roads into Los Angeles.

The painted outline of California on our "auto map" was completed on the right hood of the Model T—so our paint job now encircled the entire chassis.

Gasoline on our trip averaged 25¢ a gallon, but Los Angeles was having a gas war when we arrived, so prices dropped to 10 or 12¢—a dollar was enough to fill our tank!

Dale and I took 2 weeks to soak up the sunshine and surf of the Los Angeles area. Hollywood was just in the making, and the Pacific Ocean sprawled before us. The excitement and bustle were considerably different from what we were used to back home in Nappanee.

Our trip was the adventure of a lifetime for two recent high school graduates. In 17 days, we had driven 3,000 miles through 11 states—and patched a grand total of 52 flats!

**WHERE DO WE GO FROM HERE?** During the course of an 8,000-mile trip in this little Model T in 1926, Blen Shaver and a friend crossed the western prairie on this "superhighway". Blen, of Ithaca, Michigan, recalls they traveled through 17 states and averaged one flat per day.

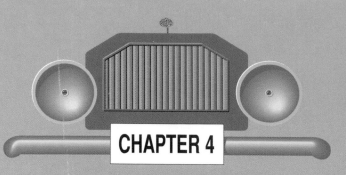

# CHAPTER 4

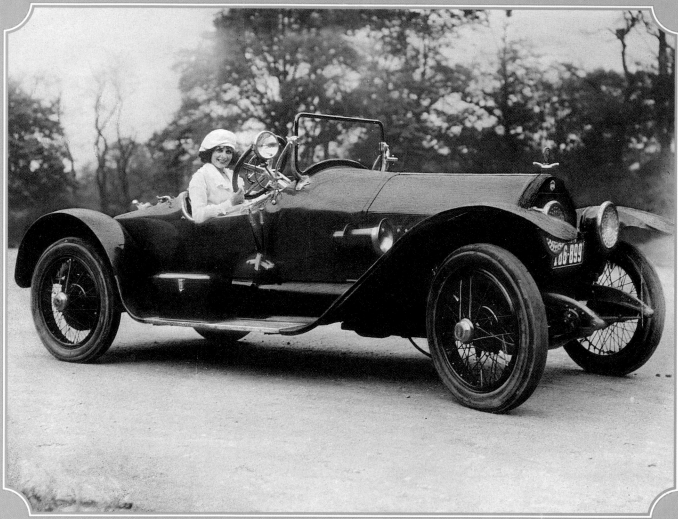

Brown Brothers (hand-tinted by Melissa Burghart)

*AGE OF OPTIMISM.* This Stutz Blackhawk could well have symbolized the enthusiasm characterizing the automobile industry in the '20s. With the economy going strong and more reliable cars coming out every year, the future never seemed brighter. After averaging over 106 miles per hour in a test at Daytona, the stylish low-slung Blackhawk was deemed the fastest production car in America in 1928.

# Roaring Through the '20s

I t's startling to be reminded that automobiles brought a whole new category of recreation into American lives. Nowadays, we think of cars as necessities that carry us to work or school or the grocery store or wherever—essential "appliances" in today's scheme of things.

But when they became part of the American landscape, autos also added a huge new dimension of pleasure to our lives. Once you had an auto, whether it was a Stanley Steamer or a Model T Ford or an Essex, your world miraculously expanded. Cars were the Seven League boots of this century.

The leap from the Horse-and-Buggy Age to the Auto Age amounted to a revolution in how we lived. Cars were still in their infancy when I was a kid in the 1920s. They were crotchety and cantankerous and prone to fainting spells.

## Those Cars Had Character

But those very flaws were what gave them a personality. Our cars were part of the family. Their quirks were mostly forgiven, just as we refused to be upset by goofy Uncle Leroy, who occasionally played the ocarina on street corners downtown.

At social gatherings, men now talked more about cars and less about politics. They compared gas mileage figures, knowing that everyone stretched the truth just a little bit. They debated the merits of different makes and models and boasted of their newfound skills as amateur mechanics.

At one gathering of the Strock clan, an uncle from Chicago showed up with an impressive new Studebaker. He alleged that it would do 60 miles per hour, a claim that was met with such massive skepticism that he finally took the doubters out for a demonstration.

I managed to squeeze into the backseat. He drove to one of the few pieces of pavement in the area and, by golly, we soon were zooming along at 60. What a tale I had for envious friends in school on Monday!

## Better Than Today—in Some Ways

With all their problems, those early cars had some features that were endearing. For example, they had no-nonsense bumpers, not today's fragile plastic ornaments.

The rear bumper on our Willys was absolutely essential for toting a 50-pound block of ice home from the ice plant. It also was rugged enough that you could push a stalled motorist until his engine kicked over. Bump into a sack of marshmallows these days and you're facing a $600 repair bill.

An earlier car—I suspect it was an Overland—had little flower vases on the post between the front and back doors. I don't recall anyone actually putting flowers in them, but it was a classy touch. That car had another feature I would welcome today, a pull-down window shade in the back window.

Those early autos also had running boards, a feature especially appreciated by ladies in long skirts as they climbed up into the high-riding vehicles.

And if the movies of that era are to be believed, running boards were essential for police chasing bank robbers. Cops stood on the running boards, blazing away at the bad guys. Today they just stick their gun hand out the window—somehow it's just not the same.

Little pop-up vents in front of the windshield were a blessing in hot weather. However, I recall the day we drove through a swarm of bees and instantly had a car filled with the angry critters. We all escaped unstung, but Mom decreed that the vent would never again be opened while *she* was in the car!

Like any other teenager, the autos of the '20s were stumbling their way into maturity, learning as the manufacturers went along. All in all, they did pretty well.

—*Clancy Strock*

**AN OWNER, BUT NOT AN OPERATOR.** Tom Davis' older brother, Perry (above), won this race car, but to his lasting regret, he never got to drive it. However, his lucky little brother did! (See his story below.)

# Miniature 'Barney Oldfield' Blasted Off on a Sunday Morning

*By Tom Davis, Colquitt, Georgia*

Back in 1920, my 15-year-old brother, Perry, had a Saturday job at a grocery store near our home in Lafayette, Indiana.

In those days, shoppers were waited on one item at a time, and he was being bothered by a fellow bent on selling him a 50¢ raffle ticket for a race car.

Perry explained that he didn't *have* 50¢. "Look," insisted the man, "this is the last ticket. The drawing's in an hour. Take it now and you can pay me back later!"

"Okay, okay," Perry replied, cramming the ticket into his pocket and turning back to take orders from his customers. An hour later, the fellow returned to the store, shouting, "Hey, kid! You won!"

### Dad Was *Not* Delighted

For some reason, our father was not overjoyed with the news that his son was now the proud owner of a race car. In fact, he warned Perry that he could get himself killed fooling with it and told him the car would have to go.

So, my enterprising brother made arrangements to sell it to a group of taxi drivers. Meanwhile, unbeknownst to Dad, Perry plotted with me to take an unauthorized early-morning spin on a stretch of pavement west of town.

I was only 10 years old, with absolutely no driving experience, yet I was the one who ended up behind the wheel of that race car that morning.

Early racers were designed to go forward and fast. There was no reverse, only a hand lever for braking, and the windshield was a metal cowling to deflect the air stream over the driver's head.

The car could be put in gear and the engine started by pushing it off. A large exhaust pipe extended from the engine manifold to the rear end without benefit of a muffler so, as you can imagine, the noise was deafening.

During pit stops, tires were changed by spinning the wheel backward, popping a spare wheel on the spindle and then going ahead (if the car were rolled backward, all four wheels came off).

### Engine Start Went Awry

At daybreak on Sunday morning, after we'd towed the racer to the site, we were ready for a trial run. The plan was for Perry to push me a few feet to start the engine, then I'd hop out and let him take over.

When the engine roared into action, I hit a few strokes on the pump in the cockpit to supercharge the carburetor. But when I stepped on the accelerator …var-r-R-O-O-o-om!

In a few short seconds, I was out of sight! To make matters worse, the cowl-

> *"The plan was for Perry to push me…"*

ing blocked my view of the road ahead —I could barely see the right shoulder of the pavement to line up with the world flying by.

Still, what an incredible thrill for a 10-year-old! Reluctantly, I took my foot off the pedal and applied the emergency brake with all my might, coasting a "country mile" before my brother finally caught up with me.

That was the end of our racing career. By mutual agreement, we decided it probably wouldn't be a good idea to tell Dad about our little trial run. And we never did.

**SHINING UP THE METZ.** It was an October afternoon in Boonton, New Jersey in 1920 when (with her father's permission) Idamay Demmers Loiselle "polished" the family's Metz with wet leaves. Idamay, who now lives in Miami, Florida, recalls that her mother was not particularly happy to see her daughter walk into the house later with a very dirty dress.

## If She'd Known They Were Coming, She'd Have Baked a Cake

ONE SUMMER in the early 1920s, we were on a vacation trip to Maine when our car broke down out in the country. While waiting for a mechanic to arrive from the nearest town, we all got hungry.

So Dad walked to a farmhouse and asked the lady there if she could fix us something to eat. She said she didn't have much, but if we would wait, she'd do the best she could.

After a while, she called us inside and we sat down to one of the most memorable meals I've ever eaten. The good lady served ham, chicken, homegrown vegetables, fresh biscuits with home-churned butter along with puddings, pies and the richest milk I've ever tasted.

After the meal, Dad asked our hostess how much he owed her. She told him she couldn't accept anything, but Dad insisted. "Would a quarter be too much?" she finally asked.

When Dad handed her a $5 bill (there were four of us), the lady almost fainted. —*Daniel Joy, Largo, Florida*

## The New Car Owner's "Badge of Honor"

UP UNTIL 1927 (when electric starters became common), most automobiles of the '20s had to be hand-cranked to start. When cranking the engine, you had to be very careful not to fold your thumb over the crank.

Instead, you cupped it down by the first finger. This was to prevent a broken thumb— or worse, a broken arm!—if the engine backfired. Yes, owning a car then was a real joy.

Once I saw a friend walking down the street with a sling on his arm and a big smile on his face. I said, "Hi—I see you have a new car."

Grinning even wider, he said, "I sure do!"
—*Fred Dawley, Williamsburg, Virginia*

*A CLOSE SCRAPE.* Claude Hyde invented "automated" snow removal in Otisville, New York.

## Was Dad's Detroiter the First Snowplow?

MY FATHER, Claude Hyde, was among the first in Otisville, New York to own an automobile. And, like most early drivers, he had a tough time in winter when roads were piled high with snow and rutted from horses and sleighs.

So, in 1917, Dad invented a snowplow that cleared narrow paths of snow in front of each wheel of his Detroiter. In 1920, he refined his design, adding a third V-shaped plow in the center of the bumper.

He even received a patent on his technological breakthrough (several publications—including *Popular Mechanics*—did stories on it).

Although it was never sold commercially, Dad enjoyed going around town when it snowed, plowing roads and driveways for friends. —*Florence House Hartford, Connecticut*

**THE CLEAN MACHINE.** Allan Wood, a Louisiana traveling salesman for Procter & Gamble, drove this Model T on his route in Plaquemines Parish in 1922. Alan's daughter, Vivienne Lindsay of Lancaster, California, says her father told her he sometimes had to take along an interpreter because the storekeepers didn't always speak English.

## Smiley Faces and "Giants" Enlivened Family Trip

IN 1921, our family of six decided to drive from Rochester to Fort Ann, New York to visit relatives. My aunt, uncle and two cousins also came along in their own car.

It was at least a 10-hour trip, which is why we left at 4 in the morning. We were all packed and ready to go when Dad came out of the garage with a can of black roofing cement and a stick. He proceeded to paint two eyes, a nose and a mouth on our headlights. That way, my uncle could be sure it was us in the car following him.

At another memorable point in the trip, our cousins in the car ahead decided to have some fun. Ray ducked his head and put his legs out one side of the car. Then his brother, Grant, stuck his head and arms out the other side. It looked like someone 10 to 12 feet tall was in the backseat! —*Donald Fisher Rochester, New York*

*ESSEX OUTFITS. Arthur Blake Jr. (the boy on the running board) and the rest of his family were dressed for the road in this '20s photo.*

### Essex Battery Made Quick Getaway

IT WAS COMMON to see breakdowns during our Sunday drives in the early 1920s. One Sunday when we were returning to our home in Atlanta, Georgia, our Essex stopped running and *we* were the ones who needed help.

A man who lived nearby walked over and asked what the problem was. He found the answer when he looked under the driver's seat—we had no battery! Apparently, acid had leaked out

*SHINY BUT SCARCE. Ellen Wilmeth of Dunnellon, Florida isn't exactly sure what kind of car this is—the license plate says 1920—but, given its unfamiliar shape, it's likely that few of them survived past the '30s. Ellen notes both the driver and the little girl (who is still living) were cousins of hers.*

and eaten away the metal straps that normally held it in place.

Glancing down the highway behind us, we saw our battery sitting in the middle of the road! We retrieved it, fashioned a cradle for it from a coat hanger and were on our way again. —*Arthur Blake Jr., Tucker, Georgia*

### Mom's Confidence Level Was a Bit Low

MY PARENTS bought a new Model T touring car in 1922.

After watching Daddy drive and asking lots of questions, Mother thought she could drive it. But, since Daddy took the car to work every day, she just didn't have the opportunity to practice.

Then one day when Daddy went to work with someone else, Mother decided to drive around the neighborhood by herself. But before she left, she gave the house a thorough cleaning—just in case she landed in the hospital!

Fortunately, her solo driving lesson went all right and she was able to tell Daddy all about it later…in a spotless house. —*Aileen Morley Willoughby, Ohio*

*OUTDOOR DINING AT ITS BEST. This trusty Model T had taken its passengers to a grove of redwoods along the Oregon coast near Sunset Bay. Ethel Briggs of New Martinsville, West Virginia (shown below with her mother and a family friend) tells us this particular camping trip took place in 1923.*

# Resourceful Duo Made Their Own Adventure

*By Renee Hermanson, San Antonio, Texas*

"California, here we come" was easier said than done in 1920—especially if you had to build a car to make the trip! But that's just what my father, Spencer Anst, and his friend Lyman Swenson did in an abandoned icehouse in Greenfield, South Dakota.

The two not-yet-20 dreamers bought a used B37 Buick and began working to transform it into what Dad called a "race car". They didn't plan on racing it, but a sporty look would no doubt add a certain flair to their adventure.

Dad, a born mechanic, rebuilt the engine, while Lyman did the body and assembly work. The modifications they made included shortening the wheelbase, installing lighter pistons and replacing the original cast-iron valves to lighten the car's weight.

### Dream Trip Was Nearly Canceled

When finished, they'd transformed that Buick into a "souped-up" roadster. The transformation took 2 years, then, just as they were about to leave, a field hand from a neighboring farm collided with their car, sending it back to the shop for repairs!

"We almost gave up," Dad recalled. "But we didn't want people to say that we'd been bragging about the trip but never intended to go."

When they finally did leave, Dad and Lyman headed south to Wichita, through Colorado, then south again to Yuma, Arizona before entering California—all without maps or guidebooks.

"We made our own route," Dad remembered, "inquiring along the way about which roads were the best." And they didn't worry much about car trouble.

"Anything mechanical can fail," Dad said, "but we made up our minds we were going to make it. If we were stalled on the road, we took any available job until we'd earned money for repairs."

A broken axle between Santa Fe and Albuquerque, New Mexico caused one such delay. While Lyman stayed with the car, Dad had to carry the broken part to the nearest railroad track and wait for the next train to come by (in those days, trains would stop anywhere for anyone).

Dad got a ride into the nearest town, where the axle could be repaired. When it was finished, he hopped another train back to where Lyman had been waiting and they were ready to move on.

Many of the roads they traveled followed railroad routes—sometimes *very* closely, as they discovered one morning when a train chugged alarmingly close to the tent they'd pitched in the dark the previous night!

### Road Went on Forever

Other times, the road was no more than tracks across vast unpopulated areas. "Choose your rut and stay there," was the driver's motto, says Dad.

**BUICK BUDDIES.** Spencer Anst (above right) and his good friend Lyman Swenson traveled all the way to California in this vehicle that started its life as a standard Buick. But by the time these two "designers" were through with it, it had been transformed into a one-of-a-kind "roadster" that attracted attention wherever it went.

*John C. Lowe Jr./Zaatsch-Hupp Photo*

*"It took those South Dakota boys 2 weeks to reach California..."*

It took those South Dakota boys about 2 weeks to reach California. They spent the winter there, working in Lyman's uncle's orchards and vineyards.

They also got a taste of the more freewheeling atmosphere of that Western state. Driving along one day, they noticed a car following closely. After a while, they pulled over and it pulled in behind them.

"We weren't speeding," Dad says, "but we figured we must have attracted the attention of the police." The car *had* attracted attention all right—but not from the police!

The two men who got out and asked how fast the car could go were bootleggers looking for a fast getaway vehicle, and Dad and Lyman had to politely turn down the men's offer to buy their car.

During his short stay, Dad fell in love with California and planned to return the following year. A broken arm (and a romance that led to marriage) postponed that trip for over 20 years.

It was 1943 when he finally returned to the land of his dreams in a Ford sedan filled with his wife and family. That trip, while still exciting, was a lot less adventurous than the first one.

At 96, Dad still loves recalling his first trip to California, usually ending with, "We sure had fun with that car!" ❧

OAKLAND FOR AN ORPHAN. Marlys Ryker of Jeffers, Minnesota says she'll never forget her first ride in this Overland in 1921. That's because she had just been adopted, and her new parents were taking her from the orphanage to her new home in Lamberton, Minnesota. Unlike the Overland in Roy Claus' story (below), this one never challenged a streetcar.

LITTLEST "RIFLEMAN". The "sharpshooter" above and at right is Janet Zimmerman of Phoenix, Arizona. When this photo was taken in 1922, automobiles enabled families like Janet's to take long camping trips. Janet says they shot their own game and caught their own fish in the wilds of Utah—so a rifle was an important part of their gear.

# Hoosier Hazards Included Streetcars and Cigars

*By Roy Claus, Sun Lakes, Arizona*

Growing up in the early '20s in Anderson, Indiana, I either walked or took the streetcar. Then one grand day in 1922, Dad came home with a 1914 Model T.

He'd purchased it from two young men for the magnificent sum of $10. It had no body, no floorboards and no glass in the windshield. The modifications he made would land him in jail today—back then, they only elicited curious stares.

For starters, Dad covered the windshield with 1-by-4-inch boards! To drive, he either looked over them or peered through a wide crack he'd left at eye level.

### Watch Your Feet!

He also installed a front seat atop the gas tank—a wooden box padded with burlap bags. It worked fine, as long as you didn't let your feet hang down— one day when she was learning to drive, Mother ran off a gravel road, and I burned my bare toe on the transmission.

One day Dad sold the Model T for $10 and bought a 1918 Overland touring car. Now we had a top we could raise, and side curtains to keep out the wind and rain.

But this car also had very skinny tires. One time, we were driving to town on a cold icy day, and the left wheels ended up in the center of the streetcar tracks. We tried moving over, but the wheels stayed inside the rail, so we just drove on toward town.

### Something Had to Give

Unfortunately, we encountered a streetcar going the opposite way and came to a stop, nose to nose. The motorman kept stomping on his bell, so Dad started blowing his horn. Finally, the streetcar passengers got off and lifted our wheels off the rail and everyone went on their way.

Our next vehicle was a 1924 Dodge touring car. At its top speed of 35 miles

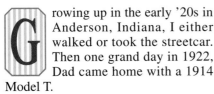

Bart Johnson/Unicorn Stock Photos

per hour, the left front fender vibrated in harmony with the engine (giving a very good imitation of a Ford trimotor plane roaring down a runway).

Motorists passing us on the left at 36 miles per hour would yell over and ask whether we could "get her off the ground"!

The next occupant of our garage was rather dainty, sort of like the well-dressed daughter of a prosperous Model T. I was told it was a 1925 Overland Redbird. On top of each rear fender was an egg-shaped light on a little pedestal, with a blue "jewel" on the front and a red one on the back.

### Forget the Brick

And—wonder of wonders!—it had a heater (actually an exhaust pipe covered with heavy mesh). The only automobile "heater" I'd seen before that was a hot brick.

Our last vehicle before moving into the marvelous new age of art-deco streamlining and advanced '30s technology was a 1928 Chevrolet two-door coach. It was dark green, with a black top and fenders, green disk wheels and green corduroy upholstery.

That car had only *one* bad characteristic: Every cigar butt Dad threw out the front window flew in the back window and hit me in the face! ♪

## Mom Lost Shoving Contest With Family Chevy

MY PARENTS bought their first car, a new Chevrolet, in 1921. With no traffic on the roads around our home near Artesian, South Dakota, learning to drive was simple.

One spring afternoon when I was about 5 months old, Mother decided to visit her sister-in-law, who lived about 3 miles away. So she tucked me into the top of my buggy and placed the buggy in the backseat.

There were no roads between our house and Aunt Josephine's, but horse and buggy tracks had worn a path for Mother to follow. However, there were fences, and one of them didn't have a gate to let vehicles through. This one required the wire fence to be let down to the ground between two fence posts.

Somehow, as Mother was letting down the fence, the car started rolling forward. Fearing for my life, she valiantly and foolishly jumped in front of the car and tried to hold it back. Of course, the car was stronger and heavier and it ran right over her!

Miraculously, the car's skinny wheels didn't touch her and, thanks to the engine's high ground clearance, she didn't even suffer a scratch. Scrambling to her feet, Mother rushed to the backseat...where she found a laughing baby who'd actually reveled in the bouncing!

Though Mother drove on to visit Aunt Josephine, it would be some 27 years before she worked up the nerve to get behind the wheel of a car again.

—*Eleanore Moe*
*Rapid City, South Dakota*

**SAFE SPOT.** Eleanore Moe's mother preferred the passenger seat after one particularly bad driving experience.

**TIME TO HIT THE ROAD.** This homemade "crutchless carriage" (see story below) looked a lot like a go-cart—and was probably just as much fun to drive.

## Crutches Couldn't Keep Uncle Housebound

MY UNCLE FRED was a shoemaker in the early 1920s, and his shop bustled with customers. Then one day, his little shop caught fire and burned to the ground. In a valiant effort to save it, Uncle Fred lost one of his legs.

After hobbling around on crutches for a while, he was determined to find some way to transport himself from place to place. Unable to afford a car, he *built* a vehicle to meet his needs.

The design was simple: Four fendered bicycle wheels were rigged upon a sturdy wooden platform with a steering wheel and a comfortable adjustable seat. An engine with a fifth fendered wheel at the rear center powered forward motion (a gas tank sat atop the engine fender).

This simple vehicle was even provided with a Utah license plate...plus it featured plenty of fresh air!

—*Fred Vreeken, Layton, Utah*

***WINDOW DRESSING.*** The shiny new car and fashionable driving clothes at left were part of a Lansing, Michigan department store display, according to Annie-Laurie Robinson of Williamston, Michigan. By the early '20s, the automobile's popularity had not only changed the way folks got around, it was beginning to influence the way they dressed.

**THE FIRST TURN SIGNAL?** Besides building race cars (see story below), Oscar Swanson invented this turn signal about 1922. It used an electromagnetic coil that activated an arrow indicating the direction of the turn.

**COLLISION IN CLEVELAND.** This little Ford coupe fared badly in a bout with a Cleveland lamppost one night in 1926, says Howard Wise of South Euclid, Ohio.

## A Race Only a "Mudder" Could Love

MY FATHER, Oscar Swanson, was born in Gothenburg, Nebraska in 1894 and was an automobile enthusiast from the time he saw his first car. For a couple years around 1915, he even owned his own Overland dealership.

He finally gave up that business after getting tired of going around town on cold mornings and starting all the cars he'd sold. After that, he built and sold race cars and also raced them.

One story he liked to tell was about a race at the Dawson County Fair in Lexington, Nebraska. It had rained for several days and the track was very muddy. After looking over the track, Dad entered his Model T truck in the race (rather than the racer he'd hauled to the fairgrounds with that same truck).

Dad suspected that the race cars were built so low that they'd all get stuck in the mud. The race committee laughed when he entered the Model T truck, but no protests were heard.

Then, once the race started, all the race cars got stuck before they'd gone halfway around the track. Meanwhile, that Model T had no problems at all. So, Dad drove the truck around the track the required number of times and went to collect the winning money.

A heated argument ensued about whether it was legal to enter the truck, but Dad stuck to his guns. After he'd pointed out that there was nothing in the rules about the type of vehicle to be entered, he collected his prize money.
—*Paul Swanson*
*Round Lake Beach, Illinois*

## "Makin' Whoopee" A Real '20s Treat

I'M NOT SURE whether "whoopee roads" were a phenomenon peculiar to the Los Angeles area in the early 1920s, but about that time, my dad, Zach Magnes, and a friend built a car out of scrapped automobile parts.

They were very proud of this accomplishment (and of their kids), so they took turns driving us around the neighborhood.

My brother was 2 and I was 4 when Dad discovered "the whoopee road" and decided to try it out. For a 10¢ fee, we were allowed to drive up and down big mounds of packed earth arranged in a semicircle on a vacant lot.

Everything went fine until the day a bolt suddenly broke loose, and the hood flipped off the car and clanged down the embankment.

Our screams of delight turned to screams of fear. Daddy stopped, calmed us down, picked up the hood and continued on.

Trips to our beloved whoopee road became a special children's treat for the next couple of years—until the day we discovered, to our dismay, that it had been leveled for the construction of a building. So much for progress!
—*Margaret Olesen*
*Gardnerville, Nevada*

**"OFF-ROAD" VEHICLE.** Zach Magnes (standing) posed proudly with a home-built auto that spent plenty of time bouncing around in vacant lots near Los Angeles, California in the '20s (see his daughter's story above).

# Dad's Delivery Team Met Every Challenge

*By Glenn Miller*
*Burlington, North Carolina*

**M**y father, a dealer for a Hupmobile Agency in Luray, Virginia, acquired a four-cylinder Monroe Roadster in 1920. At the time, my brother Guy was working in Ossipee, North Carolina, about 225 miles away.

Guy wanted the roadster, but the problem was how to get it to him. "The solution," Papa announced, "is to let Ike and Glenn deliver it to him."

Mama said she didn't want two young boys (Ike was 17, I was 15) making a trip like that by themselves. But Papa claimed it would be a good experience and he eventually won out.

The roadster's self-starter was broken, so we had to hand-crank it to start it. We left around 6 o'clock on a Friday

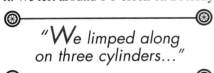

*"We limped along on three cylinders..."*

morning. On the other side of the Blue Ridge Mountains, we were sailing along on a dirt road when we came to a stream overflowing because of heavy rains.

We were just about across when the car flooded and stopped. Ike crawled out on the front fender and dried out the distributor, but he didn't realize he'd lost a small spring.

Well, it was my turn to crank! I waded out to the bank and cranked the car, but, because of the lost spring, it ran on only three cylinders.

### Boost from Little Brother

We limped along on three cylinders —Ike driving and me pushing on the hills—until we arrived at a blacksmith shop. The blacksmith looked at our distributor and said, "You lost a small spring. I'll make a replacement for you."

He did, and we left—hitting on all four once again. It began to get dark and we turned the lights on. Lo and behold, there was a short circuit and the lights

**ON THE CASE.** Back in 1924, you probably wouldn't have wanted the two sober-looking gentlemen at far right on your tail. That's because they were detectives with the Cleveland Police Department, says Howard Wise of South Euclid, Ohio. And, of course, that shiny vehicle they've just gassed up also belonged to the police department.

kept going on and off! Fortunately, we soon came to a country store, where we told the owner we needed a place to stay. "Come and spend the night at my house," he told us.

He gave us a late supper, a nice place to sleep and breakfast the next morning. When we were ready to leave, we asked how much we owed. "Not a cent, and stop in again when you are down this way," was the reply.

We got in the car and I went to crank—but there *was* no crank. We'd lost it while plowing through the mud! This same nice gentleman then got out his tractor, gave us a push and off we went again.

On Saturday, we continued all day—Ike driving and me pushing when necessary—until we came to Ruffin, North Carolina. That night, we found a bed on the second floor of a store. Sunday morning, we got someone to push us off with high hopes of getting to Ossipee by noon.

Everything went well until we were 3 miles from our destination. That's when we got stuck in

a mud hole and the motor stopped. There we were in a mud hole, motor stopped and no crank!

### Back in Business

From experience, we'd learned that you could start a car by jacking up the right rear wheel and giving her a spin or two. We got out in the mud and found a large stone and cedar pole.

We placed the stone under the axle and, using the pole for leverage, spun the wheel a few times. Soon the motor caught and we were back in business!

We got out of the mud, arriving in Ossipee at noon on Sunday, dirty and hungry. That 225-mile trip had taken us 2-1/2 days—a trip you can now do in 5 hours.

But Papa was right when he said it would be a good experience. It really was. ✎

# Crawdad 'Express' Took Snakes And Streetcars in Stride

*By Everett Ray Lane (as told to Talova Lane Jones Oklahoma City, Oklahoma)*

One day in the summer of 1925, my wife's parents decided to travel from their home in Henryetta, Oklahoma to visit relatives in Excelsior Springs, Missouri. Ma and Pa asked my wife, Ruby, and I to come along (we were 18 and 17, respectively).

Also on the trip were Ruby's younger brother, Jim, and her sister Susie, 13. Ma had traded a milk cow for an old Model T, a five-passenger touring car. After packing our bedding and clothes on the running board and putting food from Ma's garden under the rear seat, we were ready to roll.

Every tire on that Model T was almost completely worn out, so we took lots of tire patches. The first day, we had about 20 flats, but we did make it to Tulsa—a whole 65 miles!

While fixing a flat, we'd often hear the hissing of another tire losing air. Just before dark, we pulled off the side of the road.

We couldn't go too far off since, once the car cooled, we couldn't get it started again (we were banking on someone coming by to pull us every morning).

After we'd made camp, Ma worked her usual miracles with the garden stuff pulled from under the rear seat. Next morning, fortified with a campfire breakfast, we loaded the car and stepped out on the highway to hail a passing motorist.

In those days, it wasn't hard to get a helping hand. Everybody needed some kind of help and seemed to understand the other guy's problems.

Our top speed was only 20 miles per hour, but we weren't worried—we had plenty of food and plenty of time. The second night, we slept on the porch of an abandoned house along the road.

Shortly after we'd gone to bed, I looked up to see a snake hanging from a tree limb below the porch! Since everyone was so tired, I decided I'd watch it awhile and maybe it would slither off somewhere. But then I fell asleep.

The next morning, Susie told me that she had seen the snake, too, and, like me, was "just watching it". I think we were both just too scared to move!

On the third day, while the men changed a flat, we made the mistake of sending Susie to get water from a nearby well. We all had a long cool drink and felt really refreshed ...until Susie confessed that, as she'd pulled the bucket out of the well, a big frog had jumped out!

Near Lawrence, Kansas, a tire split open and neither spare would hold an inner tube. We stuffed rags in one tire, then wrapped it with baling wire to hold it on the rim.

That worked until we were about halfway across the bridge going into Kansas City, Missouri—we didn't even stop to pick up the tire; we just kept driving on the rim!

## "Perfect" Fit Meant Trouble

Unfortunately, those clincher-type wheels were just wide enough to fit over a streetcar track. As fate would have it, the wheel slipped over the track.

Meanwhile, a streetcar came up from behind and started clanging its bell. This went on for about 10 minutes, before we came to a curve in the track and I was finally able to yank the wheel off.

The old Ford quit for good 5 miles from our destination, and relatives had to come pick us up. That didn't bother us since the trip had been so much fun.

Next morning, I decided to try and fix the Ford. I took the head off the motor and the first thing I saw was a large crawdad lying on top of a piston!

I cleaned the mud off the pistons and valves, took out the crawdad and put the head back on the motor. Then I started cranking and—believe it or not—with just one little twist, that old Ford came to life and ran better than it had the whole way!

> *"While fixing a flat, we'd often hear the hissing of another tire losing air..."*

**ROCKY MOUNTAIN ROAD TRIP.** This family of eight (counting the photographer) was stopped for a break along the Falls River Road in Rocky Mountain National Park when this picture was taken in the summer of 1923. Virginia Page of Geneseo, Illinois says her father, a lifelong amateur photographer, snapped the picture. The car in the background is a Nash.

**WHAT STOP SIGNS?** Siena Feltus (the girl at left in front row above) says her dad (standing behind her) wasn't much for slowing down on family's first long trip.

## Pop Saw No Need to Break His Momentum

MY FIRST TRIP out of the state of Iowa began on a June morning in 1924. We were making the 14-hour trip from Allison to the big city of Madison, Wisconsin in our green Paige with the side curtains.

The Paige was our first car, and although Pa was driving, he had no driver's license (none were needed back then). Because of our early departure, we reached my older sister's place in Madison in time for supper.

When we reached my sister's home, Pa proudly reported how easily he'd found his way through the city. "Yep, we sure moved right along. Din't hafta stop none a'tall."

"What about those stop signs, Pa?" asked Etta. "Didn't you see them?"

"You mean those little tin signs sittin' in the middle of the street?" he replied.

"Yes, those."

"Why should I stop for them?" he explained. "There weren't nobody comin'."

After that, my sister decided *she* would do all the driving while we were in the city!

—Siena DeBower Feltus
*(as told to Rebecca Leo, Allston, Massachusetts)*

## Porch-Sitters Listened for That "Lucky LaSalle"

DURING SUNDAYS in the '20s, our father insisted on strict observance of the Sabbath. For starters, that meant all active, noisy toys—like skates, marbles, bicycles and cap guns—were forbidden.

Even reading, unless it was from the Bible, was frowned upon. My sister *was* allowed to read J.M. Barrie's *The Little Minister*, but only because Dad was favorably impressed with the title (he didn't realize the plot featured a "scarlet woman").

After completing our chores, we often sat on our front porch with the other boys in the neighborhood and engaged in a simple-minded but entertaining game we called "cars". It consisted of nothing more than seeing what model (and condition) of auto chugged by the house for each player's turn. At the end of a round, the player who got the most expensive car was the winner.

These games could get pretty boisterous since we associated the less desirable attributes of various cars with the people whose luck it was to get them.

Early on, we learned the particular grinding of gears, the sound of the motor or the unique rattle that meant an approaching "flivver" (Model T) or a "push-o-let" (as the lowly Chevrolet was then called).

Either possibility meant the player in line for that particular car would almost certainly lose the round. On the other hand, it was also possible that the town's millionaire might pass by at any moment in his liveried LaSalle limousine and win the contest for some lucky lad.

—A. Kendall Sydnor
*Lynchburg, Virginia*

**SUNDAY-AFTERNOON GIGGLES.** Obviously, everyone was in a fine mood for a drive when this photo was snapped in San Pedro, California in 1924. The laughing 2-year-old on the running board is Roberta Kent Scott, now of Kingsburg, California, shown with her parents and a family friend.

**ON THE ROAD WITH HIS HONEY.** This Haynes roadster took Lois Williams' parents on their honeymoon in May of 1924. Lois, of Whitewater, Wisconsin, recalls her dad telling her what a chore it was to wrestle tires on and off those huge Haynes wheels.

# Seattle to New York—in Only 2 Months!

*By Margaret Mannen*
*Bainbridge Island, Washington*

We bought our first car in 1924, a two-seater Chevrolet coupe. How we loved that little car!

Three years later, my husband, John, accepted a job offer in New York City. The job started July 15 and it was then May 10. Since we had plenty of time to drive, we drove to California first to visit a friend in Santa Monica, before setting out on a diagonal "east-by-northeast" route that avoided most major cities.

Heading out across the Mojave Desert, it took us all day to reach the midpoint, a little wayside station improbably named "Siberia"—the temperature was 105°!

### Hot and Bothered

The patches on one tire kept coming off in the heat, requiring John to constantly re-patch and re-inflate. Later, he'd claim that he'd "pumped his way" across the Mojave.

The next day, we crossed a river on a one-way bridge. A mile later, I watched in amazement as John started wrestling frantically with the steering wheel. The steering gear had broken and we slid off

**THE "RE-TIRING" TYPE. Margaret Mannen wasn't the kind to sit by and watch while her husband did all the work.**

the road, stopping in a shallow ditch.

Using spare wire, John fixed it in 20 minutes, but *I* was in shock. If this had happened minutes earlier, we would have plunged off the bridge and gone into the river!

Heading into the hills of Arizona, the roads were so rough that we soon broke a spring and had to coast into Kingman, then a very small town. Someone directed us to the local blacksmith, who figured out a repair.

The next day, our patched tire finally gave out, and we had to buy a new one. After less than 100 miles, the *new* one blew—a severe blow to our finances.

Driving through rain in Missouri, John noticed a sharp left turn just ahead and another car approaching at high speed. We pulled to the side, but, turning the corner on two wheels, the car skidded right into us!

The driver was an elderly lady with two small grandsons, and now she had a flat tire. John gallantly donned his rain gear and changed it. He got back in the car, wet, muddy and vastly annoyed.

"Well, we got out of it okay, at least," he muttered as he started the car. Unfortunately, we didn't go anywhere—

our steering was no longer working.

Our two front wheels had quietly parted company, each pointing in a separate direction (the collision had broken a tie rod). We had to be towed to town for repairs and, from that point on, our finances were in critical shape.

The rest of the trip was uneventful until, somewhere in Pennsylvania, a rock flew up and hit the car with a bang. "That could've been bad," John said cheerfully. "It could have broken the windshield."

### Time for the Rope Trick

But further on, he stopped the car and got out. "We got us a beaut," he said, grinning again. "There's a hole in the radiator the size of a dollar."

I sat down on the running board and, for the first time on the trip, cried my heart out. John laughed and tapped me on the shoulder. "Get in the car, old girl," he said. "This I can fix."

He stuffed rope tightly into the hole to absorb the water, filled the radiator and we were on our way again. Like the steering wheel, the spring and the tie rod, that makeshift repair somehow held up until, after 2 months on the road, we reached our destination—we even had $20 left over!

Returning to Seattle 5 years later, we rode on paved highways, ate in restaurants and stayed at motels. It was pleasant, but we both had to agree—we'd had much more fun the first time. ❧

**BARELY ROOM FOR TWO. There wasn't much space in this "hot" 1924 roadster for a young woman and her beau. Joan Crowley of Conneauville, Pennsylvania says that's her Great-Aunt Mildred behind the wheel. Incidentally, Aunt Mildred eventually married someone else.**

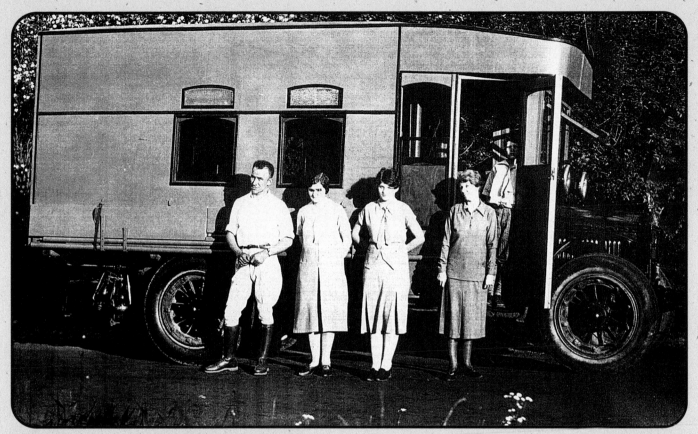

**THIS MACK CAME BACK.** This mobile home was a converted Mack truck, says Edward Mollach Jr. of Maplewood, New Jersey. Ed's father (on the left) was hired by the Henry Prior family of Short Hills, New Jersey to drive this vehicle to California and back in 1926. Besides handling various long-range travel assignments, Ed Sr. also found time over the years to teach over a thousand people how to do their own driving.

## Celluloid Surprise Had Grandma Seeing Red

OUR FAMILY'S first car, a brand-new 1922 Chevrolet 490, had side curtains with isinglass windows. Those windows were good for only about two seasons, which might have been fine in the South—but we lived in Michigan.

That meant sewing new windows into the curtains every couple of years. Celluloid was a bit lower priced and easier to work with, so that was our normal replacement (and late October was the usual time for this chore).

One fall Saturday, Dad, Mom and Grandma all pitched in and installed the new side curtains and windows. Next morning, we all dressed in our Sunday best and went out to open the garage and start the Chevy.

But Grandma had stayed behind to tidy up the kitchen. And she was just about to join us when she spotted a bag of celluloid trimmings left over from the curtain job. She tossed it into the stove, replaced the lid and started toward the door.

*KABOOM!* Dad had forgotten to mention that celluloid was made from gun cotton—an explosive! Fortunately, there was no fire, but the stovepipe blew clear across the kitchen, covering the room (and Grandma) with soot. *Very black* soot!

I can still see her in my mind, hat askew and white eyes flashing in a black face. We ended up missing church that day—Grandma was no longer in a prayerful mood.
—*Ervin Potratz*
*Athens, Ohio*

## Up the Road Without an Axle

DURING my family's move from Illinois to California in 1924, our 1916 Chevrolet broke an axle somewhere in the desert. My father hitchhiked 50 miles to the nearest town and worked in a repair shop for 2 days to earn enough to buy another axle.

Meanwhile, my mother, three sisters and I stayed in a tent we'd pitched along the road. There were no trees, and we had nothing to do but sit and wait.

When motorists stopped to ask whether we needed help, we'd give them our canvas water bag to take on to the next town. They'd fill the bag, then give it to another motorist heading in our direction. People were very helpful in those days.

Once Dad returned with the new axle, we were on our way again, arriving in California 5 weeks after we left Illinois.
—*James Jones*
*Baldwin Park, California*

# California... Land of Opportunity

*By Mary Beth Kennedy Voda*
*Wyalusing, Pennsylvania*

My elderly Pennsylvania neighbor, Earl Young, told me a memorable story about the trip he and his wife, Grace, took to California in 1927 with their 4-year-old son and baby daughter.

The first owner of their car was a man who, as Earl remembered, was afraid of the Studebaker's power. At a time when the average vehicle cruised along at 20 to 25 miles per hour, that car could do 80.

Equipped with a patching kit, torn sheets for diapers, luggage and food, the Youngs headed west—Grace said later that they could have been tracked to the coast by the trail of diapers they discarded along the way!

The only paved highways they encountered were in parts of California

## "He looked for an odd job—and found one!"

and Illinois. Everywhere else they rode on gravel. The trip proceeded relatively uneventfully until they reached the mountains west of Denver.

Crossing Hoosier Pass, two problems developed—one mechanical, one human. The car reacted to the height by becoming sluggish, and the Youngs' infant daughter simply passed out (she remained unconscious during the descent, but recovered later).

### Part-Time Job Was a Beauty

Twelve days after leaving Pennsylvania, the Youngs reached California. Since it would take some time to transact their business, Earl looked for an odd job to pay for the family's stay. And what an "odd" job he found—he and another man bought and sold bootleg manure!

It seems that farm workers at the time worked on beet ranches using their own horses and mules. They usually

**A SMUGGLER?** Earl Young certainly didn't look like the type who'd deal in "contraband". Yet, he was.

had an agreement with the ranch owners to leave the manure on the fields, but some sold the stuff to certain daring fellows who'd sneak onto the ranches at night and haul it away.

### "Honey Wagon" Needed Driver

Earl became acquainted with just such a businessman who bought the manure from the worker for $5 and sold it to the orange growers for $14 a truckload. The bootlegger hired Earl to drive what might be called a getaway truck.

The work turned out to be every bit as dangerous as driving for bank robbers (it was the rare bootlegger who didn't get shot at during a night's work). With business concluded, the Youngs turned the Studebaker eastward.

Arizona and New Mexico proved uneventful legs of the journey, but leaving Plainview, Texas, the travelers heard that the Red River in Arkansas was at flood stage—they would have to cross by ferry. According to Earl, as they'd traveled west, they forded all rivers at shallow points—and hadn't seen one bridge on the entire trip.

The final leg of the trip took the Youngs through Tennessee, Virginia, Maryland and Harrisburg, Pennsylvania, where they made one final stop.

Why Harrisburg? So Earl could buy the driver's license he'd never had!

## Brothers Left Reeling In Death Valley Daze

MY MOTHER recounted the story of a cross-country trip she took in 1926 with my father, his older brother and me. The three of them were all under 25 at the time, and I was only 3.

We drove from Meadville, Pennsylvania to California. In the middle of Death Valley, the two brothers got into a loud argument and wanted to fight each other. Since Mother was driving, they ordered her to stop the car.

Mother stopped the car and let them out. As they started to swing at each other, Mother (with me in the front seat beside her) drove off and left them in the 100° heat.

"That ought to cool their tempers and make them stop acting like kids," she commented as I began to cry. Ignoring my protests, she drove over the crest of a small hill so the two men were no longer visible.

A few minutes later, she turned the car around and drove back. As she pulled up, both of the men started yelling at her. So Mother put the car in gear and drove off—leaving them alone again!

"When they decide to be civilized, I'll let them back in the car," she said.

By the time we returned, two chagrined and sweaty men were more than ready to behave themselves. They got back into the car and there were no more fights—or even arguments—for the remainder of our trip.

—*William Keim*
*Huntingdon, Pennsylvania*

## Desert Sand No Match For Determined Dad

MY FIRST VACATION was in 1926, when I was about 10. We loaded up my stepfather's Studebaker and left Los Angeles for the Arizona ranch where he'd grown up.

As we neared the Arizona border, desert sand almost covered the road. "Don't worry," Dad said. "The plank road is just ahead."

The plank road was just that—wide, thick planks laid in two strips. When a truck approached, Dad carefully pulled the car over into the sand. The truck driver did the same but kept one set of wheels on the planks so that he wouldn't get stuck in the sand. He then eased past us slowly.

After dark, Dad noticed sand was clogging the screen that kept debris out of the car's fuel line. Always resourceful, he raised the hood on one side, folded it back out of the way and had me

**PLANK ROAD PUMPER.** Don Bronson (above right with his brother) found a novel way to help his dad drive.

sit between the fender and the motor. Golly, that motor was hot!

Then Dad gave me the tire pump and told me to blow the sand off the screen with the nozzle while Mother, reaching out the window, did the pumping.

It was dark and uncomfortable duty for both of us (once in a while I'd turn the hose up and let the air blow in my face, but it didn't help much). Although we did this for only a few miles, it seemed like a thousand.

—*Don Bronson, Placerville, California*

**BEACH PARTY.** The scene on this California beach probably looks a bit different today than it did back in 1925. Dorothy Lane (the little girl at right holding her doll) says that the Lanes had just moved to California from New Mexico and were gathered together with relatives for a picnic on the beach. Dorothy now lives in Albion, California.

**MAKING A HOUSE CALL?** That's Albert Warren, now of Paso Robles, California, in the backseat with his parents in this photo taken around 1925. Albert says this particular shot was made in Pasadena and that the driver is the family's doctor. He thinks the car may have been a Studebaker.

**ONLY ON SUNDAY.** This happy group was probably getting ready to set out on a Sunday drive when this photo was snapped around 1927, says Dottie Lonergan of Jacksonville, Illinois. Dottie is the little girl on the running board directly below the steering wheel (amid various visiting aunts, uncles and cousins).

**"K.O." AND CREW.** In 1926, Kenton O. Fowler (above left) and two of his buddies from Milton College in Milton, Wisconsin made a successful trip out to the East Coast and back in their 1919 Model T. Kenton's daughter, Marilyn Fowler of Pittsford, New York, explains that her dad's nickname was, naturally enough, "K.O." This photo was taken somewhere in New York.

## Campsite a Little Too Quiet

WHEN MY FATHER bought our four-cylinder Dodge, he practiced driving for weeks before he was ready for passengers. Finally he announced we could take a ride to Mosinee, Wisconsin—all the way from Chicago!

Delighted, we asked an aunt and uncle to come along on this grand adventure. We chatted merrily at the beginning of the trip, but after about 10 straight hours on the road, everyone was getting tired.

Night had fallen by the time we reached Mosinee's only hotel, and no rooms were available. After pondering what to do for a while, Mother said, "Let's find a quiet spot somewhere and camp outside. I knew those extra blankets would come in handy."

It didn't take us long to find a nice open spot that seemed very isolated, lay out our blankets and fall into a deep sleep. Next morning, we woke up and looked around in astonishment—we'd spent the night in a cemetery!

—*Helen Siml, Wheaton, Illinois*

## Stormy Skies Nixed Sunday Drives

AROUND 1928, we lived in Logan, West Virginia and my maternal grandparents lived 200 miles away in Ohio. Each summer, we'd visit them for a week or so.

After Sunday dinner, Grandfather would offer to take us out for a drive in his Dodge touring car. Depending on the weather, he'd carefully remove the isinglass curtains and call us to say he was ready to leave.

But if it looked the least bit like it might rain, Grandfather would just dust off the car, replace the curtains and then inform us we'd have to go another time—it was simply unthinkable to get the car wet.

And even on the afternoons that we did go for a drive in that Dodge, we rarely went more than 20 miles per hour. Yet, I can still hear my grandmother complaining, "I'll bet this would be pretty scenery if we weren't going so fast."

—*Ruth Means Reynoldsburg, Ohio*

**TOUGH WAY TO MAKE A LIVING.** According to the sign on the door of this Essex, the driver, "Daredevil Lockwood", was handcuffed to the wheel as he drove for 5 days and nights in order to win a $3,000 wager. No wonder there was a nurse riding along to ensure his safety! In 1927, Virginia Smith of Conyers, Georgia was the envy of all her classmates the day after her father took her to see Mr. Lockwood in action.

**TROOP TRANSPORT.** Robert DeBuhr of Rainier, Oregon unearthed this old photo of an enthusiastic group of Boy Scouts on an outing in Butte, Montana around 1926. Robert says the scoutmaster's pickup was called a "Rubabout", probably because it didn't run very smoothly and only got about 10 miles between flat tires. With loads like this, it's no wonder!

# Dodge Trip a 'Down East' Delight

*By Wil Powell, Warrenville, Illinois*

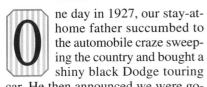

One day in 1927, our stay-at-home father succumbed to the automobile craze sweeping the country and bought a shiny black Dodge touring car. He then announced we were going on a camping trip from our home in Beaver Falls, Pennsylvania to historic New England.

Dad was undaunted by the prospect of a 1,000-mile trip with five young children in a 24-horsepower car with two-wheel brakes, no windows or trunk, and puncture-prone tires. (Mom, an invalid then, was unable to travel.)

We spent hours poring over road maps, helping Dad plot a course "down East". At last, the big day arrived. Urged on by Dad's impatient "Hurry up with those groceries!", my sisters and their friend Louise finished packing the car.

Piling in, we waved good-bye to curious neighbors and headed for the Al-

> *"We still laugh about Dad's 'rain dance'..."*

legheny Mountains. Isinglass curtains provided our only protection from the elements, and we needed them early in the trip. We still laugh about Dad's "rain dance" as he fought with those miserable curtains.

Each had to be matched to the proper rod and then slipped into the proper hole. As my hapless sisters sorted and handed out curtains and rods to our dripping dad, the atmosphere became as charged as the surrounding storm clouds.

In fairness to Dad, though, his nastiest remark was, "Child of mortality!" Predictably, as soon as the curtains were securely fastened, the sun came out and we roasted.

In a storm, it was impossible to see much through steamed-up windshields. Our distraught dad had to work the hand-operated windshield wiper while steering and shifting

**SEND-OFF.** Powells posed for a pre-trip picture. That's Wil at lower right, almost out of the photo, next to his sister Hazel. In the middle row, sisters Dorothy and Olive are flanking their friend Louise, who went along, with a neighbor boy joining in just for the photo. Their dad's in back (not wearing a hat) with a friend.

gears. As the kid who sat behind the gearshift, I frequently suffered bruised knees when the action heated up.

In 1927, every mile was an adventure. There were narrow one-lane roads and bridges; curves and tunnels that called for much downshifting and Klaxon-horn honking; and many a hill on which we'd encounter a hay wagon pulled by a sleepy-eyed horse.

And yet, when we entered a quiet village at lunchtime and smelled freshly baked bread or fried chicken, or stopped at a gas station for a bottle of pop from the water-filled cooler—life was good!

Each evening, we'd search for a campsite, usually someone's backyard. One rainy night, streams of water ran into our "bedroom". We spent the rest of the night in the Dodge, shivering and longing for the warm beds of home. But a good breakfast cooked on our gasoline stove restored our faith in tourism.

Despite my dad's gear-bashing, clutch-riding, horn-blowing technique, we never had a flat tire or fender bender. We even reached the awesome speed of 40 miles per hour once.

After many detours and wrong turns, we finally arrived at our destination—the birthplace of the nation. Our urchin-like appearance added little to the charm of New England, but what did we care?

With small-town naivete, we happily explored Lexington Commons, crossed the bridge where the "shout heard 'round the world" was fired and climbed the guns of Fort Ticonderoga.

Eleven days and 1,100 miles after it began, our tour ended when we pulled into our own backyard. My sisters and I had shared an unforgettable adventure in a vintage Dodge, and we all walked taller and straighter afterward, proud of our accomplishment. 🎺

**DAD'S MEAT WAGON.** This delivery vehicle was often seen on the streets of Lansing, Michigan back in the '20s, says Virginia Evers of Taylor, Arizona. Her good-natured dad, Howard Long, not only worked as a butcher and grocer (and deliveryman), but built and raced his own race cars. That's Virginia sitting on a Studebaker at right.

# Nightmare in Death Valley

*By George Gronemeyer*
*Naples, Florida*

At the age of 18, in 1927, I won $500 in a national essay contest. Shortly after, I told my parents I wanted to take a trip west before starting college.

They finally agreed with my plans. Looking back, I realize they had amazing confidence in my ability since most Easterners still considered the West a wild and dangerous place.

I had my own car—a 1912 Model T bought from a junkyard for $50—and I'd rebuilt the engine, using skills I'd learned in automotive school.

Starting in June of 1928, I left from Cleveland, Ohio for Seattle, proceeded down the coast to Los Angeles, then east to the California desert. Bear in mind that the sand roads had no signs —I had to navigate with a compass or by making inquiries at each town.

Arriving at Death Valley's southern entrance about noon one day in mid-August, I knew I just *had* to see it—I might never get another chance!

Large signs warned: "DO NOT ENTER IN AUGUST—NO FOOD, NO WATER, NO GAS, NO HELP!"

The air temperature in the shade that morning had been 115°. But this was the

**SURVIVAL WASN'T ASSURED.** George Gronemeyer had only himself to blame— and only his trusty 1912 Model T to depend on—when disaster struck in the heart of Death Valley during his 1928 excursion.

chance of a lifetime! So, I took it, proceeding downward on a narrow sand road into the very bottom of the valley.

After 30 miles, there wasn't a living thing in sight and the sand became fine

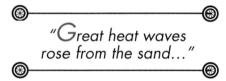

*"Great heat waves rose from the sand..."*

and powdery, slowing the car to a crawl. It couldn't plow through the sand in high gear, so I dropped into low and kept the engine racing.

There I was, wearing a black cowboy hat, long-sleeved gray shirt, gray twill

trousers and leather boots, driving with the top down in that furnace. I also was wearing cotton work gloves, since the steering wheel was too hot to touch with bare hands. And wherever I looked, great heat waves rose from the sand.

Then it happened. About 2 p.m., there was an explosion as my radiator cap blew to the sky, followed by a hissing geyser of steam. From the rivet-hammer sounds, I knew the four rod bearings had burned out as well.

I also heard the thumping of the failed front and center main bearings. With the bearings gone, the timing between the pistons and the spark from the magneto would be changed.

### A Stop Could Be Fatal

That wasn't critical at high engine speed, but if the engine ever slowed down, it would die and I probably wouldn't be able to restart it—I *had* to keep that engine running!

I knew I was in deep trouble and prayed to God to bring me out alive. For hours, I continued through the intense heat and the mirages. Finally, I found a road that took me eastward up a mountainside and out of the valley.

I reached the top at sunset but didn't dare to stop at that desolate spot either. Setting the hand lever that controlled the gasoline flow, I put the car in neutral—with the engine still racing—and filled the gas tank from my reserve cans. Then I drove on through the night.

I prayed and sweated the whole time, guided only by a compass and dead reckoning. Finally, about 4 a.m., I saw

**LUNCH IS SERVED.** That fold-down table and cabinet at the front of the vehicle was a great place for meals when the Borgelt family went on vacation in the Great Smoky Mountains in 1928. Marcia Borgelt Walker (the little girl in the middle) resides in Topeka, Illinois now, but as you can see, the family was mighty proud to be from Havana.

## "Jump Start" Backfired Badly

IN THE late 1920s, Dad overhauled the motor in his father's 1918 or '19 Overland. When he'd finished, the motor was too tight to hand-crank and, since the car didn't have a starter, Dad decided he'd get it running by pulling it.

Harnessing our two workhorses, "Nellie" and "Dolly", Dad hooked them to the front of the car. Mom got behind the wheel while my brother, sister and I climbed into the backseat.

Dad walked alongside the horses as they pulled the car out of the barn. After a while, he told Mom to put the car in gear and hold the clutch down until the engine started.

As hoped for, it did start, but when Mom released the clutch, the car backfired with a huge bang! Nellie and Dolly were immediately off and running, and the ride was so rough that my brother, John, bounced right out of the back

of the car! Fortunately, no one was seriously hurt, because after a few hundred feet, the horses broke loose and tore off for the peace and quiet of the pasture.
—Robert Archer
Garnett, Kansas

**TOO MUCH HORSEPOWER. Robert Archer's grandparents are riding in back of the car where his brother once went "overboard".**

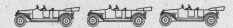

## Motoring Didn't Come Easily to Mom

ONE DAY in the late 1920s, Mom took our Model T for a spin while Dad talked with friends on the porch of the general store in Dyer, Kentucky.

As a new driver, Mom was very conscious of everyone watching her. That may be why she turned the corner and promptly knocked down a signboard. Dad and everyone else nearby came running to her aid, but the car was okay, and so was Mom—although a bit shaken up.

As she climbed back into the Model T, she started crying. "I've wrecked your car," she sobbed, "and I can't find the steering wheel anywhere."

"That's because you're in the backseat," Dad replied. —Jeanette Stavrou
Lake Placid, Florida

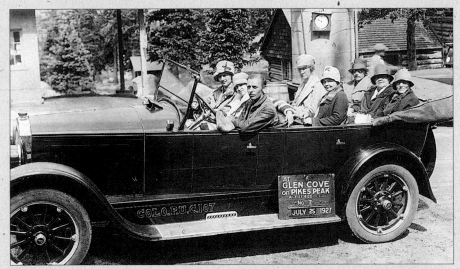

**PIKES PEAKSTERS. Even though it was a July day in 1927 when this photo was snapped, all those coats and hats among the passengers suggest that temperatures up near the top of Colorado's Pikes Peak may have been a little less than balmy. Kathryn Woerner of Glen Allen, Virginia isn't sure, but she thinks the woman next to the passenger door in the front seat may be her aunt.**

the lights of a little town that turned out to be Las Vegas—I'd been driving with the engine racing for 14 hours!

Pulling off the road, I poured water into the engine to cool it, removed the head and bottom engine pan and dumped out the molten metal remains of the bearings. I removed the pistons and connecting rods, then walked into town.

It was just a couple of blocks long then, so when I saw a store with a Ford

sign over it, I thought I had it made. But the owner said he had no parts for a 1912 Ford. They'd have to be ordered and that'd take at least 2 months.

Dejected, I walked around town, asking if anyone knew of an old unused Ford. Within an hour, I was directed to an old settler's house on the edge of town.

The man there had an old Ford in the barn and said I was more than welcome to take any parts. I removed four pistons

and rods and paid him $15, which he was happy to get.

By 5 p.m., I'd rebuilt my engine and had it running. I couldn't replace the main bearings, so the crankshaft still banged noisily, but I could live with that.

I left for the Grand Canyon the next day. And, after several more harrowing experiences, made it home to Cleveland in time to start college...and thankful to be alive. 🎺

# Dad's Vacation 'Bug' Didn't Survive First Car Trip

*By Florence Burden*
*Torrington, Wyoming*

**ROAD REGRETS.** Florence Burden (above) was excited about the family's first car trip, but her parents' enthusiasm dimmed as time went on.

**W**hen Dad suggested a family vacation in our 1925 Model T touring car, we had high hopes. Both Mom and Dad and my two sisters were happy and optimistic when we started out that summer of 1929.

We'd never taken a long trip before. Now we were going to drive 400 miles —from Scottsbluff, Nebraska east to Grandma's farm in Antelope County.

I was 10 years old, and my sisters were 12 and 14. For the trip, Mom bought each of us girls khaki pants—the latest fad. They came just below the knee and buttoned with a flap. We were very proud of them, even if Dad teased us about our "new look".

With good weather the first 2 days, we enjoyed stopping for gas at the filling stations that had soda pop cooling in tubs of ice. Dad would buy us all a 5¢ bottle of pop and we'd have to drink it right away and leave the bottle there.

One station had a sign that read, "We don't know where Mom is, but we have Pop on ice." We laughed and laughed at that one.

On the third day, we woke early, had a quick breakfast of cornflakes, milk, doughnuts and bananas. With the mattress rolled and tied to the back of the Ford, we set out through the Nebraska Sandhills toward Grandma's.

We noticed motorists waving as they passed—some were even yelling and pointing. When Dad stopped to let the radiator cool, we found out why.

## Bedding Left Behind

What was left of the mattress was dragging along the road. No wonder people had been pointing at us!

We arrived safely at Grandma's and were happy to sleep in real beds and eat good food for a week. For the trip home, Grandma gave us another mattress and a basket of goodies.

The sky was cloudy as we drove toward our campsite in Valentine on the first night. A bad storm was brewing and, by late afternoon, Mom was begging Dad not to set up the tent.

Why not rent a tourist cabin near the campgrounds? Dad said it would cost too much money. When the storm hit— complete with hail—it was impossible to build a campfire, so we ate the food Grandma had sent and went to bed.

We fell asleep with the storm still raging…and woke a short time later when the tent blew down on top of us! Scrambling out from under it, we made our way back to the car.

## Silence Was Deafening

Everyone was wet and unhappy. Taking me by the hand, Mom informed Dad she was taking me to find a hotel room. We walked the half mile to town (by the time we checked in, we were soaking wet).

Meanwhile, Dad and my sisters spent a soggy night in the car. Next morning, we all went to a cafe for a hot breakfast, then set out for Marsland (where Dad's sister lived). By then, Dad and Mom were barely speaking to one another.

Dad said it wasn't his fault it had rained. Mom didn't answer because she still had a headache from where the pole hit her when the tent blew down. At this point, we girls knew better than to talk or sing.

After 2 days at Aunt Sadie's, we drove home. Unloading the Model T, I heard Dad say to Mom, "Don't ask me to go on any more vacations." And Mom assured him she didn't *ever* want another trip like that one.

It was the only family vacation we ever took. I guess once was enough!

**CALIFORNIA BOUND.** The Hughes family was en route from Ohio to their new home in California when this photo was taken in 1923. Edith Hughes Short (next to her father) says she can't remember any roads on that trip—only ruts in dirt and mud. Edith now lives in Ranchita, California.

### When "Gumbo" Meant "No Go"

IN JULY of 1927, my mother, father, uncle, aunt and myself set out in our 1924 Hupmobile coupe for Yellowstone Park (a 1,300-mile journey from our home in Wisconsin).

We'd never been west of the Mississippi before, but farms dotted the landscape in Minnesota and we felt at home there. When we reached South Dakota, the scenery changed drastically.

Before entering the Badlands, my father stopped at a filling station for gas and asked about the condition of the road to Rapid City. "The road is a dirt road and it's impassable when it rains," the man said. "That Badlands 'gumbo mud' is very sticky."

Well, we were about halfway through the Badlands when a sudden heavy shower came up and we learned exactly what he meant. We chugged along slower and slower as the wheels became loaded down with that sticky gumbo mud. Ahead of us, we saw a line of eight or 10 cars that had ground to a stop.

When we reached them and stopped ourselves, our wheels sank even deeper into the mud. "We'll have to wait until the mud dries out," my father said.

Thus began our overnight stay in a caravan of luckless tourists. We sat cramped in our small car all night, our only food a banana and a bottle of water.

It was barely dawn when my father and uncle removed their shoes and socks and rolled up their trousers. Getting a shovel from the trunk, they freed each wheel from the mud.

Then they washed their feet with the last of the water and heaved a sigh of relief as the cars in front of us started moving. Once again, we were on our way west. —*Carol Schaech Mickowski Milwaukee, Wisconsin*

**STOPPED FOR BURGERS.** Rose, Daisy and Violet Elliot had a memorable experience one Sunday in 1928. Robert Beall of Spring, Texas (Violet's son) says they'd just left church in Cato, Arkansas and were headed home when a wheel came off this 1926 Model T, traveled down a rut and hit a neighbor's heifer right between the eyes! After repairing the wheel, the driver (Robert's grandfather) spent the remainder of the day butchering his newly purchased cow!

**A REAL STOCKING STUFFER.** It's a good bet that the Depression wasn't even a rumor when this "Santa" (you'll notice he's wearing business shoes instead of boots!) offered to deliver this gleaming new Ford on Christmas Day. George Boozer of Atlanta, Georgia shared this unusual old photograph.

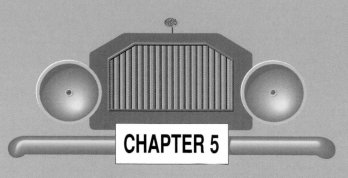

## CHAPTER 5

(Hand-tinted by Melissa Burghart)

***SUNSHINE SWEETHEARTS.*** **Pauline Corlew Underhill
was making 50¢ an hour at the Du Pont plant in Old
Hickory, Tennessee when she came up with the
down payment for this Chevy. Carolyn Elrod of Madison, Tennessee says this photo of her mother and father was taken a few months before they got married in late 1934.**

# Tough Times, Terrific Cars

T he "Dream Machine" would have been the perfect name for the automobile. And the 1930s were when it began to make dreams come true.

Two important developments were responsible. First of all, cars had finally become reliable enough to make long trips thinkable. Having a car that would get you to the next town was one thing; having a car that could take you to Yellowstone National Park or Niagara Falls was quite another.

The other essential was improved roads. Not that they were wonderful, but they were a big step up from wagon roads. There were even road maps that let you plot your course down the East Coast on U.S. 1 or along the West Coast on U.S. 101 or across the heart of the country on U.S. 30 or into the Southwest on Route 66.

Our family took two vacation trips during the '30s. One was from Illinois north to Ely, Minnesota, almost on the Canadian border. The other was all the way around Lake Michigan, made possible by a car ferry across the straits of Mackinac.

### Trip Made on Table First

Families of modest means, like ours, could now make their travel dreams come true. First you stopped at your local gas station and collected maps. Remember the days of free maps?

Then you sat around the dining room table while dad and mom charted an itinerary.

"The first day we should be able to make it to Cleveland. Then, if things go well, it looks like we could get to Pittsburgh on the second day. The next day…"

Ah, to dream! Of course, things never quite worked out as planned; you knew that ahead of time. But a road map was to the traveler what winter seed catalogs are to the gardener.

Although I didn't appreciate it at the time, I had a front-row seat for the excitement. That's because I worked one summer in a filling station on U.S. 30, the Lincoln Highway.

Those were the days when you actually received *service* at a service station. Besides pumping gas (5.6 gallons of regular for $1), I also cleaned the bug-splattered windshields, put

air in the tires, checked things under the hood and served as travel consultant. (Yes, you can make Chicago in 3 hours.)

There was a steady stream of tourists, cars packed with kids and Aunt Flo, luggage tied on top or jammed into homemade luggage boxes on the back fender.

The adventurers were often sweaty and tired, sometimes cranky…but always excited about what lay ahead. There also were scores of traveling salesmen, backseats packed with samples of their wares.

Just think, we never would have had all those traveling salesman jokes had the car not been invented…the jokes that always began with, "There was this traveling salesman, and his car broke down out in the country. So he went to the farmhouse and knocked…"

The stories that follow are wonderful chronicles of the perils and adventure that went with travel in the '30s. They give a dandy picture of how the car finally made dreams come true.

—*Clancy Strock*

Hugh P. Smith Jr.

TIME TO RE-TIRE

**BLOWOUT BUDDIES?** Contrary to what the ad at left and photo below might lead you to think, small boys usually weren't much help when it came to changing a tire. By the '30s, while tires were much more reliable, replacing them still wasn't much fun.

Archive Photos

# There's More Than One Way to Fix a Whippet

### By Alverna Anderson, Grand Rapids, Minnesota

I bought a used Whippet—a neat little car put out by the Overland Company—in 1930. I was a country "schoolmarm" in Minnesota at the time, and that little car and I had many adventures. The one I remember best happened on a summer morning in 1931.

My sister Berneill and I were headed 200 miles downstate to visit relatives, and it had rained the night before. When the motor suddenly stopped, I wasn't too concerned, as this had happened before.

Climbing out, I noticed my nice shiny car was spattered with mud—and I was all dressed up in my new spring outfit. Horrors!

Gingerly, I raised the hood and saw what I'd suspected was the trouble. Sure enough, the copper tube to the carburetor had worn through again and cut off the fuel supply.

"What in the world will we do now?" called Berneill. "You'll ruin your clothes if you try to fix it."

"Just watch," I replied. Going back to the car, I picked up a pipe wrench that lay on the floor. The jaw was broken, but the long handle fit the jack I carried under the backseat.

My brother-in-law had used it when he changed a tire for

**FEMININE WILES.** Alverna Anderson (driving above) discovered a nifty alternative to climbing under the hood and getting all dirty.

me and, tossing it back in the car, had laughingly said, "Here, take this along—you can use it as a club if anyone tries to hijack you."

Taking the wrench, I went and stood by the front of the car. In less than 5 minutes, a vehicle approached—an oil truck driven by a good-looking young man. Stopping beside us, he called out, "Having trouble, lady?"

"Yes," I answered. "I think I know what's wrong, but I can't fix it."

He climbed out of the truck and eyed the situation: stalled car, lady all dressed up and carrying a big pipe wrench. A quick look under the hood verified my diagnosis, but his lips twitched and his eyes twinkled as he looked at the ungainly tool I carried.

"We're less than 2 miles from Pine River," he said. "You get in the car and steer and I'll push you. The mechanic there can fix this in no time."

Tossing the wrench back in the car, I got behind the wheel. At the garage, the trucker explained the problem. "This lady's having a little trouble with her gas line," he told the mechanic. The mechanic took one look and said, "This is easy—I'll have it done in a minute."

### Listened from the Ladies' Room

Berneill and I got out of the car and went inside the garage to the rest room. It was clean and adequate, but there was no ceiling in the room, so we could plainly hear the conversation outside.

We heard a car door being opened and the truck driver's voice: "Take a look at this," followed by laughter. "This is what she was going to fix it with." Louder laughter as the mechanic joined in.

"Women drivers!" he remarked. "They shouldn't be allowed on the roads."

In the rest room, my sister and I had a hard time containing our laughter. In fact, we had to stuff handkerchiefs in our mouths. After we managed to control our mirth, we came out and met the smiling men.

"No charge, lady," the mechanic said. "It only took a minute. You had better have some new copper tubing put in when you get home. This could happen again."

I thanked the men for their kind help and then we proceeded merrily on our way—leaving the men grinning broadly at the helplessness of women.

Meanwhile, we girls giggled for at least 5 miles. Those gullible young men didn't realize they had been hoodwinked by a "dumb woman driver" who didn't want to get her clothes dirty.

He who laughs last, laughs best!

**NUTS BEHIND THE WHEEL.** This Ford jitney served as transportation for the Phi Gamma Delta fraternity at Hanover College in Hanover, Indiana. Wayne Kempshall of Westerville, Ohio bought the car for $50 in 1930 and says it featured a removable steering wheel. Wayne says he'd ask a girl if she'd ever driven. If the answer was "no", he'd hand her the steering wheel! By the way, the trophy Wayne's holding was the fraternity beer mug.

**JOYRIDERS.** Paul Schmidt (with hat on second from left) and his friends rounded a corner a little too fast in this vintage Model T one afternoon.

## At Least It Was A Soft Landing

IN 1936, two friends and I shared ownership of a Model T. One day, we were driving in farming country near Bridgeville, Pennsylvania. Rounding a curve, we saw a farm wagon just ahead.

I pushed the reverse pedal to stop, but the Model T didn't quite make it: We hit the back of the wagon—not hard, but just hard enough to cause the man sitting on the wagon seat to topple back into the wagon bed.

Unfortunately, the wagon was loaded with manure! I won't tell what happened next, but as you can probably guess, it wasn't pretty.
—*Paul Schmidt*
*Mt. Bethel, Pennsylvania*

about the billy goat that he'd previously tethered in the yard.

The goat, following its natural instincts, climbed up onto the running board, then the fender, then the hood and finally onto the cloth top. Of course, all four of his legs went right through the top!

We found the goat bleating loudly—with his legs doing about 30 miles an hour and going nowhere. Getting the goat out was a major problem since it was impossible for any of us to push him from below because of his sharp hooves.

Finally, after much cussing and effort, two men and three boys finally managed to lift him free. And Uncle Archie *never* parked his car in the yard with the goat again! —*Tony Blume*
*Jefferson City, Missouri*

## "Snarling" Chrysler Hard to Miss

I PURCHASED my first car—a 1928 Chrysler—in 1931, at the beginning of the Great Depression. She was a beauty, sleek and baby blue with a white top, rumble seat and interior trimmed in white fake leather.

We lived on a farm in West Texas. Since it was my last year in high school, I had lots of fun with my prized possession. Everyone knew when I was nearing our country school.

That's because it was on a slight rise and, as "Betsy" (my pet name for that car) and I began the ascent of the hill, I'd reach down on the floorboard and pull the wire that opened the "cutout" for my muffler.

Roaring into the school grounds, I'd slow to a stop with a growl, shove in the clutch and give the accelerator a couple of quick jabs, letting the cutout blast full-throated as if it were warning, "Beware!"
—*Paul Kyle*
*Yountville, California*

## Billy Goat Wasn't Half as Gruff as Uncle Archie!

ONE SUNDAY in about 1933, my Uncle Archie returned home from church and parked his 1928 Whippet on the front lawn instead of putting it in the barn. Apparently he'd forgotten all

**SUNDAY SAVIORS.** Back in the early '30s, a Sunday drive in the country always held out the possibility of getting hopelessly lost. These American Legion members set out to make that a little less likely by marking the scenic backroads of the Hill Country near New Braunfels, Texas with handmade signs. Laurie Jasinski of San Marcos, Texas says that one of the members of this altruistic crew was her grandfather, Joe Sanders (fourth from left).

# Maine Misses Piloted Model A Across the Country

*By Aileen Nile
Dunedin, Florida*

**B**ack in the summer of 1931, my roommate and I (2 years out of college) had the biggest adventure of our young lives as we drove across the country in our Model A Ford.

With a Maine license, our motto was "Portland to Portland". Our preparations included enrolling in a class for auto mechanics—we were the only females. My dad made us take a gallon jug of water for the radiator (which we never used) and a tow chain, which came in very handy—*once*.

From a caring friend, we accepted a rock wrapped in a sock for protection! And finally, with $500 each in traveler's checks, we were on our way.

## Went Where Road Took Them

We had no planned route (the one not driving studied the Rand-McNally maps and decided where we would go next). We'd promised ourselves a good $1 meal each day—but found it difficult to find one that cost that much!

We began by exploring upper New York State and Niagara Falls, then spent a night in Canada. We reached western Michigan just in time to catch the night boat across Lake Michigan.

At the Wisconsin-Iowa border, we found a ferry to take us across the Mississippi River.

From then on, there were no paved roads until we reached the West Coast—and the heat was terrific.

The roads were terrible, too—almost impassable in spots. But no matter how rough the going, our trusty Model A kept chugging along and we always found something to laugh about.

In the Rockies, we were delighted to find that our Ford could pass some of the larger cars stranded with steaming radiators on the steep upgrades.

We thought we'd be elated to reach Portland, Oregon, but when we went to the local AAA office to tell them of our accomplishments, we found an unsympathetic ear.

We were interested in seeing the sights, so we asked the man about Crater Lake. His assessment? "Just a hole in the mountain with water in it." The redwoods? "Just a lot of big trees."

He *did* tell us where the post office was, so after picking up our mail, we couldn't get out of town fast enough.

Crater Lake *was* beautiful. We rode mules down to the water's edge and back. Later, when we were driving around the rim, a tree crashed across the narrow road ahead of us (that was the time our cable tow chain came in handy).

At Union, Oregon, we saw another Maine license plate—the two schoolteachers we met were just as excited about that as we were! Union was a lovely town so we stayed the night.

The worst lodging we had was in Yellowstone Park. With only a candle for light and heat, we were so cold! The most we ever paid for a cabin was $3.75 in Reno, Nevada —we thought that was ridiculous.

## Point of Pride

Several states had huge signs at the border extolling that state's claim to fame. One in particular stands out for me—"South Dakota has more free bridges over the Missouri River than any other state in the Union."

I guess the two most memorable sights of our trip were seeing Mt. Rushmore with the unfinished head of Washington, and the spectacular firefall at Yosemite Park.

In Washington, D.C., we couldn't resist parting with some of our dwindling cash on a plane ride around the Washington Monument—our very first plane ride!

When we finally reached home after 2 months on the road, we each had $5 left in our pockets. What a trip! What memories! ✒

**FERRIES AND FIREFALLS.** Aileen Nile (at top of page) and her roommate (above left) saw about as much of the United States as two intrepid travelers could see in the summer of 1931. Above is the ferry that took them across the Mississippi at Prairie du Chien, Wisconsin. At right is one of the highlights of their trip—the spectacular firefall at California's Yosemite Park.

## That Face Looked Awfully Familiar

DAD BOUGHT a 1931 Chevrolet Cabriolet with a rumble seat in 1932. He drove so slowly that my brother Logan and I often hopped out of the rumble seat and ran along behind the car.

To get back in, we'd hop onto the bumper, climb onto the fender and return to the rumble seat. One day, Dad took my 4-year-old brother, Renny, and me on a drive into the Arkansas countryside.

Dad was a soft touch, and I talked him into letting me drive, while Renny rode in the rumble seat. Starting out slowly, I gradually picked up speed and confidence.

After a few minutes, I looked in the rearview mirror to see another car coming up fast from behind. I had just entered a very narrow bridge and asked Dad what to do.

He told me to pull over to the right as far as I could. Still, the other car sideswiped us as it passed, then came to a stop in front of us.

As soon as it stopped, a little redheaded, freckle-faced boy hopped out and ran toward us,

tears pouring down his face. I told Dad, "Hey, that looks just like Renny."

We both turned and looked in the rumble seat. Renny wasn't there! It turned out that Renny had climbed out of the rumble seat to run behind the car—just as he'd seen his big brothers do—but he couldn't keep up.

When the other driver came along and saw Renny's predicament, he picked him up and raced to catch up to us.

Dad offered to pay to repair both cars, but the stranger refused, putting the blame on himself.

In the end, they shook hands and agreed to take care of their own repairs—they were just happy that no one was hurt. It was a far different world in those days.

*—Edwin Creighton*
*Benton, Arkansas*

## Following Orders Got Her In Hot Water with Mom

WHEN I WAS 3, in 1933, we lived in Red Wing, Minnesota and my dad worked on road construction. He insisted on a hot lunch, so my mother and I took him one every day. Riding in the rumble seat of our Model A roadster was a special treat for me.

I was always told to sit perfectly still and not say a word, or I would never ride back there again. One day Mom took along a lady friend and her son, Wes, who was a holy terror.

He and I were allowed to ride in the rumble seat (after the usual dire warning about sitting still and keeping quiet). As Mom rounded a curve, she glanced back and saw only me in the

FORDS FOREVER. Jim O'Brien's first car was this 1928 Model A coupe. Jim, of Oregon, Ohio, is shown with his niece, Betty, in this 1932 photograph. This particular Ford also featured a rumble seat...as you'll learn in the stories on this page, rumble seats and kids about Betty's age did not always mix!

rumble seat. Bringing the car to a stop, she hollered, "Where is Wes?"

I said, "Oh, he fell out a ways back."

Why then, she asked, hadn't I yelled at her to stop? I replied innocently, "You said if I didn't sit still and be quiet, I couldn't ride here no more."

What more could she say? We turned around and started back, my mother mad and Wes' mother crying. Soon we saw Wes running down the newly tarred road toward us—his coattails flapping and feet sticking with every step.

Luckily he wasn't hurt, but, from his white-blond hair down to his feet, he was covered with tar.

Needless to say, after that, *neither* of us rode in the rumble seat for a long, long time.

*—Bonnie Waliezer*
*Brush Prairie, Washington*

"ROLLS" DIDN'T IMPRESS MOM. Arline Janssen of St. Louis, Missouri explains that this Model T with "Rolls Ruff" and many other sayings painted on it belonged to her father. A Lutheran school teacher in Cleveland, Ohio in the summer of 1930, he drove this car to Chicago to visit his future wife. Unfortunately, she was so embarrassed by its appearance that she refused to ride in it!

**SCHOOL SPIRIT.** Heads turned when Don Willis drove his 1927 Model T around town or past his high school in Penne Grove, New Jersey in 1932. That's Don behind the wheel. Now living in Cherry Hill, he recalls he and his friends painting this car their school colors of red and white—with house paint!

### Mom Lifted Everyone's Spirits...Except Her Own

WHEN I WAS 5 years old, we drove from our home in Watertown, South Dakota to Lake Kampeska for a Sunday picnic. On the way home, we had a flat on our mid-1920s Chevrolet Cabriolet. As Dad was jacking up the car, the jack broke.

With a long fence post, and a rock as a fulcrum, Dad was able to raise the wheel enough to clear the ground. But

he wasn't able to take off the rim and hold down the pole at the same time.

In an inspirational flash, he decided to have Mom sit on the end of the pole. She was only 4-foot-11 and barely weighed 100 pounds, so when she sat on the pole, it was more like a teeter-totter.

But Dad was innovative. He found a sizable rock and had Mom hold it in her lap for extra weight. That arrangement worked out great, but then, just as Dad finally got the rim off, a couple of young fellows approached from the other direction.

They had slowed down so they

wouldn't cover us with dust when they noticed Mom sitting with the rock in her lap. Stopping across from her, they couldn't help but grin. Mom was embarrassed at first—until her German-Irish temper started to rise.

One of the fellows picked up his box camera from the seat and took Mom's picture. Then the two drove off, laughing loudly. Dad cracked up, too—which didn't endear him much to Mom (who, by then, was livid).

We drove home with Dad chuckling and Mom mumbling. If I'd been Dad, I think I would have waited a bit longer to remove the rock from Mom's lap—lest she pick up the pole and clobber him with it!

—James Older
Pasco, Washington

### Choke? What Choke?

GRANDMOTHER was not the most accomplished motorist as she cautiously steered her 1928 Oldsmobile into town. As we rode along, we kids often wondered why she used only half of her side of the road.

"I just point the radiator cap over the white line," she'd explain. "That way, I won't run into the ditch."

For some time, she complained that the Olds was sluggish and used too much gas. Riding with her one day, I finally discovered the reason—she pulled the choke rod out and hung her purse on it!

—Marcus Orr
Columbus, Ohio

*NO RAMBLER.* This new Nash from the mid-'30s was billed as a way to take a "step up" from the "small car class". But, with the Depression in full swing, it's a safe bet that a car like this was not even a fantasy for the millions of folks struggling just to make ends meet. They, and teens like those pictured at right and above, were much more likely to be driving a small car or a "rattletrap" from the previous decade. This ad was shared with us by Curtis Norris of Norton, Massachusetts.

*BALL-PLAYING BUDDIES.* Frank Ehling (below right) and his friends were getting ready to play ball in Chicago's Humboldt Park when this picture was taken in front of their 1933 or 1934 Ford coupe. Frank now lives in Villa Park, Illinois and his wife, Lois, sent the photo.

**"FOXY" FORD.** This Ford pickup truck was helping a cameraman for Fox Movietone News shoot some newsreel footage when this photo was taken in 1933 or 1934, explains George Boozer of Atlanta, Georgia.

## Now That's a Rough Road!

WE LIVED about 1-1/2 miles from town and had to drive on terribly rough roads to get anywhere. My mother had been into town to do some shopping, but when she got home, she parked in the driveway and just sat there looking down at the floorboard.

Dad had seen her drive in, so he went out to the car to see why the motor was still running and Mother was making no effort to stop it or get out.

"You're home now, dear," he said quietly. Why don't you shut the engine off?"

"Well, now, Charlie," Mother replied, "I will…just as soon as I find the key!"
—*Joanne Gwin*
*Belle Mead, New Jersey*

## Pennsylvania "Pit Crew" Raced to School

WHERE WE lived in Pennsylvania in the 1930s, a school bus was unheard-of. My father's Model A Ford transported seven of us girls to high school, with me, a 16-year-old driver, behind the wheel.

We lived about 10 miles from the high school in Franklin and, although our local school board provided us with tuition help, transportation was our own responsibility.

Each girl contributed 50¢ a week for gas and oil (new tires were a luxury we didn't even discuss). It was understood that we would all be responsible for tire repairs when they were needed—and they were needed often!

Our old jack was stripped, so when we had a flat, one girl would scurry to find a flat stone to boost the car off the ground. Another would get out the wheel wrench, another the tire tool and another the patching material. Someone else would cut the patching to fit the rupture exactly, without wasting any material.

Each of us had a station. We could boast a complete wheel removal, tube patch, replacement, and reinflation in 15 minutes flat. Many a morning we breezed into school just as the bell rang, soiled from our labors but exhilarated at our success.

We learned self-reliance and were confident of our skills. These trials and triumphs bonded us with a camaraderie unknown to city kids who just walked to school.

That closeness remains to this day. On the rare occasions when we meet, we still laugh about the blowouts on that old Model A.
—*Shirley Borger*
*Franklin, Pennsylvania*

## Close, But No Cigar

OUR 1928 Reo Wolverine was a big, tough family car. One unusual feature was the cigar lighter, which attached under the dashboard with a spring-loaded, retractable power cord.

We four kids delighted in sitting in the backseat, allowing the lighter to zip back into the dash. But our fun was over the day our baby brother pushed the lighter's "little red button" and burned his finger.
—*Marcus Orr*
*Columbus, Ohio*

# Were Gangsters on Their Tail?

### By Sam Zickefoose, Ames, Iowa

There were two loves in my life in the early '30s—my future wife, Helen, and my first car, a 1930 Model A coupe.

Helen and I had just spent the weekend with her folks in Battle Creek, Iowa and were headed home on a smooth stretch of highway east of Sioux City.

There'd been a big snowstorm and the ditches on the sides of the road were level full, but the road was clear and the weather was fine. As usual, Helen was sitting quite close to me—for we were in those wonderful courtship days.

*"We went under the snow like a mole!"*

All of a sudden, the Model A started gaining speed, even though I wasn't pressing on the foot feed. As the speedometer approached 60, I thought something must have gone wrong under the hood, causing the throttle to stay open.

### Failed to See Humor

But then I heard Helen cry out, "Somebody's pushing us with a big car!"

To my horror, I looked in the rear-view mirror and saw a huge yellow Cadillac with four men all dressed in black suits and black hats. They seemed to be laughing their heads off at our predicament.

Faster and faster they shoved us—I told Helen that they didn't care if they killed us. I knew at this speed something would happen—we'd either have an accident or blow our engine.

But I was afraid to take the car out of gear with that much pressure on the drive train—I'd probably lose what little control I still had.

"There's one thing they don't want to do," I said to Helen, "and that is take the ditch with that big car. The road veers a little to the left just ahead. When it does, we must take a chance and turn into the ditch full of snow, hoping it'll act as a buffer and stop us."

At that high speed, I knew I'd have to make only the slightest adjustment of the steering wheel, so I hung on with all my strength. At just the right moment, with a prayer in my heart, I turned just a bit to the right into that unknown ditch full of beautiful white snow.

**SURVIVED SOMEHOW.** Sam and Helen Zickefoose narrowly escaped disaster on an Iowa road in the '30s.

We never even saw their car leave because we went under the snow like a mole! But the snow stopped us so gently that neither of us was thrown forward against the dash.

Our next problem was getting *out* of the car. I finally was able to wiggle free and work my way to the trunk, where I always kept a scoop shovel.

### Needed "Wiggle Room"

First I had to clear room near the rear wheels so I could jack up the car and install the chains. Then I started to shovel the packed snow from the front of the car. After making a couple of short tracks, I started the engine and went as far as I could in low gear.

After repeating this slow process many times, we made a slow angle up toward the pavement. In a couple of hours, that sturdy little car took us over the hump and we were back on our way—2 hours late, but grateful to be alive.

I've since learned that the gangster John Dillinger had a hideout about 40 miles west of Sioux Falls, South Dakota (around that time, he robbed a bank in Mason City, killing one man and wounding my future wife's uncle).

It was a time when men like Dillinger or Pretty Boy Floyd could shoot up a small-town bank and be hundreds of miles away before anybody could get on their trail.

Although I'll never be able to prove it, I'm convinced that Helen and I survived a hair-raising encounter with Dillinger or some of his men.

**BONNIE AND CLYDE?** No, they aren't desperadoes, just Janet and Ed Rodda posing in front of their beloved 1929 Model A roadster in 1935. They now live in Hemet, California, but back then, this little car took them all over Michigan's Upper Peninsula. Although the Roddas weren't gangsters, there were some pretty unsavory characters traveling the nation's roads back then (see story on this page).

# Flats Kept Dad Fuming

*By Ethel Davis, Beaver, Pennsylvania*

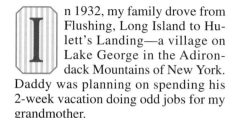

In 1932, my family drove from Flushing, Long Island to Hulett's Landing—a village on Lake George in the Adirondack Mountains of New York. Daddy was planning on spending his 2-week vacation doing odd jobs for my grandmother.

Meanwhile, Mama, sister Betty and I would stay in one of the cabins Grandmother rented out to city folks.

After Daddy strapped the luggage and boxes on the running board, he put the spare tire on the back of our '29 Chevy and we were ready to go.

From our home, we drove to the ferry, which would take us around to the New York City side, where we'd begin our long trek of 250 miles to Lake George. Once we were on the ferry, we

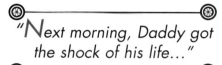

*"Next morning, Daddy got the shock of his life..."*

were allowed to get out of the car and watch New York Harbor come into view.

Maybe it was getting up after midnight and standing in the cool night air or the excitement of the trip that made me tremble so, but I'll never forget Daddy's hand holding tightly onto mine as we stood by the railing of the boat together.

Once we left the ferry and began our trip, Betty and I tucked our dresses under our legs so the prickly mohair cushions wouldn't scratch our legs as the day grew warmer.

On our way up Route 9W, we had many problems, but flat tires were the biggest! Each time we got a flat, Daddy would get out his old faithful can of patching material. After removing the tire tube, he'd scrape the tube where the hole was with a metal scraper before applying cement and a new patch to the tube.

Every so many miles of driving over the hot macadam roads would melt the patch off the tire and he'd have to do a patch job all over again. That little cardboard kit with the metal scraper lid would be his companion for the whole trip.

This went on all day long until we reached Saratoga Springs—200 miles from where we'd started. Having driven since 2 a.m. and having fixed *eight* flats, Daddy was not in a very pleasant mood by this time.

As the sun sank behind the mountains, everyone was hot and exhausted, and Daddy and Mama had a heated discussion as to what we should do.

Looking around, Daddy saw we were near the Saratoga battlefield, so he just whipped that old '29 Chevy into a

**RUNNIN' MATES.** Those old running boards were just the right height for kids to sit or stand on, recalls Bernard Holub of Westlake, Ohio. He's third from the front on this 1927 Chevy, which took these kids from Cleveland to Pennsylvania to spend the summer with their grandmother. Bernard says the vehicle belonged to his Uncle Mike and was unique in that it had solid bright red wheels.

secluded section of the park. We didn't mind sleeping in the car for the night because we knew Daddy couldn't face fixing another flat just then! Curling up inside, we slept soundly until the morning sunshine woke us up.

Next morning, Daddy got the shock of his life when he got out of the car and found *all four* tires were flat! Out came the trusty old tire patch can one more time.

Although we only had 50 miles to go, our trials were far from over—we had to constantly worry about the car's radiator boiling over. Many times Daddy would have to stop at a farm to ask for water in order to get us up the next hill.

My sister and I rocked back and forth (and crossed our fingers, arms, legs and eyes!), hoping to get that Chevy up the next mountain road without the radiator boiling over again.

I can still hear the grinding and shifting of gears as we slowly crept up each hill waiting for the descent, which meant we were that much nearer Grandmother's house and our hard-earned vacation in the country. ✆

**COOL DOWN.** Dad had calmed down and was teaching daughter Ethel (in inner tube at left) how to swim when this photo was taken. Ethel's mom is shown in front of the family's flat-prone '29 Chevy below.

# Rail-Ridin' Brothers Brought Home a Beauty

*By Richard Pohl, Seabeck, Washington*

y older brother, Gordon, was 19 and I was 16 in 1934. We lived on a farm outside Kent, Washington. Our father was a building contractor, but Gordon and I raised vegetables for sale to restaurants.

After three summers of farming, we'd saved up enough for a brand-new car—a 1934 Plymouth coupe. We planned on hopping a freight train to Detroit to pick it up (thereby saving $200 in shipping costs).

After many long conversations, our parents agreed to let us go. A neighbor, a switchman at the rail yard in Auburn, offered to help get us on an eastbound train in late August.

We planned to visit our grandparents en route. They lived in South St. Paul, Minnesota, and we'd already shipped them a suitcase of clean clothing. It was cool that night as we crossed the Cascade Mountains, arriving in Yakima, Washington the next morning.

We stayed on the edge of the rail

## "What a thrill for two farm boys!"

yard all day (there were a lot of bums and hoboes, and it was quite scary). With some difficulty, we finally found a small branch line that was leaving Yakima at 5 p.m. By the time we got to Spokane, there was just an engine, a coal car and a caboose.

About 12 of us were stowed away on the coal car. Gordon and I arrived about 4 a.m., neither of us having had any sleep. After the train stopped, we were fortunate enough to find an empty boxcar and finally got a few hours' sleep before hopping the next train.

Quite often we passed westbound trains. There'd be perhaps 100 men like ourselves on top of the train. As the trains passed, we'd yell out, "Go East!" while the westbounders yelled back, "Go West!"

After 6 days, we finally arrived in Minneapolis. From there, we decided to hitchhike the rest of the way.

**DREAM TEAM. Gordon and Richard Pohl were more than pleased with their 1934 Plymouth.**

An uncle took us to Red Wing, Minnesota by car, but our efforts at finding rides weren't very successful—I'm afraid we did much more hiking than we did hitching!

Running short on time, we had no choice but to take a bus from Madison, Wisconsin to Detroit. At the factory showroom in Detroit, there were rows

**HOMEWARD BOUND. This brand-new Plymouth probably made one of the fastest Chicago-to-Washington trips of 1934 as the Pohl brothers hurried home.**

and rows of shiny black cars lined up in formation.

Our hearts jumped when we looked down one particular row and spotted *our* glossy, jet-black two-door Plymouth coupe with the polished chrome and the rumble seat. Gordon and I stood there with the hugest grins anyone could wear! What a thrill for two young farm boys!

Being older, Gordon got the honor of driving first. What a difference it was to ride on cushions! Next stop was Chicago, Illinois, where we planned to visit relatives and the World's Fair.

But disaster struck in Gary, Indiana, when a teenager just learning to drive went right through a stop sign and hit our front fender and wheel! We were too embarrassed to call our aunts (we figured they'd think it was poor driving on our part).

So we stayed at a nearby hotel until the car was repaired, then proceeded to Chicago, where we spent a pleasant week.

Traveling west from Chicago, we drove 12 to 14 hours a day and slept in the car at night.

### Heard Them Coming
The closer we got to home, the faster we drove—we just couldn't wait to tell everyone about our trip and show off our new car. Coming through Kent, Washington, we honked and waved to everyone.

Then, heading down the long dirt road toward home, we started honking again—our family said they could hear us coming a half mile away!

I can still remember the first thing Gordon and I saw: A cheering crowd (all family members) waving their arms—it reminded us of the final lap of the Indy 500.

Everyone was so glad we'd had a safe trip, and they all took turns driving around the yard and honking the horn. No one could believe how shiny and smooth that Plymouth was—they all had to run their hands over it.

When I took the car to school, I was more popular than some of the football players. That only lasted a couple of days, but I didn't mind. We'd had a wonderful trip—one we'd never forget. ❧

## Snake Outsmarted Dad

DADDY'S first car was a used Star that started with a crank kept under the front seat. One day while we were out for a drive, a big bull snake crossed the unpaved road ahead of us and slithered into the grass.

Carter County, Oklahoma had plenty of snakes, and Daddy didn't like them. So he stopped the car and got out to kill it.

When he found the snake, it stopped and coiled (I could hear the blowing and hissing from the backseat).

Daddy searched for something—anything—he could use to kill that snake. Unable to find anything better, he finally decided to use the crank to make the kill. Getting as close as he dared, he hurled the crank.

It came close but landed harmlessly beside the coiled, hissing snake. Now the snake had the crank...and we weren't going anywhere without it. The snake had won!

All Daddy could do was sit on the running board and wait. He sat there until the snake finally simmered down and decided it was now safe to move on. After it did, Daddy retrieved the crank, started the car and we resumed our journey.

Not one word more was ever said about killing that snake.

—*Lavin Farrar, Fort Worth, Texas*

## Diminutive Mom Was "Master" of Her Big Buick

MY MOTHER was a tiny lady, standing about 4-foot-10. But the way she dealt with flat tires in the early '30s still amazes me.

Our car was a 1928 Buick "Master Six" with huge wooden-spoked wheels. When Mother drove, she sat on a pile of cushions and peeked under the enormous wooden steering wheel to see the road.

One day when I was about 10, we had a flat. Mother stopped the car, got the tools out of the trunk, crawled under the car and placed a mechanical jack under the axle. After jacking up the car, she took off four lug bolts and clamps to remove the rim. Since we had no spare, she took the "clincher"-type tire off the rim using two tire irons. She found a nail in it, and she removed it with pliers.

She then took out the patching kit, roughed up the tube where the nail had penetrated, applied patching cement and covered the hole with a patch. She pried the tire back onto the rim, bolted it on, pumped in air with a hand pump, lowered the jack, replaced the tools and drove home. I was impressed.

The whole job had taken about half an hour, and it obviously wasn't the first time she'd done it. She was a capable lady and took things like flat tires in stride, always wearing a smile.

Mother was still driving in her 80's (delivering Meals on Wheels to "old folks"), but she didn't have the same kinds of tire problems she'd had with that old Buick Master Six.

—*Harvey Cook, Fort Myers, Florida*

***FLIVVERS ON THE FAST TRACK.*** In some parts of the country, Model T racing was very popular during the '30s, says Jean Schwarzlow of Janesville, Wisconsin. That's her father, Ed (second from left), in the top photo. He and two of his brothers had wonderful times racing on weekends on tracks all over Wisconsin and northern Illinois. Jean says her father once won a state championship in Milwaukee driving a car named "Tin Buc Two"—and his brother Louie came in second in "Tippy Tippy Tin".

**AUSTIN GAL.** Bob Britton's future wife, Pauline, took a spin in his tiny automobile.

## Little Car Had Big Hero at the Helm

I BOUGHT a 1931 American Austin roadster for $300 in 1936. It was a great little car, and I drove it for 3 years. It had a four-cylinder engine and averaged over 50 miles per gallon.

But the tank only held about 5 gallons, so I ran out of gas often (I always kept a half-gallon can of gas behind the seat). At the time, I was in the enlisted reserve of the Army Air Corps in Cincinnati.

One Sunday, a couple of brand-new AT-6 planes landed at our field to "gas up" at lunchtime. The two pilots were hungry and asked where they could get a bite to eat, so I offered to drive them to a restaurant in my Austin.

They were tickled by that idea, asking, "Can the three of us really get in there?" We did, and they were surprised at how well the car ran.

On the way back from lunch, one of the pilots asked if I would let him drive the car back to the field. I did—only to learn later that he was future World War II hero Capt. Jimmy Doolittle!

—*Bob Britton, Cincinnati, Ohio*

## A Cloud of Dust And a Hearty "Wahoo!"

IN THE early 1930s, my brother had a Model T of unknown vintage he fondly called "the ol' strip-down".

Ed spent lots of time working on that vehicle. When driving it, he'd usually sit on an old car seat placed atop the gas tank.

After work, Ed enjoyed driving on the dirt roads around our Kansas farm, watching his wheels stir up dust. There were five other farm families living within 2 miles of us. Whenever Ed saw any of them, he'd holler "Wahoo!" and, of course, get a "Wahoo!" hollered in return.

When the nearby town of Pawnee Rock had a celebration, Ed drove his strip-down in the parade. Across the back, he painted the words: "Constipated—can't pass a thing."

This drew lots of laughs from bystanders, especially our cousins—although if our parents had known about it, I'm sure they wouldn't have approved.

That car is no more and Ed has passed away, but family and friends still recall those wonderful "Wahoo strip-down days".
—*Marjorie Andrasek Garden City, Kansas*

## You Load 70 Tons And Whaddaya Get?

WHEN I was a sophomore in high school, in 1935, I saw an ad in a Minneapolis newspaper for a Bantam automobile dealership. Dad was an implement and scrap dealer and said if I could fill up a 70-ton railroad car with car engines, he'd buy me the initial car required for a dealership.

That was a busy and interesting summer. I had to remove all of the valves, camshafts, crankshafts, rods, pistons and everything else from the engines (I learned a lot about how they worked in the process). And, by fall, I had 70 tons of clean cast iron.

The Bantam Car Co. made a convertible, a sedan and a pickup. We chose the pickup because it was the least expensive—$485 wholesale plus a $39 freight charge.

In the spring of 1936, the depot agent told us our car was on the siding, ready to unload. It was strapped down in the middle of a boxcar. I filled it with oil and gas, cut the straps and drove it away.

**A BOY AND HIS BANTAM.** Orval Peickert was 16 and 6 feet tall when this photo was taken of his green and black Bantam pickup. Orval says that there were times when he actually fit three people into the cab.

Light green with black fenders, the Bantam was a cute little truck. But I could feel every bump as I drove—until I discovered that the springs had been strapped down so that they wouldn't bounce in the box-car. After removing the straps, I had a much smoother ride.

We never sold any of the Bantams, but I sure had fun with that little truck.
—*Orval Peickert Browns Valley, Minnesota*

# Stove Oil, Fly Spray And a Franklin Fanatic

*By Ted Rischard, Santa Ana, California*

**LION IN THE DESERT.** The Rischards' trusty Franklin (with its pawing lion on the hood) seemed right at home at the Natural Bridge in Death Valley, California when this photo was taken in 1937.

**D**ad thought the Franklin car was the greatest thing on wheels. I used to kid him about it whenever we'd have a vapor lock on a mountain grade. "Was that pawing lion hood ornament trying to climb its way up the mountain or what?" I'd say.

Then he'd tell me about a Franklin dealership in Pasadena, California (where we lived) that had driven a Franklin in reverse up Mt. Wilson. "No other car could do that," he'd assert.

Dad was a self-taught mechanic. In fact, in 1909, at the age of 30, he built a car of his own design with parts he'd either made or scavenged! He patented several automotive service tools and was operating a repair garage when I was born, in 1919.

### Diesel Oil Was Depression Bargain

My own recollections of our Franklins are intertwined with memories of the Great Depression. Money was scarce, but Dad loved exploring the Pacific Northwest in our 1928 four-door model.

Although gas was only 15 or 20¢ a gallon, Dad observed that diesel fuel (usually called stove oil then) could be had for half that. Since the Franklin ran quite hot, he figured it might run on stove oil.

So, he bored a hole in the side of the intake manifold for a small brass tube and elbow, then mounted a second carburetor beside the original one. A second vacuum tank was installed and a second foot throttle mounted on the floor between the clutch and brake pedals. An extra tank on the back completed the installation.

At slow speeds, the stove oil didn't work too well—but at 30 miles per hour or better, it worked great and didn't even smoke. You drove with both feet using the fuel of preference or maybe a little of each depending on the conditions.

For our camping trips, Dad built a metal rack with spaces in it the size of food cans and mounted it on the exhaust manifold. All we had to do to heat supper was to punch holes in the cans, place them in the rack, drive for 15 minutes and supper was ready! Or it could warm while we were setting up camp.

Camping in those days was certainly different. If public campgrounds weren't available, we'd just pull off onto a farm or logging road and set up our tent. It never occurred to us that anyone might bother us.

### Kept Bugs Out of the Engine, Too

Once, driving in central California, we ran out of both gas and stove oil. Luckily it happened near a little country gas station. But it was Sunday and no one was around.

Dad, always the improviser, scouted around the back of the building and came back with a can of something he said smelled like it might burn.

So he put some in the tank, and we got the engine started. We made it to the next little town, although with frequent loud reports from the muffler. Dad later admitted that the can had been labeled "fly spray"!

After I'd finished high school, a friend had a Model T Ford I was seriously considering buying to use for driving to college. Dad said, "You don't want that old car. I'll buy you a fine, safe car instead."

Naturally, his choice was a Franklin—a 1929 Model 130 coupe with a rumble seat. This was in November 1937, and the car cost $175. It was a nice-looking little car, repainted a light cocoa color with red pinstripe, black top and lots of chrome in the front.

She came to be fondly known as "Betsy" and, of course, Dad immediately installed his "Dieselization Kit" for me. Amazingly, I still have that 1929 Franklin—but that's another story! ❧

**SCHNECKSVILLE SPORT.** Charles Stopp of Sun City, Arizona was living in the little village of Schnecksville, Pennsylvania when this photograph of him and his classy Plymouth Sport roadster was taken. The roadster is a 1930 model. With the top down as above, Charles' sunglasses undoubtedly got plenty of use.

# Panic in the Pasture

*By Don Payne, Alameda, California*

Shortly after my ninth birthday, on a hot July day in 1936, I had my first driving lesson. On our rural East Texas farm, going to the city for supplies was a major undertaking that occurred every 2 months and took all day.

I'd been left home alone to look after the chores. As I stared at the tail end of the Model A Ford sitting in the garage, it was like a magnet. Who would know?

Who would see or care if I took a little spin around the barnyard? After all, I'd ridden with Grandfather hundreds of times, and it looked easy!

Staring out from under the rim of the steering wheel, I started the Ford, lurched backward out of the garage and took a grand tour of the pasture. Then I stopped and walked around the Model A, admiring it from all angles (and feeling rather proud of myself).

That's when I noticed our milk cows grazing in the shade of some pecan trees and decided I'd herd them to a better pasture. A couple toots on the horn got them moving, and all went well until I tried to fit the Model A between two closely spaced pecan trees.

Suddenly there was a soft smushing sound, and a very rapid stop. My door wouldn't open, so I crawled out the window to assess the problem.

### Going Nowhere Fast

The fenders were sharply creased and the running boards were angled up about 45 degrees and firmly wedged against the trees. Crawling back inside, I started the engine and tried backing out, but the wheels spun uselessly.

My grandparents would be home in a few hours and I was in *big* trouble! I was too embarrassed to ask anyone for help, so the only thing left was to go home, pack my bag and clear out before my grandparents returned!

Then I had an idea. Harnessing "Joe" and "Maude"' (our two giant Percherons), I marched them back to the scene of the disaster. Once there, I hooked them to the rear bumper of the Ford.

When I called out "Giddyap!", they leaned into the load. I watched the bumper stretch out flat, then stared aghast as it ripped from the frame with a loud crunching noise!

I ran back to the house to get a length of log chain for the next pull. Returning, I wrapped it around the rear axle. Maude and Joe gave it their gentle best. They pulled and pulled, but that Ford wouldn't budge.

Then I noticed the rear wheels were pointing in opposite directions. Something had given way underneath the Ford, and it sure wasn't the running boards!

I was defeated. As I waited to face the music, I wondered what it would feel like to die. From the front porch, I could see the cloud of dust, but it seemed like an eternity before the car pulled into the driveway.

While unloading the groceries, my grandfather asked, "Where's the Ford?"

"Well, I...um...took a drive and got stuck down in the pecan grove," I stuttered.

"You what?"

"I got stuck between two trees, and it wouldn't come out," I squeaked.

"Well, help carry this stuff in and we'll go down and have a look," he said quietly. As I carried in the lion's share of the bags, I remember thinking I might get out of this alive after all.

### The Silence Was Unbearable

Things were very quiet on our walk down to the trees. Grandfather circled the Model A twice before readjusting his hat lower over his eyes and going around it again, only the other way.

I waited anxiously for a sound—*any sound*. Finally, looking at me with his one good eye, he muttered, "Well, she's stuck all right! We better go back up and tell the old woman."

The trip back up the hill was endless. Once there, my grandfather and "the old woman" had a conversation beyond my earshot. After that, Grandfather took an ax and headed back to the Model A.

Meanwhile, Grandmother gave me a spanking that ensured I wouldn't be able to sit comfortably for a couple of days! Afterward, I was busy trying to stay out of her way when I heard the familiar sound of the Ford grinding its way up from the pasture.

It was a sorry-looking sight. I was grateful no mention was made of my punishment at dinner that night (al-

---

### *"They pulled and pulled, but the Ford just wouldn't budge..."*

---

though the meal was consumed in total silence).

On Saturday morning, I volunteered to milk "Old Blue", the meanest cow in the herd and one that Grandfather hated because she swatted him in the face with her tail.

When we were finished, he said, "Let's get changed. We're going into Whitesboro this morning."

To make the Model A go straight, the steering wheel had to be turned a full half turn to the right. We got more than our fair share of stares—drivers we met either gazed in amazement or started laughing.

Rather than face the embarrassment of Main Street, we took back streets to the Ford agency. I was still in the Model A when my grandfather came driving out of the alley in the prettiest thing I'd ever seen—a shiny new Ford V-8 four-door sedan with gorgeous maroon paint and whitewall tires.

### Time for a Joyride

"Get in, son," he said with a grin a yard wide. "Let's take a little spin!" We spun down Main Street and pulled up at Larson's Drugstore, where we ordered two double-scoop ice cream cones. We took them back to the new car, trying not to let the ice cream drip on the mohair upholstery.

We took the long way home, covering twice as many miles as necessary for the 10-mile journey. I was licking the last of the ice cream into the bottom of the cone when Grandfather broke the silence.

"You know, for the last 4 years, I've wanted one of these new V-8s, but the old woman just wouldn't hear of it!"

He speeded up to 50 miles per hour, reached over and gave my knee a good squeeze, then said, "Now this is a real automobile!"

I had to agree, but, secretly, I was thinking I'd *never* get to drive this one!

**HILLSDALE HONEYS.** It was a pleasant Sunday afternoon in Hillsdale, New Jersey when this good-looking pair posed in front of what looks like a snazzy Model A roadster. Barbara Palmisano of Toms River, New Jersey tells us that the couple would one day be her parents, Rosemarie and Bob Rawson. She also notes that, given the look in her mother's eyes, it probably wouldn't have mattered what kind of car Bob was driving that day.

**AN UNFORGETTABLE MOMENT.** Even though she was only 3, Doris Rock of Ripley, Ontario clearly remembers what was going on when this picture was taken. The family farmed near Kincardine, Ontario and had just bought their first car—a 1934 Chevrolet. That's Doris' dad standing proudly behind her above. Meanwhile, her brother, Lorne, seems to be checking for loose lug nuts.

# Dad's Death-Defying Ride

*By Linda Debski, Comstock Park, Michigan*

Cars weren't the only vehicles on the road in the late '20s and early '30s—the trucking industry was just getting started as well. At age 19, in 1928, my dad, Jim Vickrey, started as a trucker and drove until 1937 (the year I was born).

In his later years, Dad loved telling trucking stories to anyone who would listen. And, in the telling, I could see how privileged he felt to have seen so much of this country before it was developed.

Of course, not all of his experiences were positive. He also witnessed the turmoil of forming unions and the crime connected to bootlegging. Once he was offered a bribe to pull over for some

## "The clutch let go and the huge vehicle was out of control..."

hijackers (he took his truck in the opposite direction—which might have saved his life).

But the greatest risk to his life (and the wildest experience he ever had) occurred in 1937. The following is quoted from an account in a Pennsylvania newspaper:

"Jim Vickrey is still wondering why he is not in a hospital or the morgue, instead of a local hotel, following a wild 2-mile ride down Pennview Mountain at 100 miles an hour. The truck left the road at the foot of the mountain and ripped through trees and brush for a thousand feet before coming to a stop, but the only damage was a broken headlight lens and bulb.

"Jim had left New York with an 11-ton load and newly installed brake linings. In third gear, he started down the west slope of the mountain. The truck gained speed and the brakes failed. The clutch let go and the huge vehicle was out of control. Jim pulled around a sharp S-curve and barely missed an oncoming truck."

"The speedometer was at the maximum, 80 miles per hour, beyond that he must have been going 100 by the time he reached the bottom. Two cars veered off the road to avoid the speeding truck.

"Jim was sure he was a goner when the truck left the road twice, but he managed to bring it back both times. He ran it into a thicket, guiding it between two telephone poles so close together that the average driver wouldn't attempt to drive between them at a slow speed.

"When he came to a stop, small trees and brush covered the front of the truck and windshield."

"Persons who went over the scene of

**HE LIVED TO TELL THE TALE.** When Jim Vickrey's truck lost its brakes coming down a mountain in Pennsylvania, his chances of survival didn't look good at all. That's Jim in the top photo and above, next to the passenger door of his truck after it finally came to rest following that incredible ride.

his wild and fearful ride, and measured the distance he traveled leaving the highway, declared they would not have believed the driver's story had they not been able to follow the marks on the highway and seen the truck before it was towed away.

### Dad Had Company

"Jim does not know how he did it. He said, 'I just hung on to the wheel and fought it the whole way down.'"

Unknown to the reporter who wrote this newspaper account, Dad had another reason for concern while careening down that mountain—he had two passengers (a man and a woman) in the cab with him.

It was against company regulations, but times were tough, so it was not uncommon for people to hitch a ride when they didn't have the fare for a bus or train. The young couple who experienced the terror of that ride and had their lives in the hands of a stranger knew that he'd risked his job by giving them a ride.

They were grateful for the lift—and even more grateful that he had the skill to get them to the bottom of the mountain alive!

When Dad, a married man who would soon be a father, gave up life on the road, that harrowing experience was the deciding factor. But his days as a trucker were always "Dad's Great Adventure".

**THE GUYS WHO KEPT 'EM GOING.** Sunlight was streaming through the windows when the mechanics stopped work for a moment to pose for this picture at the Ford garage in Ionia, Michigan. Donna Teichman of Battle Creek supplied the photo and tells us that her father, Elmer Walters (below arrow), worked there during the '30s.

## Gal "Grease Monkeys" Tuned Up Their Skills

I LOVED CARS as a teenager and am convinced that I started the country's first auto mechanics class for girls. I was always sticking my head into the auto shop at the Manual Arts High School in Los Angeles, California to see what was going on.

In 1936, I asked the teacher, Harry Meyers, if I could take the class. He said if I could find 13 other girls willing to join me, he'd do it. It took some arm-twisting, but I managed.

The rumor around school was that we girls tore the cars down, and then the boys in the next class put them back together. That might be partly true, but we accomplished a lot.

We learned how to drop pans and replace gaskets, run a lathe, smooth pits in valves and set the gap on spark plugs.

Mr. Meyers also taught us an unusual way to change tires. We weren't strong enough to lift the wheels and place them on the bolts, so he had us sit on the ground and place our hands and *feet* on the wheel. We'd lift with all four, and on the wheel would go! I later changed many a tire that way.

We did give Mr. Meyers a few headaches. One day during class, I was under a car, dropping a pan, when he suddenly grabbed my ankles and pulled me out. Another girl had started the car above me, and he had to explain that you *never* work under a car with the motor running.

Another day, I removed a battery and was carrying it against my chest. Mr. Meyers grabbed the battery, then ripped away my coveralls from the collar down. They were already in shreds, but thanks to his quick thinking, no acid touched my skin.

Much of what we learned was put to good use. In 1939, when I bought a 1929 Model A, I could set the spark plugs, regulate the carburetor, change gaskets and patch tire tubes. I learned more in Mr. Meyers' class than in any other I ever took.

Of course, when we started out, we didn't know *anything.* —*Edith Short Ranchita, California*

**MECHANIC IN A BATHING SUIT.** Edith Short was 19 and headed for the beach in her 1929 Model A when this photo was snapped in 1939. And, as mentioned in her story above, if anything went wrong, she could probably fix it.

# Cross-Country 'Scooters' Savored Life On the Road

*By Jesse Smith, Ona, West Virginia*

**GRANDMA WAS GRAND, TOO.** That's Rosemary Palmer (above right), Jesse Smith's mother, at the Grand Canyon on a trip taken a couple years after the one described below. Above left is Clara Palmer, Jesse's grandmother and an adventuresome traveling companion who dressed nicely—even on the road.

Starting in the summer of 1938, my widowed grandmother, Clara Palmer, took a series of automobile trips across the country from her home in Maryland. Accompanying her was my mother, her only child, Rosemary.

My grandmother (a spry 53 years old at the time) was an adventuresome sort, undaunted by the prospect of unpaved roads and uncharted horizons.

Purchasing a used 1935 Ford panel delivery truck, she modified it for sleeping and travel. Before the summer was over, she'd also made a lean-to tent that rigged up against the outside of the truck.

A college graduate and former Latin teacher, Granny named their traveling motor home "Scootie Hoosie" (loose translation: moving house).

### Library Idea Didn't Pan Out

Originally, she'd planned to loan books out to country folks on the way west, then retrieve them on the way home. That's why the driver's door was neatly lettered "The Lucian Palmer Vacation Library" (named after Clara's late husband).

But Granny and Rosemary quickly discovered the book-lending idea didn't work—people either didn't care about reading or already had access to books.

Although the traveling library didn't last long, it provided the incentive for a series of trips that ultimately took my mother and grandmother across 48 states, through Canada and over more than 30,000 miles of primitive roads.

In letters home to her uncle, my mother wrote of the sense of adventure present in everything they did. Every evening, they'd look for a night spot that offered both seclusion and a view.

Parking miles from the nearest paved road, they'd build a campfire, put up the netting in Scootie Hoosie's windows and cook dinner. For entertainment, they'd brought along an autoharp, and Rosemary learned to play it.

Under wilderness skies lit by a million stars, Rosemary wrote that they, "took down the curtains, opened the back doors of Scootie Hoosie and let the night air flow in with the prairie wind."

Well-versed in nature, Granny used the trip to teach Mom about astronomy, geology, birds, plant life and evolution. Their 1938 route took them west through South Dakota, Wyoming and on to Glacier National Park in Montana (at 14, Mom also learned to drive on the trip).

At the Grand Teton Range in Wyoming, they discovered what would become their favorite spot on Earth. Those spectacular snowcapped mountain peaks, crystal lakes and the flat cowboy country around Jackson Hole captured Mom's love forever.

### Memories to Last a Lifetime

In the Tetons, they hiked up Death Canyon and watched the sunset from high above emerald-green Phelps Lake.

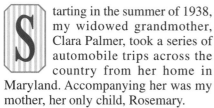

*"In a flash, Scootie Hoosie careened across the oncoming lane..."*

That night, they heard the song of a coyote, and saw the stars shine with a brilliance only Western stars have.

From Yellowstone, Granny and Mom headed for Glacier National Park in Montana, then west to Oregon and California, where they camped beneath giant redwoods and watched the Pacific surf.

The long drive home to Maryland would take them through the Southwest, where they'd experience the trip's most thrilling moment—as well as a near-tragedy.

At the south rim of the Grand Canyon, they made arrangements to take a mule trip down into the canyon. Granny later wrote home, "I am still out of breath from my first gasp as my mule took me over the edge and down into the canyon.

"That first mile is terrific from the back of a mule. How I wanted to be on my own legs," she wrote, "or on all fours crawling along the inner edge of the path, rather than perched atop the canyon mule, looking three or four thousand feet straight down."

Several days later, in the blink of an eye, their spectacular trip would change violently. In 1938, Route 66 across Arizona was a two-lane road of blacktop, flat horizons and sagebrush isolation.

*THE THRILL OF THE OPEN ROAD.* Rosemary was only 14 when she drove over Logan Pass in Glacier National Park (above). In Wyoming, she sat on the running board with her autoharp. At left (top to bottom): Rosemary and her mother were headed to Banff, Alberta; they drove through a giant redwood in California; they camped along the way.

Scootie Hoosie was headed east, making about 50 mph with Granny at the wheel, when a leaf-spring behind the truck's left front tire snapped, causing the steering wheel to instantly cut hard left!

In a flash, Scootie Hoosie careened across the oncoming lane, plunged off the road into a gully and rolled over onto its roof. When they came to a stop (upright again), Granny was caught beneath the steering wheel under the dashboard, her back injured and several ribs broken.

### Long Wait Had Happy Ending

Bleeding and shaken, my mom climbed out to flag down a passing car. Emergency response out on the Arizona desert was almost nonexistent back in 1938. When help finally arrived, it was discovered Granny's injuries were serious, but not critical.

Mom wired an uncle in Maryland for money, and the $100 he sent paid the hospital bill, as well as the repairs for Scootie Hoosie. Within a week, they were on their way east again. Granny, still in pain, drove the 2,200 miles home.

By the end of August, they were back home in Norbeck, Maryland, ending their magical summer of extraordinary adventure. ✍

## Blown Fuse a True Miracle of Timing

IN 1937, my brother-in-law, J.W., was given a 1926 Pontiac as partial payment for helping a family move onto a farm near ours outside Flatwoods, Pennsylvania. The car was in fair shape, and we had it running after a few weeks.

The only problem was the wiring. We kept blowing fuses, and the lights would go out. All we could do was change the fuses and jiggle wires until the lights came back on.

One evening we got the lights to *stay* on and decided to take my four sisters along on a trial run in the country. The WPA had just black-topped a new road, so we decided to try it out. Everything worked fine…for a while.

Then, just as we rounded a curve, the lights went out, J.W. brought the car to a screeching halt. While he started checking fuses, I went around front to jiggle wires.

As the lights came back on and I turned to get back into the car, I could not believe my eyes—not 8 feet in front of us, the road had disappeared!

An old coal mine had collapsed, and the road had sunk with it, leaving a

*A GIRL ON THE GO.* Carolyn Hamilton was a secretary at the Oconee Textile Company in Athens, Georgia when this photograph of her blue Ford V-8 was taken in 1936. Carolyn, now of Clarendon, Texas, says she absolutely loved this car with its steering knob and greyhound on the hood. After her marriage in 1938, she and her husband both drove the car until after World War II ended.

crater 6 feet wide and very deep. If we hadn't stopped when we did, we'd have run head-on into it.

We quickly drove back to tell the WPA foreman, and he put up a roadblock and lanterns. I often think back to that dark night…and a blown fuse that saved our lives.    *—W. Ray Skiles*
*Weirton, West Virginia*

## Not Exactly the Best Time To Be Choosy

WHILE DRIVING in their hometown of Franklin, Indiana in the late 1930s, my parents and a friend ran out of gas. Dad noticed a filling station about 200 yards away, so he and his friend got out and started pushing while my mom steered.

After pushing quite a while, Dad and his friend looked off to the side and noticed that they'd passed the station. They stopped pushing and asked Mom why she hadn't pulled in.

She explained that the station had cheap gas and dirty rest rooms, and she didn't want to use their services! With no other filling station in sight, Dad eventually persuaded Mom to settle—just this once—for cheap gas and dirty rest rooms.
   *—Steve Van Antwerp*
*Wildomar, California*

*A DEVIL OF A CAR.* Lillian Howe Patterson of Lansing, Michigan says it was June of 1938 in Vermontville, Michigan and Stanley Howe had just asked her if she would like to spend the rest of her life with him when this photo was taken. Note the "thumbing nose" devil hood ornament (inset) on Stanley's car (Lillian thinks it was a Chrysler). Lillian's mom hated that ornament, but ironically, she was the one who took this picture, silhouetting it against a tree and unintentionally preserving it for posterity.

# Trailer Travel Suited 10-Year-Old Just Fine

*By Don Andersen*
*Lenoir, North Carolina*

In 1938, my father sold his Packard agency in Chicago and we moved to Florida, pulling a 16-foot house trailer he'd taken in trade. Mom called it "the covered wagon".

It was a swell-looking rig, sort of streamlined in front with Masonite covering outside. Inside it had linoleum floors, two double seats flanking a table and a kitchen with sink, icebox, kerosene heater and even a two-burner gas stove.

### A Traveling Rumpus Room

There was a bed and closet in back. To me—just 10 years old—this was really something! It took us 5 or 6 days to get to Florida, and on the way down, Mom and Dad let me stay in the trailer.

Sometimes Mom and my 2-year-old brother would be back there, too. Once a toaster fell off a shelf and hit him on the head. No damage—just tears!

If we had to stop when we rode back there, we would put a red flag or piece of red cardboard in the left window, where Dad could see it from the big fender mirrors on his '38 Packard (now that was some car!).

**DON'S DELIGHT.** Don Andersen (shown here with his mother and little brother) discovered that he loved traveling.

While we were traveling, I built a Curtiss-Robin flying model airplane, almost finishing by the time we reached Naples, Florida. We arrived in Naples at night and stopped at a gas station.

The owner (who lived above the station) was just closing up. He said we could park the trailer at the side of the station. Then he went upstairs and threw down an extension cord and we were in business.

Next morning, he asked if we wanted to go fishing on the big wooden pier that stuck out into the gulf. With cane poles, we caught two big snook weighing 8 to 10 pounds *and* on the way back to the station saw two 6-foot rattlers!

I'm afraid that era is gone. It didn't matter where you stopped—people were always friendly. "Where you from?" and "Where you going?" were the questions they'd ask.

### Bitten by the Travel Bug

And I must have been born to travel: I was so wound up at night my folks had to holler at me to go to sleep!

When we were ready to leave Naples, Dad asked how much we owed. The station owner replied, "Do you think 75¢ is too much?"

Dad gave him a few dollars, but the man gave some of that back, saying, "You folks stop in again anytime you come through." 

---

## The Life of Riley?

I WAS POPULAR during the Depression because (at age 17) I had my own car, a 1929 Model A. My father, a schoolteacher, had summers off and we had a summer home on Lake Winnipesaukee in New Hampshire.

Nearby was a campground filled with kids my age. One day I'll never forget, a buddy and I drove with two girls to a super swimming pool in a stream near the well-known Mount Washington Hotel in Crawford Notch.

As we parked, I noticed a tire going flat. The girls offered to change it—so we let them. All I did was start the jack and loosen the lug nuts slightly. They did the rest while my buddy and I sat on a big rock next to the car.

The real fun was listening to the comments from people driving by. The men called out things like, "What's your secret?", while the women said, "Shame on you!"

—*Edwin Judd, East Greenwich, Rhode Island*

**SUMMER FUN.** Owning his own car at age 17 made Edwin Judd (driving the Model A at left) a very popular fellow. But when the two girls above left changed a tire while Ed and a friend lounged nearby, it created a stir.

BOB'S "BOMB". Not every 15-year-old can boast of owning his own car, but Bob Lauters (above with a giggling cousin) could. Bob says he didn't even need a driver's license.

### Blind Father "Saw" Amazingly Well

MY FATHER, a South Dakota machinist for years, lost his eyesight shortly before I was born. When I was 15, in 1937, Dad decided I needed a car.

He'd heard of a farmer who had a Model T for sale because he couldn't get it started. So, for $20 and my bicycle, a deal was made.

Before going out to the farm to look at the vehicle, my father instructed me to look for something like a spark plug under the floorboard and see if there were a wire connected to it. If there wasn't, I was to reattach it.

Well, when the time came for my inspection, I found just what my dad had expected—the wire had fallen off.

After reattaching the wire, it was time to try and start the engine. With a few twists of the crank, it came alive with a roar.

Needless to say, the previous owner was just about fit to be tied—he'd been taken in by a a blind man and a 15-year-old kid!

After a few weeks, Dad decided it was time to overhaul the engine. With him coaching me from a nearby nail keg, I dismantled the engine with the famous Ford wrench (designed to fit every nut, bolt and screw on a Ford).

After some machine work done at a shop plus the addition of some new parts, the reassembly began. When our overhaul was complete, that Model T ran perfectly.

About a year later, someone offered us $40 for the old Lizzie and we sold it. That's when the master mechanic and his young apprentice began dismantling a 1928 Chevrolet coupe. After a bearing, ring and valve job, it, too, ran perfectly.

Profit was never an issue in fixing up these (and other) cars, but experience sure was. Those times spent with my dad were among the most precious of my youth.

—Bob Lauters
Cupertino, California

LIZZIE NEVER LOOKED LIKE THIS! That's Paul Cowgill behind the wheel of his homemade roadster. The picture was taken in Balboa Park at the 1935 World's Fair in San Diego, California. Paul, now of Eucha, Oklahoma, purchased a 1925 Model T for $10 and converted into a "racer" that was the envy of every boy who saw it.

GRIND ME A POUND. This mid-'30s Ford did double duty as a sausage grinder, says Andrew Kuhnline of Carrollton, Illinois. Andrew's dad (on the left) and his friends look quite pleased with themselves at having found a way to take most of the work out of a tedious job.

# 'Mothballed' Pontiac Taught Local Speed Demon a Lesson

*By John Ralph, Enid, Oklahoma*

I will never forget one of the cars my dad bought when we lived outside of Platteville, Wisconsin. It was a deluxe, fully equipped, specially ordered 1937 Pontiac, and we took delivery on it just before Christmas of 1936. That was a big Christmas!

In return for a promise to keep it serviced and clean, Dad generously let me use it almost any time it was free—a happy arrangement that contributed greatly to my high school and college social life.

### Got the "Squaw" Up to Speed

My schedule was often tight, so it wasn't long until I ascertained that the "Squaw" (as my brother and I irreverently named the Pontiac) topped out at about 85 miles per hour.

There was no numerical speed limit in Wisconsin then. The law simply stated "reasonable and proper" speed. (To a teenager, that meant "anything it'll do if the road ahead is clear.")

In the fall of 1939, as a college freshman, I started commuting 15 miles daily on the new smooth, fairly flat concrete highway between our farm and Platteville State Teachers College.

Soon, I noticed that the same new Ford V-8 passed me each morning—even though, at a respectable 65 or 70, I certainly was not obstructing traffic! I found out the guy's name was "Fluffy".

A sophomore, he was always in a hurry and quite disdainful of anything other than a Ford V-8. For some dumb reason, it wasn't long until I tried to race him. Of course, I was humiliated—there weren't many cars around then that could stay with a new Ford.

But I had dreams of somehow redeeming the Squaw's embarrassment, so I tried all the known remedies—new plugs, points, etc. I gained maybe 3 miles per hour.

Finally, in desperation, I told the Pontiac dealer the whole sad story—adding that the Pontiac's reputation at college was in jeopardy. Exhaling loudly, he allowed, "I probably shouldn't tell you this, but there might be a way to teach that guy some manners."

I was all ears as he explained that when he'd raced on dirt tracks, some guys gained an edge by dissolving mothballs in a couple gallons of gas. He

**PONTIAC PRIDE.** The 1937 Pontiac in this old car ad—sent by Curtis Norris of Norton, Massachusetts—was much like the one John Ralph's father bought.

said the ether in those mothballs made tigers out of the little Ford 6's he used to race and should do the same for me.

A few days later, my tank was close to empty, so I poured in a sample of the dealer's recipe, then took the Squaw out to test the results.

Well, let me tell you, that model of Pontiac had a long perfectly horizontal speedometer that went from 0 to 100 across the top of the instrument cluster. That needle went past 100 and buried itself over on the right-hand side!

### A Surprise for Fluffy

Next morning, I was lying in wait for Fluffy. I saw him coming a mile away, so I pulled out and spooled up to about 70 (there was no other traffic).

I timed it so, as he got even with me, I was staying with him. Then, when I could tell he floored it, I did, too. I'd have given a fortune to have seen his face at that moment!

By the time he got to school, I was already parked. Fluffy sauntered over and said he'd like to see my engine. Of course, I was glad to oblige.

He didn't say anything more for a few days, but I knew it was killing him. Finally he asked "What'd you do to that engine?"

"Fluffy", I told him, "all it needed was a good tune-up." ✎

**CRACK-UP IN CLEVELAND.** Even Cleveland's quiet residential neighborhoods occasionally experienced car crashes. Howard Wise, a retired Cleveland police officer now living in South Euclid, Ohio, shared this sharp photo of a vehicle involved in a 1939 collision.

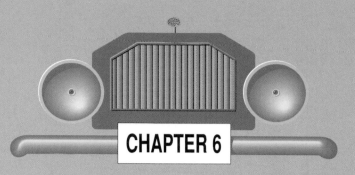

# CHAPTER 6

(Hand-tinted by Melissa Burghart)

**DROVE (AND DANCED) LIKE A PRO.** Jim Foulis and his wife, Jeanne, appear to be dancing with happiness over their new Buick in 1941. Jim was the golf pro at a country club in Hinsdale, Illinois when this photograph was taken. That's Jimmy Jr. standing in front of his parents. He and his wife, Mary, now live in South Miami, Florida, and Mary shared the photo.

# Comin' in on a Rim and a Spare

By the time America entered the '40s, automobiles had gone from a luxury to a necessity in most families. We wondered how we had ever gotten along without them. They took us to work, they toted home our groceries and they turned us into a nation of vagabonds.

Then came Pearl Harbor. Cars stopped rolling off the assembly lines. The giant Detroit factories were swiftly converted to the production of Jeeps, trucks, tanks and other military vehicles.

Need a new car? Forget it!

Suddenly gasoline was tightly rationed, doled out in accordance with your demonstrated need and your involvement in the war effort. Doctors, for example, got a more generous monthly allowance than the man who ran the dress shop.

To get new tires, you made a trip to the local rationing board and pled your case. Likely as not, you were turned down and went home to do the best you could with bald tires and oft-patched inner tubes.

### A Time to Tinker

As a result, civilians became experts at improvising—whatever it took to keep Old Bessie running. And keep in mind that, compared to today's cars, Old Bessie hadn't been much of a machine to begin with.

Radiators rusted out in a few years, brakes and clutches needed frequent replacement and engines were chronically balky. Cars of the '20s and '30s needed lots of tender loving care.

The good news was that those Whippets and Packards and Essexes and DeSotos were fairly simple. Even if you weren't personally much of a mechanic, it wasn't hard to find a neighbor or brother-in-law who delighted in repairing cars.

My dad was perfectly equipped for the era, having been to an auto mechanic's school in his younger days. Our town had one junkyard. It was where old cars went after they died.

Sometimes I went along with Dad on one of his trips to search for repair parts. During the war years, the place was crowded with men hoping to find a wheel or an axle or a carburetor or a bumper that could be salvaged to keep the family car running. I suspect that few autos on the road during that era would have passed the sketchiest safety inspection. Somehow they choked and gasped and rattled down the road, barely able to keep up with the reduced speed limits imposed to save gasoline.

One of the No. 1 musical hits of 1943 was a song called *Comin' in on a Wing and a Prayer*. Paraphrased to "Comin' in on a Rim and a Spare", it could have easily served as the theme song for anyone who had to drive anywhere during those years of wartime austerity.

When you came to a crippled car pulled off beside the road, the civil thing to do was stop and ask if you could provide assistance, or at least give the stranded victim a lift to the next town. But if he was out of gas, he also was out of luck. No coupons, no gas.

Which is why so many people hitchhiked and carpooled. You hoarded gas whenever and however you could.

In just 40 years, we had come to regard the family car as a necessary part of 20th-century life. Few inventions so totally pervaded our lives in such a short span of time.

In much the way that we don't appreciate electricity until the power goes out in our home, the World War II years reminded us just how profoundly the automobile had changed our world.

—*Clancy Strock*

**MAKIN' IT LAST.** With parts hard to obtain during the war, backyard mechanics improvised whenever possible.

# Late-Night 'Landscapers' Lucky to Not Be Caught

*By Vincent Sudela, Dickinson, Texas*

I acquired my first car, a 1923 Model T Ford, in 1941. It was a four-door sedan and cost $8. While pedaling my bike to and from high school, I spotted this classic at the Mobil Oil station on the corner of 39th and Avenue O in Galveston, Texas.

The 3-mile bicycle trip to Kirwin High School was getting to be a drag, especially when pumping into the cold north wind, which seemed to persist always. Why do we only remember the painful?

Heading home, the same wind was at my back—and a smile was on my face. The school day was over (I hated school!).

I had the $8 for the car, but Dad's permission was mandatory. So, when he consented, I was ecstatic!

The service station owner chauffeured me to the county courthouse on 20th Street in downtown Galveston. That Ford just "Cadillacked" down Broadway, the engine chugging in perfect harmony.

As I recall, the transfer of title cost about $1.50. The Model T lacked a spare tire, and a 30- by 3-1/2-inch tire cost $5.35 at Western Auto. But who could afford that kind of money?

One night, when a few of us were cruising the east end of the city, the inevitable happened. A tire blew out. With this vehicle, I never had flats—I had explosions. Before I got out to inspect, it was a foregone conclusion that the tire was wasted.

I had searched and scavenged every

## "I never had flats—I had explosions..."

friend's garage and chicken yard to find spare rims. The rim held the tire but was a removable part of the wooden-spoked wheel. In the past, we would just pull off the blown tire and ride home on the rim. But driving down the cement-paved streets ruined the rim.

Usually, that was no problem. We would just put on another rim from Ivan Kopecky's chicken yard. But on this oc-

casion, I knew of no other source for a replacement rim.

Since it was rather late at night, and most of Galveston was tucked away for the evening, we decided to drive down the center of Broadway's esplanade. This esplanade was soft dirt covered with softer grass.

We drove the full length of the turf, from Second Street all the way out to a dirt cross street near 49th Street. Well, our "ingenuity" saved the rim and, some way or other, I eventually scraped up $5.35 and bought another Davis tire from Western Auto.

But I've often wondered what the police would have done to us had they caught us driving some 40 blocks down the esplanade with the sharp-edged tireless rim cutting a nice furrow through the well-manicured grass.

Would we have been complimented on our resourcefulness? I seriously doubt it. ❧

**YOUR HUDSON HEADQUARTERS.** If you were looking for a new Hudson or a Packard in Laredo, Texas in 1940, Ed Ramirez (above left) and his brother, C.H., had them. Ed, who still lives in Laredo, says he and his brother were commemorating the successful remodeling of their car dealership with a handshake. They also sold Terraplanes.

*THE COOKIE DIDN'T LIE!* On the memorable night she won this 1941 Plymouth, Clara Askew opened a fortune cookie in a Chinese restaurant that said something good would happen to her in the near future. Although Clara never went to the movies, she decided she'd go to a local theater in Seattle that was holding a raffle that evening. Her son, Bud, of Mill Creek, Washington, recalls his father thinking that she was overreacting, but, sure enough, later that night, she won this car!

## Terrier's Leap of Faith Made Him One Hot Dog

I GOT MY DOG, a terrier mix named "Rex", in 1941. We bought him from a fellow who worked at the neighborhood Standard station in River Grove, Illinois. I remember the trip home like it was yesterday—Dad, the pup and me in the front seat of our 1941 Dodge business coupe.

Not long after that, we set off on a trip to visit relatives out of state. Mom,

*HOODWINKED. George Anderson's dog had a major problem with this 1941 Dodge.*

Dad and I jammed into the front seat, and Rex happily rode along in the huge trunk.

At gas stops, Dad would open the trunk, and Rex would hop out, run to the rear of the station and take care of business. He'd return to the service island for a drink from the radiator can, then hop back into the trunk and wait for Dad to close it.

After letting Rex out at one stop, Dad went around the front of the car and raised the hood to check the oil. Rex came trotting back from behind the station and took his usual drink.

If you've ever seen a 1941 Dodge business coupe with hood and trunk raised at the same time, you can probably understand what happened next. Instead of jumping into the trunk, Rex

jumped under the hood and onto the hot engine. That pup came out of there like a rocket!
—*George Anderson Rolla, Missouri*

## Human "Fuel Pump" Blew Them Home

ONE EVENING in the winter of 1940, I took friends ice-skating in my pea-green 1932 Ford convertible. On the way home, the fuel pump failed (they didn't last long in those days).

Since there was gas in the tank, I decided there was only one way to get us moving again. While one of my friends drove, I laid across the Ford's rear bumper, blowing as hard as I could into the gas tank.

That effort, plus some downhill driving, took us the final 3 miles home.
—*Robert Wagner, Dover, Delaware*

*PERFECT DAY IN EVERY WAY. Just before Jerry and Grace Gumbinger got married in May of 1941, they accepted delivery on this new Pontiac.*

## Plateless Pontiac Turned a Profit

OUR NEW CAR was delivered on the morning of May 20, 1941—shortly before we were married. It was a Pontiac town sedan painted an oyster color on top and robin-egg blue on the bottom, with red wheels and chrome hubcaps.

After the wedding in Kenosha, Wisconsin, we drove to Manitowoc to board the new car ferry *City of Midland*. We

spent our wedding night crossing Lake Michigan and arrived in Ludington, Michigan at 6 a.m. the next day. Then we drove to Detroit for a 3-day honeymoon.

While returning from a visit to the Ford Museum, a Detroit police officer stopped us and took us to the station. The offense? Our car had no license plates!

The Wisconsin motor vehicle office had been closed the day we got the car,

but a Milwaukee police sergeant had told us it was okay to keep driving. A Detroit police captain gave us a "to whom it may concern" letter stating our car was new and not stolen.

We kept the Pontiac until January 1943, when we sold it to a dealer who was looking for cars in "like-new condition". Although it had 13,000 miles on it, he gave us $100 more than we'd originally paid for it.
—*Jerry Gumbinger, Tucson, Arizona*

**CLEANUP CREW.** Robert Longfield took this photo of his buddies just before they all pitched in to help wash the mud off his new car.

last, however. After Pearl Harbor, I received a letter from my "uncle" saying he couldn't win the war without my help, and the De Luxe and I had to part company. I *still* miss it.

—*Robert Longfield*
*San Luis Obispo, California*

## This Model A Was About 60 Years Ahead of Its Time

IN THE EARLY '40s, very few high school kids owned a car. I was lucky to be one of two boys in Newcomerstown, Ohio who did. I'd worked two summers to earn $50—the full price of my 1930 Model A Ford coupe.

We did a lot of fun things with that car, like sneaking three or four kids into the Friday night football games by hiding in the rumble seat. We also loaded it up at Halloween—we once had as many as 13 kids "riding" in (or on) it.

But the main thing that attracted attention to this car was the "car phone". What I did was take a house doorbell, hook it up to the car's electrical system and put a push button on the bell.

Then I mounted a telephone handset on the dash of the car. Whenever we'd stop at an intersection where a group of people were, we'd push the bell button to make the phone ring. People would look over as we picked up the handset and pretended we were having a conversation.

Needless to say, we received lots of stares.

—*Frank Bartholow*
*North Baltimore, Ohio*

## Trip to Cabin Left Prized Ford a Deluxe Mess

THREE DAYS before Labor Day 1941, a long-held dream came true when I became the owner of a beautiful new Ford Super De Luxe station wagon.

My buddies wanted to spend the holiday weekend fishing, so on a sunny Saturday, we loaded up the car and left Minneapolis for a friend's cabin on Leech Lake in northern Minnesota.

After lunch, nasty black clouds began rolling in. We drove through a cloudburst, but the rain had stopped by the time we reached the gravel road leading to the cabin.

Within a couple of miles, the road turned to clay and mud, and the car sank to its hubs. My buddies removed their socks and shoes, rolled up their pants legs and ran ahead, trying to spot the deepest ruts, but it was no use.

We were bogged down completely and about ready to leave the car and wade back for help when a highway truck approached. It towed us out in no time, allowing us to get to the cabin just before dusk.

Next morning, my De Luxe was so covered with clay and mud it wasn't even recognizable. We dug in with rags and pails of water, and after a couple hours, when it became clear nothing had been damaged, I was one happy guy.

My love affair didn't

**SALUTE FROM A 16-YEAR-OLD.** Hazel Henson of Street, Maryland says she drove this 1933 Chevy from 1940 until 1950, then sold it for the same amount ($50) that she originally paid her brother for it. While it's unclear why Hazel is saluting, with patriotic fervor at an all-time high during the war years, she was not the only one doing so.

**WAS IT THE FIRST CAR PHONE?** Frank Bartholow (standing on the running board at right) and his high school friends from Newcomerstown, Ohio had a surefire method for attracting attention to his Model A (see his story above).

# Gas Rationing Began in Midst of 2,200-Mile Trip

*By Mildred Hazelo*
*Stratford, Connecticut*

**A MOHAWK MOMENT.** A dollar's worth of gas could get you a long way in Salinas, California in 1941. Barney Sieber of Goleta, California says his uncle owned this Mohawk station. Even though gas was cheap, that didn't necessarily mean you could actually buy it (see Mildred Hazelo's story on this page).

The war in Europe hadn't affected us much yet in the summer of 1941. My husband, Claude, was working overtime a few days a week at the Underwood Typewriter Company, and the extra money enabled us to visit his family in Rockford, Illinois.

Rockford was 1,100 miles from our home in Bridgeport, Connecticut, but we made it in 2 days, stopping overnight at a tourist court. Our two young children slept on a mattress laid over the backseat of our 1933 Ford V-8 sedan.

While visiting with Claude's family, we talked about the war. We'd heard of price controls to come and knew that an Economic Defense Board had been formed.

Then on July 31, Interior Secretary Harold Ickes recommended that filling stations be closed from 7 p.m. to 7 a.m. to conserve gasoline. This could be a problem on our trip back to Connecticut since we usually did some driving in the evening.

We started home on Friday, August 8 and were delayed twice by road construction. The next morning, Claude said, "We're running late, so we have to get on the road fast."

I tumbled clothes into the suitcase, quickly made up the children's bed in the car and we were off.

Around 11 a.m., I noticed a rash on 2-1/2-year-old Robert's legs. By noon, it had spread and I was in a panic. We had to find a doctor. But where would we find one at noon on a Saturday?

We were on the out-skirts of Sandusky, Ohio, so Claude drove around 'til he found a pharmacist. "Hives," he said. "Is he allergic to wool?" I didn't think so, but we bought some calamine lotion and returned to the car.

And there it was—in my hurry to make up the bed, I'd put a wool blanket on the mattress. I quickly stripped the bed and remade it with a sheet.

The afternoon drive went smoothly. We stopped for supper at 6 and filled the gas tank at 6:45. We'd hoped to be closer to home by now but were in the Catskill Mountains, using lots of gas. Would we have enough to make it home?

Claude thought about it for a long time, then said, "We're on the down side of the mountains. Whenever I can, I'm letting the car coast. Anything to save gasoline." With us coasting much of the way, we did make it home that night.

But we didn't go on another trip until the war was over and the gasoline shortage was a thing of the past. ❧

**NOW THAT WAS A HOOD!** John Eyler of Leechburg, Pennsylvania posed on the distinctive hood of his 1936 Hudson Terraplane. John bought the car for $180 in 1942 and says it was worth every penny.

**SUMMER OF '42.** Gene Anderson of Magalia California was looking pretty pleased with his shiny '41 Ford when his future wife snapped this photo on a sunny day in August 1942. They were at Whiting Beach on Lake Michigan, a spot where all the kids from Hammond, Indiana went for summer fun.

# It Was a Car Only a Teen—
# Or a Junk Dealer—Could Love

*By Wallace Johnson*
*Crescent City, California*

My first car cost $4. I bought it from two brothers who lived on the other side of the railroad tracks in Eagle River, Wisconsin. I was 16 years old and my father had died the year before, so he wasn't available to advise me about this investment.

Three other boys in my neighborhood had recently acquired cars (two Model T's and an Essex), so it was a proud moment for me to join their ranks.

My Model T had a peculiarity all its own. We could crank it all day and get nary a spark or cough. But push it 15 feet with hands on the left door, reach inside and flip the high-gear lever, and off it would go.

Then I'd jump on the running board, hop over the door and drop into the driver's seat. I hadn't even thought about acquiring a title, so getting gasoline turned out to be a problem.

This was during rationing, and to obtain gasoline stamps, you had to present your title to the ration board. I solved that by using the title to our old Model B, which was resting in the garage. Oil was no problem. My friends and I bailed it out of the used-oil barrel behind the service station.

### Lizzie Just Wouldn't Move

All went well until a fateful Sunday afternoon when some of us drove to a lake about 5 miles out of town for a swim. On the way back, a mile or so out of town, the Model T quit. Try as we might, we could not get it started again.

While we were trying to figure out what to do, a county patrolman pulled up right behind us. He sauntered up and asked whose car it was. One of the boys who'd sold it to me pointed in my direction. I nodded assent.

The cop asked where the license was. I didn't know. What about the title? I didn't have one. "Let's see your driver's license," he said. I didn't have one. "How did you get gas to put in the tank?"

After I'd explained, the cop left, saying, "I'll see you in my office after school Monday." I don't remember how we got the car home, but I do remember worrying all through school on Monday. Would I end up in jail?

School out, I trudged to the patrolman's courthouse office. He wasn't in, but a family friend who worked there was. His face was stern and hard. He chewed me up one side and down the other, until I felt my sins were so grievous I would surely end up doing time.

After what seemed an hour, he gave me an opening I hadn't expected. "Get that car down to the junk dealer right away and we'll forget all this."

*Forget it?* I was out the door and got that car to the junk dealer pronto.

"I want to sell this car," I told the dealer. He said, "I'll give you $6 for it." Sold!

Later, I found out the dealer had owned the car in the first place and was supposed to junk it, but had sold it to the brothers I'd bought it from. The policeman had censured him and told him he'd better get that car back. No wonder we'd come to an agreement on the price so quickly.

The car proved profitable in more ways than one. I made $2 in a short time plus had the two spare tires I kept. *And,* more importantly, I learned a lesson about getting myself on the wrong side of the law. ✒

**THE $2 TOUR.** Richard Breeden and his friends in Buena Vista, Virginia would put $2 worth of gas in Richard's '29 Model T and then joyride all weekend. Richard recalls the time they had a blowout and had to wait a week to order a new tire since no one had one. This photo was taken in 1940.

**GET ALONG, LITTLE DOGGY!** This Model T belonged to Happy Mitchell and his brother, Mick, of Sprott, Missouri (a little town that no longer exists). That's Mick behind the wheel and the boys' dog, "Pal", beside him. Happy now lives in Altoona, Iowa.

**THE LAST OF THE NEW.** When the first new cars of 1942 came out (like these Nashes), few people would have guessed that it would be another 4 years before they'd even *see* another new car.

---

### Blackout Nearly Landed Her in the Bay

DRIVING during World War II was severely limited by gas and tire rationing. Those of us who lived along a coastline faced added complications.

I lived in Pleasantville, New Jersey, across the bay from Atlantic City. One evening a week, I drove my '38 Plymouth to Atlantic City to work at the USO.

Atlantic City was true blackout territory. No lights facing the ocean were permitted. There were no streetlights or store lights, and windows were covered with blackout shades.

Car headlights had to be covered with black paint, except for a 1- by 3-inch slit that shed nothing on the road ahead, only a little strip of light when another car approached.

One night I left the USO to return home, driving slowly down Atlantic Avenue toward the boulevard leading to the mainland. Then I found myself following a dimly lit trolley car. What luck! I could just follow the trolley home.

But suddenly the trolley turned off, heading for the bay. After following it for several blocks, an awful realization hit me—this trolley crossed the bay on a trestle!

Quickly turning around, I drove back to Atlantic Avenue and groped my way to the mainland in the dark. As I headed west, I saw a little light chugging along over the bay…my trolley.

When the war ended, you can bet that the first things I did were fill my gas tank and scrape the black paint off the headlights.
— *Elizabeth Patton*
*Seminole, Florida*

### Procastination Put Dad in Mom's Doghouse

IN NOVEMBER 1941, Mom began warning Dad about the thinning tread on the tires of our 1939 Oldsmobile. But every time that she mentioned it, Dad always said he had something more important to do.

Then came Sunday, December 7, and Dad had to agree that, yes, maybe he'd better get into town and buy some tires. But when Monday came, there was one more chore he just *had* to finish that day.

On Tuesday, he finally made it to town, only to find that all tire sales had been frozen for the duration of the war. For the next 3 years, we had to travel *very* carefully—and Mom never let Dad forget it.
— *Ivan Pfalser*
*Caney, Kansas*

# Driving Lesson Ended with Mad Dash Around Farmyard

*By Nunzio Cotrone, Cincinnati, Ohio*

During World War II, my Italian-immigrant parents owned a 1932 Plymouth two-door sedan. One day, Dad stopped the car on a road near our home in rural Waushara County, Wisconsin and told me, "Today youra gonna learn-a to drive!"

I was scared and excited all at once. At 13, the eldest of nine children, I had driven our John Deere D. But the tractor's top speed was only 3-1/2 miles an hour—and that was going downhill with a tailwind.

I was too short to reach the Plymouth's pedals sitting back in the driver's seat, so Dad told me to sit between his legs. This way, he could "shim" me up so I could drive (and he could also take over the controls if an emergency arose).

At least four of my brothers and sisters were in the car that day, and they became very quiet. I think they were scared, too.

I jerked the car and killed the engine a couple of times, but finally we lurched and lunged forward, our heads whipping to and fro. I managed to shift the

⊙————————⊙
*"Dad lunged for the emergency brake..."*
⊙————————⊙

gears awkwardly and keep the old Plymouth on the road.

There was no other traffic on the road, so no lives were jeopardized. This was fun! My siblings stayed silent. For a moment, I think they were proud of their elder brother.

As we approached our driveway, Dad told me to take my foot from the accelerator and prepare to apply the brake. I obeyed. As we turned into the drive, he said, "Now you push-a da brake pedal."

I pushed, but the car seemed to speed up. "Push-a wit' all-a you might!" Dad ordered. I did, but now the car was gaining even more speed! While Dad lunged for the emergency brake and then the ignition, we sped around two barns, missed the chicken coop and an oak tree, and knocked down my mother's freshly hung wash.

Finally the car lurched to a stop, covered with a bed sheet. We had been stopped by the outhouse (which now lay on its side). Dad turned off the ignition and we all piled out. No one was hurt. "You push-a da wrong-a pedal," Dad observed. My foot had been on the accelerator!

We righted the toilet, repaired the clothesline, gathered the dirty wash and tidied the area. The Plymouth had a bent bumper, which we straightened with a big wrench. A headlight glass was broken, too.

To my surprise, Dad didn't give me a whipping or a tongue-lashing. Mom told him, "He's too young and too short to drive. He might have hurt someone!"

Dad replied, "He's-a gotta learn-a sometime!"

A few days later, Dad took me out in the Plymouth alone. We found a lonely road, and he instructed me in the finer points of motor vehicle operation.

At age 16, I took the state test for a motor vehicle operator's license in my 1930 Buick. I guess old habits die hard: I failed the first time because I didn't come to a full stop at a stop sign. ❧

**BITTERSWEET MOMENT.** When Leroy and Bertha Hunter of Unity, Maine celebrated their first wedding anniversary in June of 1942, they had no idea what the future held. Leroy had been given a very short pass from his duty station at Fort Williiams. Even so, Bertha says it was so good to have him home. The couple would end up driving this '35 Chevy coupe until 1950.

**THE BEST GAS-SAVER EVER.** With World War II rationing in full effect during the summer of 1942, everyone was trying to come up with new ways to save on gas. Meanwhile, this horse-drawn Sealtest Ice Cream truck in Washington, D.C. was getting great mileage the *old-fashioned way.* This photo was shared by R.B. McAtee of Arlington, Virginia.

# Tiny 'Tillie' Taught Aviator How to 'Hop'

*By Mac Grisham, Oxnard, California*

I was 18 in 1943 and in the Navy, stationed at Yellow Water, Florida. My first love was flying, but my little 1941 Crosley ran a close second. Since my name is Mac, I affectionately named the car "Tillie" in honor of the popular comic strip *Mac and Tillie*.

That little Crosley had a 12-horsepower engine and an advertised top speed of 60 miles per hour. That speed could be attained, but getting there was an exercise in patience.

My next-door neighbor once asked me to take her 5-year-old daughter to church. I opened the door for her to get in, but after looking inside, she began backing up and shaking her head.

She refused to get in and ran home. Later, I discovered the reason—she was afraid she'd have to help pedal!

The Crosley was supposed to get 50 miles to the gallon, so I was a bit disappointed to find Tillie only got 36. Still, having a car made me quite popular with my Navy shipmates and I usually had a car full of passengers whenever it was time to go into town on liberty.

But the added weight drastically reduced the car's forward speed. To enhance our acceleration, I instructed all of my passengers to throw their bodies forward on command as I called out a cadence.

With about five forward thrusts, our speed quickly increased to near-maximum. It must have been an amusing sight to anyone watching my little car "hop" along.

Little did I know that those hops would help me avert a serious accident while flying a jet 11 years later. On an instruction flight, my student and I found ourselves inverted at 26,000 feet with zero airspeed.

The jet began falling (why it didn't enter a spin, only the Good Lord knows). As our altitude passed 13,000 feet, I told my student to thrust his body to the left on a cadence count of three, followed by a slow movement back to the right.

Using this "body English", the aircraft rolled, and I regained full control at 8,000 feet. We could have bailed out, so it wasn't really a life-threatening situation, but we did avoid destruction of a valuable jet.

## Misbehaving Children Got Lift from Dad

WE LIVED 5 miles from Gadsden, Alabama during the war, and with rationing, there simply wasn't enough gas to transport us between home and school.

That left Dad no choice but to keep us with him at his store in town until it was closing time.

He'd converted his Chrysler-Plymouth showroom to a paint store but kept the body shop, used-car lot and filling station, which had a lift for servicing cars. But Dad also used that lift as a disciplinary tool.

If we were naughty, into a car we would go. The lift would go up and we'd sit there for 30 minutes…thinking over our transgressions.

—Jo Ann Moore
*Sylacauga, Alabama*

**HOIST 'EM HIGH.** During the war years, Jo Ann Moore (left) and her little sister (right) had a "time-out" room like no other when Dad came up with a novel disciplinary tool. The girls and a friend were getting ready to go for a Sunday drive.

**SERVICE WITH A STOOL.** The "pump jockey" at this California service station sometimes needed a little help reaching the gas tank! Grace Graunke of Lawndale, California says this is a favorite family photo. The station was managed by her husband and that's their oldest son, Curley, wearing a suit she made to match his father's.

## Rules Bent for Tireless Customer

MY FIRST real job was working as a clerk for our local War Price and Rationing Board. It proved to be a fascinating education in human behavior.

I remember patiently explaining to an elderly gentleman how to get a new tire. First he needed to have the old tire inspected at an authorized garage, then attach the inspector's form to an application and submit both to the Tire Panel.

If the panel approved his request, it would issue a certificate. Then he could actually start hunting for a new tire—but tires were in short supply, with or without a certificate.

My customer looked pretty unhappy when he left. About an hour later, we heard a commotion in the building, then saw the same man rolling a huge tire across the floor. He plopped it on the counter in front of me.

He'd struggled up two flights of stairs with this tire to show me the hole. In fact, he insisted I put my hand through it, which I easily did—right up to my elbow.

I telephoned a board member to get verbal approval to issue a certificate, on my guarantee that the tire was indeed useless. With certificate in hand, the man went off, still grumbling.

He made it clear he was plenty annoyed at having to have a young girl inspect his tire in such an inconvenient location.

I don't think he ever knew he got preferential treatment that day—and I've often wondered if he ever found a tire to buy.
—*Lois Leston*
*Durham, Connecticut*

## Remember the Days Of "Bumper Jumpers"?

DOES ANYONE recall "bumper jumpers"? That's the term we used in the late 1930s and early '40s when cars locked bumpers.

When a slow-moving car stopped suddenly, its front end would dip down and its rear would rise slightly. If the car behind it braked too late, its front bumper would slip under the first car's rear bumper. With bumper guards protruding above and below, the bumpers would be firmly locked together.

**FROM CCC TO THE "BIG C".** Before he got a job in Chicago in 1942 and purchased this '34 Chevrolet sedan, George Schwark had been working in a Civilian Conservation Corps camp. And, although it was a used car, it was his pride and joy, says his wife, Lucille, of Friendship, Wisconsin.

To unlock them, one or two people would stand on the rear car's bumper brackets while others tried to lift the front car's rear end. Once they had established a bouncing rhythm, the bumpers would usually part enough to be separated.

I watched this ritual often, and even participated in it a few times. The cars were never harmed...most people took it with a resigned sense of humor...and the insurance companies never had to be called.
—*Wesley Phillippi*
*Des Moines, Iowa*

**ROMANCE, BUT FEW RIDES.** Like other young couples during the war years, Doris and Bill Turner didn't spend a lot of time driving around. Gas was just too precious to waste on anything but essential trips (note the "A" sticker in the windshield). The couple, who now lives in Clyde, North Carolina, has fond memories of this '36 Ford sedan.

# Dad Fell for Tire Scam...But Not for Long

*By Peter Combs, Ennis, Montana*

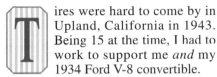

Tires were hard to come by in Upland, California in 1943. Being 15 at the time, I had to work to support me *and* my 1934 Ford V-8 convertible.

The gas station where I worked was combined with a repair shop, and one day, I found four brand-new 21-inch Model A tires in the storeroom. I talked the owner out of them, then went to a junkyard to find four rims.

But my car was built for 16-inch tires and wouldn't look very good with these. So I convinced my father—"for the war effort", of course—to let me put the new tires on his 1934 Ford coupe.

I'd get his old ones, which would fit my car perfectly, and he'd have new ones to go to work. Dad was a bit non-mechanical and fell for this bait-and-switch.

A buddy came over to help me change the eight tires that night, before Dad changed his mind. There was a major problem, though. We only had one jack and one lug wrench.

We had to jack up one tire, remove it with the wrench and take it to the other car. Then we put a rock under the brake drum of the first car and lowered the jack until the drum rested on the rock.

We took the jack to the second car, jacked *it* up, removed a tire and put it on the first car. We tightened the lug nuts, jacked up the tire, removed the rock—and started all over again. Switching all eight tires took 2 hours.

When Dad drove to work the next

---

⚙ *"His car made three complete circles..."* ⚙

---

morning, everything was fine until he had to turn a corner. The 21-inch tires met the restraint of 16-inch fenders, and he had to "back and fill" to make the turn. But that was the least of his problems.

After "backing and filling" around two more corners, Dad noticed a tire passing his car on the left. Then the left rear end of his car dropped to the road. It was *his* tire that had just cruised by—

in our haste to change the tires, my buddy and I had failed to properly tighten the lug nuts!

Dad's car made three complete circles, careening toward a filling station. The owner was pumping gas when he saw my father circling toward him, out of control, and frantically waved him away from the pump.

Dad managed to stop the car safely at the station. A few minutes later, a truck driver came walking up. A rolling tire had just chased his truck into a ditch, and now it was stuck there!

When my father got home from work at 5 p.m., his normally calm demeanor had vanished. He was livid. He spent the next 15 minutes reminding me of my wayward past.

Then Dad looked at his watch and said I was to have his tires back on his car by dinnertime—and I was not to be late for dinner, which was always served promptly at 6 o'clock.

I quickly called my buddy to help me. Within 40 minutes, Dad's tires were back on his car, and my car sat propped up on four big rocks. 📯

**ON THE BEACH IN BROOKLYN.** These photos were taken at Gerritsen Beach in Brooklyn, New York in the summer of 1942. Stanley Lundy, now of Manchester, Connecticut, is shown above with his cousin and at right with his "best gal" (wife Dorothy) and his first car—a Chevy Opera coupe. Stanley sold the car when he went into the Marines in February 1943 and for months afterward, Dorothy saw this vehicle all over Sheepshead Bay in Brooklyn with a "Special Delivery" sign in its window.

My husband was drafted in 1943 and sent to San Luis Obispo, California. Expecting our first child in September, I stayed behind in Iowa.

When Ann was born, Howard longed to reunite our growing family, but housing was scarce near most Army camps and he looked in vain for a room or apartment. Christmas was lonely that year.

In jest, I wrote to Howard that maybe I'd buy a house trailer and pull it to California. "If you can get a trailer with the money we've saved," he replied, "get one and come on out."

What a shock! I'd never even been outside Iowa—and had certainly never pulled a trailer. But I took Howard at his word and bought an 18-foot mobile home for $250.

A neighbor attached a hitch to the bumper of our 1936 Model A Ford, and gave me flares, a map and much-needed advice on maneuvering my new rig. Aunt Madge, my mother's sister, offered to go along to help with the baby.

I was frightened and wondered if I should wait until winter was over. But by then, Howard might be overseas—it was now or never!

### Security in the Backseat

On January 16, 1944, we set out. Aunt Madge rode in back with Ann and attended to all her needs. That wise silver-haired woman was a true blessing. Whenever a problem arose, she'd say, "Now, Melba, we can easily take care of this."

As we drove southwest toward Oklahoma City, the road was rough in many places, and we replaced two flat tires. One was an oversized truck tire that was too big for the trailer's wheel well.

Each time we hit a bump, another piece of rubber flew off. We knew it didn't fit, but with wartime rationing in effect, what could we do?

# Trailer-Towing Mom Set Out For California

*By Melba McDermott, Boone, Iowa*

**MOM'S MISSION.** Melba McDermott was determined to find a way that she and Ann could spend time with Dad Howard.

After 4 days, we reached my parents' home in Oklahoma City.

When Dad saw the house trailer, he exclaimed, "My God, girl, are you crazy?" Though skeptical, he found us a better tire, and soon we were back on Route 66—the only road to California in those days.

We made steady progress through the Texas Panhandle and New Mex-ico, where we were thrilled to see our first cactus and all those wide-open spaces. To my surprise, we hit snow outside Flagstaff, Arizona—I hadn't realized it snowed that far south.

Soon we were stuck, so I hitched a ride to Flagstaff, bought tire chains and hitched back. I had no idea how to put them on, but Aunt Madge had used a pancake turner to chip gravel from in front of the trailer, then spread it in front of the wheels for traction. It worked!

In Flagstaff, we had the chains put on at a gas station, but then, of course, the snow stopped for good. We constantly watched the gas gauge, hoping our precious book of ration stamps would last.

### Lost Ration Book

After a fill-up in California, I realized I'd left my ration book at a gas station. I turned the trailer around—how, I'll never know!—and headed back. But the station attendant denied seeing the book and I left empty-handed.

Our last tank of gasoline got us to San Bernardino, where, with Aunt Madge at my side and Ann in my arms, I tearfully pleaded my case to the board. They gave us enough stamps to make it to San Luis Obispo.

After 15 days on the road, we met Howard at the USO in the midst of a downpour. What a happy reunion!

Howard was thrilled to see his precious daughter and couldn't believe how much she'd grown.

Six days after our arrival, Howard learned his unit was going overseas. Although disappointed, I thanked God we'd arrived before he had to leave (as it turned out, we had another 4 weeks together).

After Howard left, I sold the trailer for $400 and rode back to Iowa in the Ford with another soldier's wife. Today my grandchildren laugh in disbelief at stories of Grandma pulling a trailer on Route 66. And I laugh with them. Why not? ✍

## Owning '36 Ford Put Teen On Top of the World

WHEN I turned 18, my brother and I pooled our money to buy a '36 Ford for $350. But he never let me drive it. In 1942, my boyfriend enlisted in the Navy and gave me *his* car, which was identical to my brother's.

Finally, I had my own car! As a teenager, getting "a set of wheels" was my primary goal. Having my own car was synonymous with being emancipated, and I drove around town as if I owned the world.

I polished my car every day, never regretting any of the time or money I spent on it. There was such prestige in having a 1936 Ford with black paint and white sidewalls, complete with a tailpipe filled with spun glass—even though they were illegal.

I loved that car and wish I still had it. Even though I've had many automobiles in my life, I never fell in love with any of them as I did with my '36 Ford.  —*Bea Milan, Tigard, Oregon*

## He Solved the "Ping" Problem

WHEN I was working at Boeing's plant in Seattle, Washington during World War II, we experimented with various ways to get more power from aircraft engines.

One method involved injecting wa-

**MODEL "BEA" FORD.** Bea Milan loved her black '36 Ford with its white sidewalls and an engine that had a distinctive (but illegal) sound.

ter directly into the cylinders to keep the engines from overheating at full throttle. I got to thinking about this and wondered if it might work on cars —so I devised a system to put on my 1940 Plymouth.

It consisted of a 1-gallon jug of water under the hood and a tube that ran through a metering valve. The tube had holes on the underside, and the plugged end was inserted into a hole in the carburetor. Suction from the carburetor pulled water into the carburetor intake, then into the cylinders.

A shut-off valve was controlled by a choke cable in the driver's compartment. The low-octane gasoline sold during those war years made car engines ping terribly, even on small hills. My system didn't seem to affect the Plymouth's power, but it completely eliminated all pinging the minute it was turned on! A couple of years later, I pulled the head and found no carbon buildup in the cylinders (an unheard-of condition in older engines).

With the strict gas rationing enforced then, anyone stopped by the police had to have a good explanation for being too far from home. My plan was to say that I'd found a way to run my car on water after starting it on gas…then I'd raise the hood to prove my point.

Maybe it's just as well that occasion never arose.

—*Joe Oliver*
*Kent, Washington*

**THE TRUMAN MOBILE.** Missouri Senator Harry Truman was one of the lucky Americans who purchased a new automobile early in the '40s (while new cars were still being made). Truman bought this '41 Chrysler "Royal" coupe in November of 1940 and drove it until he became President in 1945. James Swords, Tonkawa, Oklahoma, shared this photo.

**BUMPER CROP.** Virginia Davis (second from left) and her two brothers (third and fourth from left) loved Sundays in the early '40s—that meant they got to go visit their uncle and aunt's farm in Pennsylvania. Virginia, of Whiting, West Virginia, says even though they had to get dressed up, they enjoyed playing with their country cousins.

## Trip to Woodpile Almost Landed Her in the Woodshed

OUR FAMILY of seven lived on a one-horse tobacco farm in rural North Carolina in 1944. On cold winter mornings, when Daddy's '37 Pontiac wouldn't start, he'd call us outside to help.

Daddy or my older sister would sit behind the wheel while we pushed the car out of the driveway and down the dirt road until it finally cranked up. I was 13 and wanted to learn to drive. Then I could sit behind the wheel and not have to push.

One day when Daddy was working in the back field, the car was parked near the barn and needed to be moved into the yard. I begged my sister to let me do it. She reluctantly said, "Okay, but don't you dare tell Daddy."

Happily, I climbed behind the wheel and started the motor. But, as I rounded the barn, I proceeded to drive through our grapevines and right up onto the woodpile. My brothers, who'd

**IGNORANCE IS BLISS.** Mary Thrower's dad (above) never learned about her driving this Pontiac.

been stacking wood, saw me coming and ran for their lives!

There I sat, on top of the woodpile in Daddy's forbidden-to-drive Pontiac! My sister grabbed the wheel, backed the car off the woodpile and parked it in the yard.

Then we grabbed a hammer and nailed the grapevine posts back together. After that, we got the rakes and began removing the car tracks. Whew! Did I sweat those moments out.

When Daddy finally came up the lane a few minutes later, he was impressed that we were raking without being told (thankfully, he never learned what really happened).

And—you may not be surprised to learn—it would be many years before I had the urge to drive again. —*Mary Thrower Rockingham, North Carolina*

**HE THUMPED HIS WAY TO THE BAY.** Home on leave in 1943, Edward Manning of Wild Horse Plains, Montana drove this '41 Dodge from Southern California to his new duty station in Oakland. Ed says new tires weren't available to the likes of him back then, and the tires he did have tended to fall apart since they'd been repaired by inserting what was called a "section". He had to scrounge up a new sectioned tire on the way.

# Dream Durant Turned into 'The Heap'

*By Torben Torngren, Vacaville, California*

It was 1943, I was 14 and had just finished my first driving lesson in my buddy's father's 1935 Ford. It wasn't a roaring success—I'd knocked out one of the supports that held up the roof of the front porch of their house near Grand Rapids, Michigan.

Luckily, his dad was out of town, and we managed to get everything back together (more or less). In spite of this incident, my lessons continued whenever the coast was clear, and I was soon driving like a pro…at least, that was my opinion.

When I told my dad I wanted a car when I turned 15, he said he had no objections, providing I used my own money for the car and insurance.

My mother (whose response had been, "What does a 15-year-old kid need a car for—he'll just kill himself!") was relieved to hear the conditions.

In her mind, there was no way I'd come up with that much money so soon. From that moment on, I saved every penny I earned from my two newspaper routes and any odd jobs I could find.

No one was unhappier than Mom when, shortly before my 15th birthday, I told Dad I'd saved up almost $100. Soon I'd found a 1931 Durant coupe that looked great and sounded good, and the owner only wanted $50.

Against Dad's advice, I bought it—he didn't think it was too bright to buy a make of car no longer made.

The car was named, believe it or not, after William Crapo Durant, actually an important figure in American automobile history. Although I would later believe his *middle name* would have been more appropriate for my car!

I was excited about the Durant's six-cylinder engine, which I figured would make it a "killer" of the four-cylinder Model A

Fords my peers drove. That was true the few times it was running well.

When I turned 15 and got my driver's license, I was in heaven: I had a neat-looking car, a few extra dollars and lots of girls wanting to go for rides.

Unfortunately, all too soon, I was broke, my neat-looking car (now named "The Heap") was barely running and all those girls, once again, were being chauffeured around in Model A's.

Worst of all, I had to admit Dad was right. I'd had a real tough time keeping the car running, the tires were bad—

---

> "Worst of all, I had to admit Dad was right…"

---

and no replacements were available to a kid with only an "A" gas ration sticker.

When it finally occurred to me that I was doing more pushing and walking than riding, I decided to put an ad in the *Grand Rapids Press* and sell it. Luckily the car wasn't running badly

then, although the radiator leaked like a sieve.

At the gas station, I found what I needed—a giant "stop leak" capsule. After filling the radiator, I stuffed the capsule in and fired it up. As advertised, the leak stopped after a few minutes of squirting and bubbling.

I'd just hosed off the front of the car when the first customer showed up. He walked around it, kicked the tires, then fired it up. It sounded good, and I thought I had him hooked.

Then he got out of the car and lifted the side panel of the hood. The look on his face when a giant gob of "stop leak" foam slid out of the engine compartment onto the fender was a classic.

By the time the second customer showed up, I'd cleaned up the engine compartment and moved it to a drier part of the driveway. That fellow gave me $50 for it and I never saw the car again.

Shortly afterward, I bought a huge 1928 Buick, and I once took 13 buddies to a football game in it…but that's another story. ✌

**LIBERATOR FLEW—DURANT WAS GROUNDED.** Torben Torngren (see his story above) learned that the demands of military hardware, like the B-24 Liberator pictured here, made it next to impossible for a 15-year-old kid to keep a 13-year-old car running. This Lincoln might have been a better bet. Photo was shared by George Boozer of Atlanta, Georgia.

### Ride with Surgeon Was Hitchhiker's Dream Come True

THE FASTEST RIDE of my life took place in 1945. At the time, I was stationed at Camp Carson in Colorado Springs and was trying to hitch a ride to Denver for the weekend.

After several cars passed me by, a Cadillac convertible swung out of a side street and stopped. The driver, a distinguished-looking white-haired gentleman, said, "If you're going to Denver, get in. If not, I can't stop on the way."

I got in. There were about 12 more blocks to the edge of town, and the speed limit was 25 miles an hour. Before we'd gone two blocks, the Cadillac was doing 80, and I was wondering what I'd gotten into!

When a car started to poke out at an intersection, I heard the scream of a siren and figured my ride was over. Wrong! The siren was on the Cadillac's left front fender, accompanied by a large flashing red lamp.

It turned out that my driver was the chief surgeon of Denver General Hospital and had been called in for an emergency operation. Once I understood, I relaxed and enjoyed the ride.

Even if the doctor didn't care about me, I was sure he wouldn't jeopardize his own chances of reaching his destination. Besides, it was clear he knew exactly what he was doing.

Two miles outside Castle Rock, he turned on the siren and we drove through the main street of that little town at 105 miles an hour.

A few minutes later, the doctor let me out in front of the hospital. I thanked him and took a trolley downtown.

We'd traveled 70 miles on an old two-lane highway in 50 minutes!

—Donald Robinson
North Billerica, Massachusetts

**READY TO BLAST OFF.** Even parked in front of the housing project at the Sand Point Naval Air Station in 1943, this Graham Supercharger looked like a powerful machine. Its owner then, Raymond Kirlin of Seattle, Washington, says the car's acceleration was terrific. He recalls getting it up to 85 miles per hour and estimates it would do 100 easily.

**WADIN' IN THE WATER.** No, this '38 Ford is not floating down a river. Actually it's driving across a concrete causeway in Trexler Game Preserve Park in Lehigh County, Pennsylvania. Albert Schantz of Reading, Pennsylvania says the picture was taken in the spring of 1944 and his girlfriend, Jennie (now his wife), was in the passenger seat beside him.

**BUSTER RODE IN BACK.** Art Woldt enjoyed driving his '28 Chevrolet roadster around his grandpa's farm in 1945. Along for the ride, says Art, who now lives in Wynantskill, New York, are his cousin Gerry and a dog named "Buster". The Chevy also had an "ah-ooh-ga" horn.

# Navy Men 'Sailed' Down Volcano with No Brakes!

*By Melvin Hess, Dunbar, Wyoming*

Today it's a great thrill to bicycle down the slopes of Haleakala, a dormant volcano on the island of Maui. No one ever dreamed of doing that when I was stationed there with the Navy in 1944.

But there were dreamers back then —my friend Mort and I among them. We purchased a very old Model T and made it run by all sorts of adaptations, such as cutting the top off to make a convertible and welding on Jeep wheels so we could find tires for it.

After taking it on one successful trip, we were ready for our assault on Haleakala. We tightened the bands on what then passed for a transmission, checked the cable brakes (which were a never-ending source of trouble) and gassed up. Prudence dictated that we gather up baling wire, tools and rope. We also carried extra gas, water and oil.

On a bright Sunday morning, Mort and I picked up two friends and headed for the "up-country". We packed Spam baked with fresh pineapple and brown sugar, bread, cheese and a supply of Primo beer.

The radiator spouted steam, and we stopped several times to tighten bands and add water, but we chugged around all the hairpin turns quite well.

Around noon, we arrived at the crest of Haleakala. We were astounded at the size of the crater. After admiring it for a while, we prepared for our descent. How little we knew about getting a Model T down 38 miles of steep, winding curves!

Thirty minutes down from the summit, the brake cables snapped and the car took off like a rocket. I plowed into the side of the road to stop the careening hunk of metal. The two men in back were thrown out—no seat belts then—but sustained no life-threatening injuries.

Now we faced a serious problem: How to get down this volcano without killing ourselves. But Navy men are resourceful. We wired up the brake cable and started down again. It broke after 10 minutes. Once again we were hurtling downward at an alarming rate. Once again, "bam" into the hillside.

This, we finally realized, was not going to work.

So out came the rope, which we tied to the rear axle. We geared the bands to their lowest position and eased down the road with one sailor walking behind, hanging onto the rope.

This worked fine until the bands burned out, sending us into another near free-fall. The sailor on the rope couldn't hold back, and we slammed into the hillside again. If one sailor couldn't hold back the car, perhaps three could.

This worked better, except that now and again one of us would tire, and the car would again gain speed. With shoes skidding, we tugged to hold the car back.

When we reached Kula, we persuaded a Jeep driver to tie onto us in the rear and ease us slowly down the slope. About a mile from the valley floor, the rope parted and we were set free to whistle through the cane fields.

There wasn't much to bump into, so we settled down to ride it out. The car shook at speeds it was never designed for, but in the end, we coasted to a stop on beautiful level ground. When the Jeep driver caught up with us, he towed us back to the base. ✍

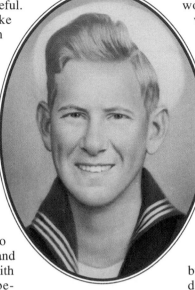

**WILD RIDE. Melvin Hess had reason to smile after surviving Model T trip.**

**HE WENT OVERSEAS—THEN OVERLAND.** In June of 1945, Robert Kashnig of Sheboygan, Wisconsin had just returned from combat duty as a pilot in Europe. Stationed in Sioux Falls, South Dakota, he bought this 1924 Overland for $45 for local transportation. Although riders had to wear goggles and put up umbrellas when it rained, the Overland was still better than riding the "GI Bus", recalls Robert, who's behind the wheel in this photo.

# CHAPTER 7

**A HUDSON—AND NO WAITING!** When Jim and Helen Wilcutts left the military in 1946, it was nearly impossible to buy a new car of any vintage. Then a friend helped them get a Hudson dealership—which meant that they could also buy a brand-new vehicle every year! That's Jim above showing off the new 1948 Hudson in West Chester, Pennsylvania (where the couple still lives).

# On the Road Again

When World War II came to an end, the pent-up demand for new cars almost amounted to national hysteria. Not only had Detroit produced nary a new car in 4 years, but several million servicemen and women were eager to spend their mustering-out pay on a car of their very own.

It was easy to spot a car dealer in a crowd. He was the one with the permanent smile on his face.

The car business was topsy-turvy. You didn't walk into a dealership and haggle over how *little* you were willing to pay. Instead, you hinted at how much over the official price you were willing to shell out.

Officially, autos were under price controls. But there were ways around that. A dealer who had a rare new car in his showroom might say, "Charlie, I'll bet you $200 you can't throw your hat up and make it stick to the ceiling."

If Charlie wanted a new car, he'd take the bet—and, of course, lose. But he also would be the proud owner of a new car.

Quick to spot opportunity, new manufacturers got into the carmaking business. A man who had become a legend for building Liberty ships fast and cheap during the war boasted that he would break Detroit's near-monopoly on the auto business.

He was Henry J. Kaiser, who was soon marketing three models, The Kaiser, the Frazer and the smallish Henry J. As things worked out, he should have stuck to building ships.

A man by the name of Tucker took over a former wartime armament factory and, with great fanfare, announced a car he said would forever change the industry. People rushed to Tucker dealerships to put down deposits long before the assembly line began to roll.

## Steady as She Goes

A friend of mine actually met Mr. Tucker, who insisted on taking him for a ride in one of the first models. He pushed the car up to 100 miles an hour, sat back and, to my friend's horror, took his hands off the steering wheel. "See, it's as steady as a rock," Mr. Tucker crowed.

But, in the end, only 34 were built and few actually ran. Today they are museum pieces and collectors' treasures.

The Studebaker company turned to a famous industrial designer, urging him to take a whole fresh look at car designing. He did, and turned out a sleek beauty!

But, like the Chrysler Airflow of the '30s, the car was at least a decade ahead of Americans' ideas of what a car should look like. The popular joke was that you couldn't tell if the new Studebaker was coming or going. Eventually, it went.

While the car-buying public fretted and fussed and waited, it was urgent to keep those weary prewar clunkers running. It took limitless ingenuity, as the stories on the following pages attest.

Just think what a market there would have been for duct tape, had it been on the market back then! —*Clancy Strock*

**BLUE TORPEDO.** The Tucker Torpedo was one of the more stylish cars to come out of the postwar period. It was a powerful car, too—with a top speed of 120 miles per hour.

H. Armstrong Roberts

# 'Green Monster' Had Motorists Doing Double Takes

*By Philip Horn, Jonesboro, Arkansas*

As children of the Great Depression, my friends and I developed survival skills growing up in Akron, Ohio. We also learned to repair almost anything—including automobiles.

While hunting rabbits in 1946, we'd found a 1928 Hudson S abandoned in the brush. The farmer, surprised someone had used his property as a dump site, offered it to us free if we'd remove it.

We originally planned to sell the car for scrap, but after a little tinkering, we realized that a lot of labor and a modest amount of money would turn it into transportation.

We wanted to drive to Washington, D.C. and visit all the places we'd read about. So, in less than 10 days, we had the frame and engine disassembled. The engine was in pretty good shape except for two broken springs that operated the valves.

The springs cost less than a dollar. No other engine repairs were needed. The sheet metal was in bad shape, but we found replacement parts at local junkyards.

In less than a month, we had a very strange vehicle that looked nothing like anything that ever came out of Detroit. The rear wheels were bigger than those in front, which made the car look like it was going downhill (an effect we liked).

When we started it up, we were surprised—and our families disappointed!—that the contraption actually ran.

Next we hand-painted the car with red primer, followed by several coats of

---

### "No respectable girl would be seen in it!"

---

paint and lacquer—bright orange, yellow, pea green and apple green. We sanded out the brush marks between coats, ending up with a rippled effect.

The car looked like a chameleon imitating a spoiled apple, so we called it the "Green Monster".

In those days, no insurance, inspection or proof of purchase was required for a license. We listed one of the junkyards as the owner and identified the make and model as "experimental".

The Green Monster received lots of attention but was never the "date-mobile" we'd envisioned—no respectable girl would be seen in it!

Our trip began in early summer, with all stops marked on a map. It wasn't much help (we were lost most of the time), but we didn't care. We had over a month for the trip and a primary belief God would continue to protect fools.

### Paint Job Had "Depth"

Road conditions took their toll on the Green Monster's paint job. By the time we reached Washington, D.C., sand and stones had deteriorated the finish so much that each layer of paint was visible in spots. Our car had become a "tie-dyed original".

We'd assumed the sophisticates of Washington wouldn't be surprised by much, but most of the motorists we passed seemed shocked by the Green Monster. We saw lots of smiles and waves, too.

On July 19, we visited the Smithsonian Institution and left the car in the parking lot. When we returned, a large crowd was gathered around it, taking pictures. Some of the people were speculating that the car was an art exhibit of unknown deep significance.

Until we climbed inside, no one seemed to suspect the car was actually a means of transportation. The crowd cheered as we drove off in a cloud of dust, smoke, thumps and rattles.

After meandering for nearly 1,300 miles, we returned to Akron and gave the Green Monster to a junkyard. We often wondered if some of that scrap metal was reincarnated into another vehicle.

If so, I hope the new owner got as much enjoyment out of that pile of iron as we did.

**FINALLY—A NEW CAR!** This Nash "600" was one of the first new cars available in 1946. Its owner, Jess Baudour of Salinas, California, says its 85-horsepower engine wasn't strong enough to take it up the steeper hills. By the way, the pretty girl, Gladys, was Jess' fiancee at the time, and she's now his wife.

## Mom and the Phaeton Had a Falling-Out

THIS is a photo of me, at age 16, in my third (and favorite) car, a 1931 Chevrolet Landau Phaeton. It was the only one of my cars my mother ever rode in with me—and then only once!

A civic-minded person, my mother was president of the band mothers for our school outside Grand Rapids, Michigan, as well as president of the local PTA.

One day, she asked me to drive her to Grand Rapids to attend an important PTA dinner at the very prestigious Pantlind Hotel. I told her I would, quickly washed off the car and away we went.

When we pulled up in front of the hotel, there were lots of important-looking, well-dressed people milling about. Being a well-mannered kid, I jumped out of the car, ran around and opened the door for my mother.

But to my surprise, the door came off the car and fell onto the sidewalk—with me still holding the handle! A little flushed, but still reserved, my mother stepped out of the car and calmly announced, "It won't be necessary for you to pick me up after the meeting."

So, after picking up the door and putting it in the backseat, I drove home. Later, when I told my dad what had happened, he laughed 'til there were tears in his eyes!

And Mother never rode with me again.

—*Torben Torngren*
*Vacaville, California*

**GREAT SHAKES!** Margaret Ellingham (on the left) says that when her brother-in-law, Don, came home from overseas duty as a B-17 gunner and radioman in 1946, one of his dreams was to have ice cream again. That's Don with his girlfriend in the front seat of this '37 Plymouth. Margaret, now of Lake Havasu City, Arizona, recalls that gas was still being rationed so they couldn't go far—but what a welcome treat those shakes were! Don's dad is on the right.

## Hudson Had Unique Features

MY FIRST CAR, purchased used when I was 19, was a 1942 Hudson Commodore "6" business coupe. For those too young to remember, business coupes were three-passenger, two-door vehicles with a shelf behind the single seat.

A friend helped me convert the Hudson into a "club coupe", doubling its seating capacity. We took out the single-back seat and replaced it with a split-back front seat from a junked 1940 Chevrolet. Then we removed the rear shelf and made a seat from the original front-seat cushions.

The Hudson was black with a red pencil stripe down the side. The long chrome parking lights with white-milk glass atop the front fenders added to its striking appearance.

One interesting feature was the Hud-

**COMMODORE CLUB.** Sheridan Johnson loved his 1942 Hudson.

son's "vacumotive" drive. By pushing a button on the dashboard, you operated the clutch pedal electronically. The car even had a foot-operated station selector for its eight-tube Zenith radio.

—*Sheridan Johnson, Worthington, Ohio*

## They Could've Had a Working Honeymoon

WHEN I returned from World War II, there was a huge selection of autos available where I lived—exactly *one* long-used car! Of course, I took it.

Although it was a gorgeous rusty green, I arranged for the dealer to repaint it a pale yellow. It came out a bold taxicab yellow instead. Still, it had four wheels and was faster than walking, so I kept it.

Later that year, on our honeymoon in San Francisco, my wife and I passed a lady on the street who hailed us—and looked quite surprised when her "taxicab" didn't stop for her!

—*Walter Hanson, Hemet, California*

Archive Photos/Hammond

## "Suicide Doors" Proved a Menace on Runaway Ford

WHILE attending the University of North Dakota after World War II, I bought my first car, a 1933 Model B Ford. The 1934 B had a new V-8 engine—mine still had the old four-cylinder, a bad combination.

But I wouldn't say the car was a total failure—it could always be used as a bad example!

The Model B's "suicide doors" hinged at the back. With any hinge malfunction, the force of the wind would pull the door open, exposing the driver to considerable risk.

One day of the first winter I owned the car, I started the B to go for a drive. The road was covered with snow and ice, and my inadequate tires were spinning uselessly. Knowing the car just needed a little nudge, I left it in low gear and got out to give it a push.

The car did start to move. But then I slipped and fell, and the car kept going! I got up to chase it but had to get in *front* of the suicide doors before I could climb in and regain control.

Slipping and sliding all the way, I managed to get into the car just before it reached the "T" intersection at the end of the road. I learned two lessons that

*SUICIDE SPECIALS.* **Cars like William Warner's '34 Plymouth (above) or Ralph Long's Model B could be extremely dangerous. The worst moments (as Ralph attests on this page) came when trying to exit or enter a moving vehicle. William's wife, Theresa (at right in 1948), shows how it was done when the car was parked. The couple now lives in Naples, Florida.**

day: Never leave a moving car and *never* buy a car with those crazy, front-facing doors.
—*Ralph Long*
*St. Germain, Wisconsin*

# New Chevy Blazed Its Own 'Oregon Trail'

*By Eula McGee, Dowling Park, Florida*

Even before my husband and I married in 1943, I knew that Dave's dream was to move to Oregon. By 1946, I'd already been discharged from the Navy and was living in California.

When I heard Dave's ship was returning to Virginia and that he'd be discharged soon, that was all I needed. I headed back East and ordered a new Chevrolet two-door sedan.

When the car came in, I left our apartment in Portsmouth, Virginia for what should have been a 1-hour flight to Wilmington, Delaware. My family would meet me at the airport, then take me to pick up the car. Easy, right? Wrong!

### Any "Port" in a Storm

A freak snowstorm prevented a landing in Wilmington. We tried to land in Albany, New York, but that airport was closed, too. We finally landed in Cleveland, Ohio and took a bus to the train station.

After a 20-hour trip on a crowded train, I arrived in Philadelphia and boarded a bus for the long trip to my sister's in New Jersey. My 1-hour flight had turned into a nightmare!

When we finally picked up the car, my sisters were as excited as I was. After the war years, a new car was a thrilling sight.

On the trip back to Virginia, I was

**WESTWARD HO!** Eula and Dave McGee had always wanted to move to the Northwest. In 1946, they made their dream a reality.

joined by my 6-year-old niece, who was going to visit us for a few weeks. Along the way, we stopped near a farmhouse for a picnic lunch.

When we got back in the car, it wouldn't start. This was supposed to be a brand-new car, just serviced and ready for the road!

With a prayer, I walked to the farmhouse and related our tale. That wonderful farmer called someone to check out the car. We learned the mechanic had shorted out the generator. With a little adjustment and a push, we were off again. The Lord is good!

### Time to Hit the Road

For our trip West, Dave designed a baggage trailer with a canvas cover to hold household goods and furniture. It looked like a covered wagon—and it definitely wasn't aerodynamic (as we later discovered).

We were on our way at last, following our own "Oregon Trail". The car performed beautifully, despite a tendency to boil over on long mountain climbs. We solved that by taking on the mountains in the cool of the evening.

One day we'd attacked the approach to Little Big Horn but had to back up, fill the boiling radiator with water from a nearby stream and wait for evening. By then, several cars were being towed up the incline by tractor.

But our Chevy went right to the top in low gear. With a full moon overhead, it was one of the most beautiful moments of our trip.

### Trailer Nearly Did Them in

Our "covered wagon" obstructed the rearview mirror, which didn't cause as many problems as we'd feared. But it did contribute to one very harrowing experience.

Descending a steep mountain grade, the trailer seemed to be pushing the car instead of following it—we were coming down much too fast! Just ahead, the highway made an abrupt left turn, with a seemingly bottomless drop-off to the right.

When Dave turned the wheel as hard as he could, the trailer seemed to take flight out into space. I'm not sure what kept us from going over. Maybe a band of angels lifted the trailer, and the car with it, for we miraculously came to rest just around the curve.

Finally we reached Bend, Oregon and Dave's dream was realized at last. There were other moves after that, but through all of them, that trusty '46 Chevy served us well. ❧

**COVERED WAGON.** This homemade baggage trailer with a canvas cover "followed" the McGees' 1946 Chevy all the way to Oregon, blocking the view behind them the entire way.

**TINY BUT TOUGH.** This Crosley got Homer Metz and wife Iva halfway across the country in the summer of 1946—on a 4-gallon tank!

# Crosley and Jeep Bailed Them Out During Car Shortage

*By Iva Metz, Bothell, Washington*

My husband, Homer, was stationed near Cocoa Beach, Florida in 1944. Cars were hard to come by, so we felt very fortunate when we eventually found a 1939 Crosley convertible.

Our little car got 52 miles to the gallon, so even with rationing, we always had enough gas (although the tank held only 4 gallons).

When Homer was placed on inactive duty in July of 1946, we loaded up the Crosley and mapped out a route to Kansas, where our folks lived. With an average speed of 25 miles per hour, the trip was slow and arduous.

From Kansas, we planned to drive to California, where Homer had been accepted at school. There was no housing available, so we'd take our own—a new 27-foot Elcar trailer home.

There was no way that little Crosley could pull a trailer, so now we needed another car. But it was impossible to buy a new car or truck of any kind in Kansas at that time.

### Time to Cash in the Crosley

But we could—and did—purchase a brand-new Jeep! It had no top, so Homer bought a tarp and installed grommets to snap it into place before we set out for California in August.

We were only 22 (if we'd been older, we probably never would've attempted it). Our route took us across Kansas, Oklahoma and into Texas, where we caught Route 66. Disaster struck outside Holbrook, Arizona when we had a blowout on the trailer. We'd never even thought of getting a spare—after all, everything was new!

Leaving me with the trailer, Homer walked to Holbrook to look for a tire. It was about dusk, so I used a flashlight to warn other cars away. As it got darker, I began hearing noises in the desert. I was scared to death.

Then an old car stopped, carrying two sailors and a young woman. They, too, had broken down in Holbrook and had spent all their money on repairs. All they'd had to eat for the past 2 days was a cheese sandwich and a pint of milk.

We had plenty of food in the trailer, so I made them a good meal. They were kind enough to stay with me until Homer returned—without a tire. The sailors helped him get the trailer off the road, where we'd be safe for the night. We sent them on their way with $10 in dimes for gas.

### A Tale of Woe

The next day, we drove to Winslow, Arizona to look for a tire. No one had them. As we drove around, we passed a trailer park where trailers were sitting up on blocks.

We saw one with the size tire we needed, so we knocked on the door and told the man our sad story. The gentleman felt so sorry for us that he took the tire off and let us have it.

After that, we looked in every town we came to for another tire. Finally, we found a recapped one and bought it —just in case we had another flat.

We'd been advised not to drive over Oatman Pass in Arizona—the hairpin curves would not have been kind to a Jeep pulling a 27-foot trailer! So we left Route 66 and drove north to Las Vegas.

It was so hot there that we were afraid to travel during the day. So we spent the day in an air-conditioned theater, then drove all night across the desert to California.

We probably should have had more sense than to start out on that trip. But we made it and will never forget our journey or the kind people who helped us along the way. ❧

**SHOEBOX ON WHEELS.** Helen Campbell (on left) says this Crosley was not a car you wanted to challenge a Percheron in.

### Crosley No Match for Real Horsepower

MY MOTHER learned to drive in our Crosley station wagon in the late 1940s. Watching the car jerk and hop—or, worse, being *in* it as Mom tried to shift—was quite an experience. She tore up two transmissions ( at a cost of $36 each) before getting the hang of it.

One time in New York State, we came upon two gigantic Percheron horses walking loose along the highway. We couldn't think of anything to do except drive slowly, hold our breath and hope for the best.

When the horses walked up to the car, we had to stop. They gave us a good looking-over, took a sniff or two and wandered off.

Encounters like that were cause for concern when you were riding in a car the size of a bedroom slipper!

—*Helen Campbell*
*Sandpoint, Idaho*

SITTING WHERE THE FUHRER SAT. After the war in Europe ended, Hitler's personal car was taken on a nationwide savings bond drive. John Baumberger of Johnson City, New York provided this photo taken in the showroom of the Toledo Edison Company. If you bought a Victory Bond, you could sit in the car for a moment—which is exactly what John is doing above.

## Postwar Waiting List Caused Patience to Wear Thin

WHEN I was discharged from the Army in early 1946, I wanted a car so badly that I put in orders at three different dealerships—Pontiac, Ford and Studebaker.

I realized my name would go on a waiting list but was shocked to find at least 20 customers ahead of me—and new cars were coming in very slowly.

Every week I made the rounds of the dealers, always finding my name still far down on the list. I was losing patience. Then one day when I stopped at the Pontiac dealership, a customer drove in with a 1941 Plymouth two-door sedan. He was trading it in for a new car, so I immediately asked the salesman about the Plymouth.

He said they'd have to inspect it and make minor repairs before selling it.

I replied that if it was drivable, I'd take it "as is". I paid $700, the going price for that year's model, and drove it home that afternoon.

Then I put in almost $500 more for an engine overhaul and new brakes, tires, shocks and seat covers. That Plymouth had only cost $650 when new, yet I spent nearly twice that on it.

But I had no regrets—I drove that car until 1954.

—Howard Knab
Amherst, New York

## Butyl Tube "Blow-Up" Became a Daily Ritual

AFTER I got out of the service in 1946, I bought a 1934 Ford coach that had been parked all through the war for lack of tires. I bought new tires but couldn't find decent rubber inner tubes (synthetic butyl tubes were all I could get).

We lived about a mile from the main road, and after the first snow, I couldn't be sure of getting the car out there. So I started parking close to the road, which worked fine until the weather turned really cold.

Every time I walked out to the car, I'd have one to four flat tires. On inspecting them, I'd find tiny leaks in the inner tubes. Soon I tired of fixing flats, so I just pumped up the tires and found that they stayed up until I needed to use the car again.

Finally a mechanic explained that tiny gas bubbles formed in the butyl tubes, and when the tubes got too cold, the bubbles would break and cause a leak.

I then went out and bought myself a new air compressor powered by a Briggs and Stratton gas engine and mounted it in the trunk. That way, while I was warming up my car, I could start the gas compressor and pump all my tires up, too!

I used this system until rubber inner tubes were available again.

—William Plate, Wasilla, Alaska

THE PRICE WAS LIKE NEW. In 1946, Howard Knab paid the going rate for a new car for this '41 Plymouth, then fixed it up to last.

**"A" WAS FOR AVALANCHE.** In the summer, Meg Letterman's Model A forded many a mountain stream in the high country of the West. In the winter, Avalanche took Meg and her friends on skiing trips. That's Meg standing by the car door above on a trip to Alta, Utah. That's her again below staring up through the car's chicken-wire "sunroof".

# 'Avalanche' Took Them On Many an Adventure

*By Meg Letterman, Goldendale, Washington*

A 1929 Model A Ford four-door sedan, which I acquired during World War II for $50, was my first car. Some friends named it "Avalanche", which was appropriate since it went downhill much better than it went up, you could always hear it coming—and it took everything with it!

For my friends and me, the "everything" was camping gear. We liked to hike, ski and paddle when we weren't working 60-plus hours a week at our defense jobs in Schenectady, New York.

Avalanche got 20 miles to the gallon, more than most other cars, and enabled us to go to Lake George for canoeing and ice skating, the Adirondacks for hiking and Vermont for skiing.

In 1946, I decided to return to college in Colorado for my master's degree. First, I packed my belongings into (and onto) Avalanche and set out in a cloud of rust for my folks' home in Philadelphia. Tied to the outside of the car were my canoe, bicycle and skis.

At the entrance to the Hudson River Parkway near New York City, an attendant looked at Avalanche with its load and declared it wasn't a "pleasure vehicle", which meant I couldn't use the parkway! Instead, I had to drive through the city. There we were—a country girl not used to heavy traffic, and Avalanche, with lots of play in the steering wheel—surrounded by big hulks.

The trip was terrifying and slow, but somehow we got through without being crushed.

Then, in New Jersey, one of the tires went flat. The spare was a tire that had previously gone flat and now had a "boot" in it.

I finished the trip home slowly, bumping along on the spare. In Philadelphia, I made sure I had a couple of replacement tires before setting out for the University of Colorado.

### See-Through Roof Was Handy

In Colorado, Avalanche again collected a group of devotees, and we made many unforgettable trips into the Rockies. In the mountains, half the scenery's up high, so I turned Avalanche into a convertible.

I replaced the original roof with a roll-up canvas cover laced around the edges, with the original chicken wire left in place for support.

Climbing steep hills with a 30-horsepower motor was a slow process, and more powerful cars often zoomed past. But Avalanche did have its advantages. Since gas was fed to the carburetor by gravity, it wasn't susceptible to the "vapor lock" that plagued bigger, fancier cars with fuel pumps.

Whenever we drove by a car with its hood up, and the driver scratching his head, we'd yell helpfully, "Get a good car!"

We also began seeking out lesser-used roads. My friends and I saw some beautiful countryside that way—although moving forward sometimes required not only Avalanche's

**UP, UP AND AWAY.** Meg says that she and her little Model A conquered many a mountain backroad on their frequent weekend getaways. That's Meg (on bumper at left in the photo at far right) with some friends. They supplied the "eight-leg drive" that was sometimes necessary on the steeper grades. Avalanche was often loaded down with bikes as in the picture above. Photo of friend at right was taken near Telluride, Colorado, while the lonely shot below was snapped on a road near Ouray, Colorado.

two-wheel drive, but "eight-leg drive" as well!

Some of those old mine and logging roads are now open only to Jeeps. On one trip deep into the mountains in May, a wet heavy snowfall sheared the pin connecting the windshield wiper to its motor. Without wipers, I couldn't see to drive.

I tried hanging my head out the window, but the snow just plastered my eyes. Finally, one of my friends tied two strings to the wiper blade, running one through each of the side windows.

### Wipers on "Manual" Setting

Then the person in the middle of the front seat pulled the strings alternately, wiping the windshield! With the heavy snow, it took 5 hours to drive the 50 miles out to civilization—with someone pulling the strings the whole way!

When it came time for me to leave Colorado, my mother and brother decided I needed a newer, safer car, so they bought me a new 1949 Ford truck as a present. But what about Avalanche?

It had been a beloved companion, and I felt downright disloyal to even contemplate selling it. Luckily, one of Avalanche's other devotees offered me $75 for it. Since I'd bought it for $50 and used it hard for 5 years, I decided to take him up on it.

He drove it to Ouray, Colorado and sold it after a few years. Fifteen years later, I visited Ouray and tried to find out what had happened to Avalanche, but no one recognized my description.

I could only assume it eventually went to a junkyard, which saddened me. I loved that car more than any other I've ever owned. ✍

**A STARS-AND-STRIPES CHEVY.** In June of 1946, Daniel Meigs and his wife, Barbara, accepted delivery of this brand-new 1946 Chevrolet from City Chevrolet in Charlotte, North Carolina. Daniel, who still lives in Charlotte, had won a contest sponsored by the GI newspaper *The Stars and Stripes*. In his entry, he told of his plans for postwar savings. Daniel was one of only 14 GI's (out of 36,000 entries) to win, and his car was one of the first two new Chevys delivered to North Carolina after the war.

# Teen's Streamliner Was a Secret That *Had* to Be Kept

*By Don Williams*
*West Harrison, Indiana*

In the fall of 1945, my father told me I'd be getting a new car as a high school graduation gift. Although I wasn't due to graduate for another year and a half, and had seldom driven our 1937 family car, I knew Dad meant what he said.

I'd worked on our farm (without an allowance) since I was 11, and the promised car was my folks' way of showing their gratitude. Mother and Dad talked about it as the months passed, but I didn't dare get my hopes up.

New cars were available in southern Indiana by mid-1946, but they were awfully rare. Seeing one drive up the lane seemed about as likely as having an airplane land in our pasture.

### Moving Up in the World

When spring of 1947 arrived, Dad told me he'd been talking with a car dealer, and my name was on a list for a new Pontiac Streamliner. Then, early one evening in May, the phone rang.

Mother answered, then handed the receiver to me. It was Mr. Metzler, the car dealer. He told me there were two names ahead of mine on the list.

Those buyers were willing to take any model, but a Streamliner had just come in, and Mr. Metzler knew how long my parents had planned to give me a new car for graduation. So he had a proposal.

He'd meet me later that night at his garage and give me the car—on the condition that I drive it straight home and leave it in the shed until he "gave the word"!

He'd move me ahead on the list, if I promised not to drive my car before the other two buyers got theirs.

That night was even more exciting than I could've imagined. At the car dealer's, we walked back through Mr. Metzler's dark offices and entered the garage.

There sat the most beautiful car I'd ever seen. That two-door white Streamliner had a wide chrome strip, accented in black, down the center of the hood. I kept thanking Mr. Metzler, but the $1,765 check Dad had sent seemed to be all he expected.

That gorgeous shiny car sat in the shed from the night I drove it home until Mr. Metzler called to "give me the word".

Meanwhile, for 3 long weeks, I went to the shed every night after chores and supper and slid behind the steering wheel. Then I settled back into the gray upholstered seat and started the engine.

As a favorite song played on the radio, I'd fix my eyes on the Pontiac Indian chief perched on the tip of the long hood, rest my hands on the steering wheel, lay my head back, close my eyes and see myself driving down the lane and cruising past my friends' homes.

### No More Hiding

Finally, at the end of the third week, the long-awaited call came! Mother and Dad wore smiles as big as mine as I backed out of the shed. I motioned for Dad to crawl in back so Mother could sit up front with me.

It was our busiest season of the year, but we were off for a "Sunday drive" on a Wednesday morning. The farm grew smaller in the rearview mirror as we made our way out the lane and down Drewersburg Road.

I kept that beloved Streamliner until the late '50s. Mother and Dad are gone now, but I still live in our family farmhouse and have been in and out of that lane too many times to count since that morning in 1947.

But every once in a while, I can still see Mother out of the corner of my eye and hear Dad's laughter in the back, and once again it's a Sunday drive in the middle of the week. 🎺

## First Driving Lesson Left Dad in the Dust

ONE SUMMER in the late '40s, my dad made up his mind to teach me how to drive. My lessons would take place in northern Michigan, where traffic was almost unheard-of.

Mom climbed in back, I got behind the wheel and Dad sat beside me, giving instructions. Poor Mom had a bumpy ride, as I couldn't shift our 1946 Plymouth without jumping all over the road. Then the car stalled (I can still hear Dad yelling at me in German).

"Enough of this," he said at last. We would start over, but this time he'd get behind the wheel, shift into low, then jump out, run behind the car and jump back in on the passenger's side while I moved to the driver's seat.

For me, this worked just fine. I shifted into second and said, "How'd I do, Dad?" No answer. I asked again. Still no answer. Then Mom said, "Dad's not here."

I pulled over and stopped and saw Dad limping to the car. He'd fallen off the running board and never made it to the passenger side. I hadn't noticed because I didn't dare stall the car or look over to his side—God forbid I should drive off the road!

Now Dad had plenty to say to me in his fine fast German! To make matters even more embarrassing for all concerned, a car had appeared out of nowhere and stopped to see if Dad was all right.

From the way he was sprawled out on the highway, they'd assumed I'd hit him!
*—Mrs. R. Ratowski*
*Prudenville, Michigan*

**ON MANEUVERS?** The Faulkses (shown at left with visiting relatives) used a former Army reconnaissance vehicle (behind them) as a family car. It served them well after the war, especially on long vacations and camping trips.

## Purchase of "Blunder Bus" Was No Blunder After All

OUR old Ford sedan piled up lots of repair bills during World War II. One spring morning in 1946, my husband took it to town for repairs but didn't come back that afternoon as expected. Then suppertime came, and Glenn still wasn't home.

As the rest of us ate, I glanced out the window and saw him driving up in a huge vehicle. I knew it was ours, and I was horrified.

"How could he?" I exclaimed. "What a blunder he's made this time!" Everyone laughed, and my sister immediately christened our new car the "Blunder Bus".

It was olive drab and had been an Army reconnaissance car during the war. Glenn found it at a used-car lot in Caldwell, Idaho. He said he chose it because good used cars were hard to find.

The Blunder Bus sat high off the ground, had a trouble-free Dodge motor and was very roomy—one summer my sister drove it to Vacation Bible School with *19* of us packed inside!

We often took the Blunder Bus on vacation. On one trip back to Homedale, Idaho from Eugene, Oregon, we stopped for a lot of sightseeing in the high desert. The next evening, we learned three prison escapees had been captured just north of Homedale. They had been traveling on the same road with us the day before!

With all the stops we made, our guardian angel must have been watching over us—or maybe the prisoners saw the Blunder Bus and figured the Army was out looking for them.

Eventually we bought another car and converted the Blunder Bus to a pickup, and it served us faithfully for many more years. Buying it was not the blunder I thought it was.
*—Ella Faulks, Homedale, Idaho*

**THE DUCK HAS ARRIVED.** When Clarence Baker got out of the Army in 1946, he drove this four-cylinder '42 Willys. When his girlfriend saw him, she told him he looked like Donald Duck coming down the road. He now lives in Midland Park, New Jersey.

**WAS IT A TANK—OR A CADILLAC?** William Wagner of Eugene, Oregon says this '37 Cadillac that he owned back in 1948 weighed over 5,000 pounds. The fenders made him feel like he was driving an Army tank. It had a big "flathead" V-8 engine to push all that weight around.

# Terraplane Was Terrific Buy for This Teen

*By Esther Olson, Clay Center, Kansas*

**TERRAPLANE GANG.** Esther Olson took this 1947 picture of three cousins and a friend posing atop her beloved Terraplane.

I n 1947, I was working in a small Kansas town when a co-worker bought one of the rare new cars just then becoming available. I quickly asked what she was doing with her old one and learned she was going to sell it for $160.

It was time for my supper break, so Edith suggested I drive the car home and try it out. I had never actually driven a car, but I was sure there'd be no problem (after all, I'd had my driver's license for 4 years), so I didn't mention this minor fact to Edith.

Key in hand, I floated out the door to the most beautiful car I'd ever seen—a tan four-door 1935 Terraplane. The long car was angled in at the courthouse square, and the street behind it was busy with workers heading home.

As I reached for the door handle, I heard someone call out my name. Mr. Anderson, an old family friend, was right across the street. I yelled to him that I was probably going to buy this car.

I climbed in, started the car, shifted into reverse, stepped on the gas pedal and excitedly let out the clutch. After that, everything happened too fast. When the car finally stopped, its rear wheels were against the curb on the other side of the street—very near where Mr. Anderson stood, mouth agape!

Thankfully, I'd managed to miss all the cars traveling down the street. Mr. Anderson came over to see if I needed

> *"I prayed that I could drive this contraption away gracefully..."*

help as I prayed that I could drive this contraption away gracefully.

I reassured him everything was under control and this time, my getaway was flawless. By the time I'd driven the four blocks home, I'd already named the car "Betsy"—but had no idea how to pay for her.

At 19, I knew nothing about borrowing money. But then, my generous landlady offered to loan me the $160, and I went back to work with stars in my eyes.

I quickly learned to drive Betsy and cure a few of her ailments. Tires were still in short supply, but several friends donated used tires and tubes, and I carried all of them with me. On one trip to Bible camp, the Terraplane was crammed with seven girls, our luggage for a week and three spare tires.

Later that summer, I decided I was going to move to Chicago—without Betsy. My brother came to Kansas to help me drive the car to our parents' home in Wisconsin. Around midnight in St. Joseph, Missouri, I discovered I couldn't shift gears when the car was in motion.

## Shiftless Pair Made It Home

My brother insisted we had to have it fixed. I pointed out that neither of us had money for that, so we'd just have to keep going. I think I willed that car to work. Twenty-five hours later, we made it to Wisconsin, tired but intact.

Dad knew some young fellows who were interested in buying Betsy, but I was hesitant. After all, Dad was their pastor and I didn't want any hard feelings.

When they came by, I told them the car wasn't running quite right, but if they still wanted it after a test drive, the price was $260. (You've heard of inflation, and besides, cars were in short supply.)

They drove away in Betsy, and within 30 minutes, I stood with a check in my hand—and lots of memories in my mind. ✒

**DESOTO HAD TO GO.** Raymond Kirlin of Seattle, Washington bought this 1941 DeSoto in February of 1946, when he returned from overseas duty in Saipan. After his honeymoon 3 months later, he sold it in order to furnish a new "GI home" for his bride.

ROLLOVER. This dramatic photo of a 1949 car crash may have been taken in North Carolina, says Jesse Smith of Ona, West Virginia. Jesse's great-uncle, Herbert Barber, was an avid amateur photographer who happened by soon after this accident occurred.

## He Drove to the Beat of A Different Drum

ONE Sunday afternoon in 1946, a very strange-looking vehicle pulled into my two-pump gas station in western New York. It was accompanied by a huge cloud of steam, and at first, I thought it was a steam-powered car.

The vehicle had something in front that looked like a vertical boiler. Then the driver jumped out, asked for a gaso-line fill-up and water (lots of water!) and told me his story.

An accident in a small town with no car dealer, garage or even a junkyard damaged his radiator beyond repair. That's when the village handyman stepped in and mounted a 55-gallon oil drum on the front bumper and frame, securing it with braces, straps and ropes.

He attached the radiator hoses to pipe fittings he'd welded into the top and bottom of the drum. When the drum was filled with water, the driver was on his way.

Forward visibility wasn't great, as the drum sat at least a foot higher than the hood and the front springs almost bottomed out from several hundred pounds of extra weight.

After 20 miles or so, the barrel would start to boil, and clouds of steam would reduce visibility to zero. Then it was time to stop and let the "radiator" cool.

That driver was still 100 miles from home when he rolled out, but I'll bet that he made it—and gave a few more folks a sight they wouldn't soon forget!
—*Robert Milby*
*North Palm Beach, Florida*

## Teenage Driver Suffered The Ultimate Embarrassment

IN THE spring of 1948, when I was 17, I talked my dad into buying a 1929 Chevrolet for $50. It was my first car, and I was elated. I hung so many trinkets and gadgets from the dashboard and ceiling it's a wonder I could see to drive.

That fall, when school closed for the customary 2 weeks so we kids could help with the harvest, I loaded up my friends and headed for the sugar beet and potato fields. It was a real status symbol to be able to offer kids rides.

One day after work, I'd taken everybody else home and had only my best friend with me. I'd just turned my head to look out the rear window and, without realizing it, turned the steering wheel, too.

The car came to an abrupt stop—we'd run head-on into an electric power pole! Although no one was seriously hurt, my pride was destroyed.

And so was my Chevy! It had to be towed home the next day.

The incident even made the front page of the weekly paper, with the headline "Driver Looks Back, Snaps Off Pole". My friends still tease me about it whenever we reminisce about the good old days.
—*Richard Sorensen*
*Hyrum, Utah*

POLE-SITTER. Richard Sorensen's car and this telephone pole made headlines in the local newspaper.

A BEVY OF BEAUTIES. When Peter Combs came back to California after the war, he drove this 1932 Model C Ford roadster. Peter, who now lives in Ennis, Montana, loved those old cars—almost as much as he did filling them up with young lovelies like this giggling group!

## Silver Swan Was Just the Start

THIS PHOTO was taken in 1949 (could I ever have been that young!) in Cleveland, Ohio. The car is a 1946 Ford with all the "extras" of the day. The thing that was really special about it was almost everything that was metal was chromed.

Luckily for me, the father of one of my friends owned a chrome-plating factory and I could get all the chrome-plating I wanted done for next to nothing!

So I ended up with chromed window trim and knobs, a chromed dashboard—you name it, if it was metal, it got chromed. Of course, everything under the hood also got "the treatment".

This particular Ford had a stock V-8 engine with "Smitty" dual mufflers and the always popular swan hood orna-ment—which came with lighted wings, no less!

I bought the car used in 1948 and kept it until 1950, when I bought my first new car—a 1950 Ford convertible, which as I remember, cost $2,000 "loaded"!

—*Dave McDill, Beaumont, Texas*

## Brake Test Nearly Broke Cop's Composure

AFTER our marriage in 1948, my wife and I graduated from a one-speed bicycle to an ancient 1919 Grey Dort that had been converted into a small truck. Although it had no starter, no turn signals and no speedometer, it did have instant-lock rear brakes.

I drove it to work in Winnipeg, Manitoba every day with a passenger named Ken—and a 25-gallon drum of water to replenish the leaky radiator. One day a city cop pulled us over and asked how the brakes were. I said, "Fine." He said, "Let's give it a test."

Ken moved into the truck box, alongside the drum of water, while the burly cop slid in beside me with a box on his lap that would register how many yards it took me to stop at a given speed.

"Okay," the cop said. "You tramp on the gas, and I'll tell you when to brake."

I'd gotten the Dort close to its maximum speed, about 25 miles an hour, when the cop hollered, "Brake it!"

The combination of dry paved streets, instant-lock brakes and a somewhat apprehensive driver all contributed to what happened next. I hit the brakes a little too forcefully and sent Ken tumbling to the front of the truck box.

Meanwhile, the drum of water came sliding forward to the area directly behind the officer, soaking him from head to foot!

Removing his glasses, the cop carefully wiped them dry, brushed the water off his uniform, turned to me very slowly and said, "Your brakes, sir, seem to be responding satisfactorily."

He then checked me and my truck over *very* thoroughly. When he finally noted that the truck had no windshield wipers, his stern warning almost came as a relief.

Then, with a faint smile, he waved us on our way. God bless our men in uniform!

—*Lawrence Anderson Winnipeg, Manitoba*

**ALL THIS—AND A RADIO, TOO!** Loretta Heffinger of Oceanside, California fondly recalls this 1949 Mercury—the first new car her family ever had (that's her mom and brother ready for church above). For Loretta, the best part was Sunday drives with the radio playing the soothing sounds of Guy Lombardo or the "swing and sway" music of Sammy Kaye.

**PANIC STOP.** Lawrence Anderson (on the right) braked this Dort a little bit too well on a Winnipeg street.

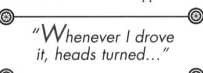

# Battered Phaeton Made Him Big Man On Campus...Temporarily

*By George Denardo, Camarillo, California*

Two years after World War II ended, I entered high school. At that time in New Jersey, cars of any kind were in great demand. Adding to this dilemma was the fact that I was the youngest of five children and my family had only one car.

Dad used the car for work on weekdays. Jack, the second oldest, got to use it on Friday nights, and Matthew, the oldest, got it on Saturdays. On Sundays, I got to wash it.

My chances of getting to drive Dad's car were negligible, and I went through my sophomore and junior years without wheels. Whenever I had a date, I either walked, took a bus or double-dated. It was a drag and I hated it.

My senior year came and went, and I was still a pedestrian. Just as I became resigned to my fate, a stroke of good fortune hit. A friend had bought a 1934 Ford Phaeton touring car for $50, used it for a few months and sold it. The car passed through three more owners before it was offered to me for $50.

I'd started college, and when school was in session, I bussed tables, washed dishes and ushered at football games. During Christmas break, I worked as a mail carrier, saving every penny until I could afford to buy that car.

By the time I got the Phaeton, it was a total wreck. The rearview window was broken, the canvas top was full of holes and none of the wheels had caps. The paint was so faded it was difficult to tell what color it was.

The muffler was so shot that I had to stuff steel wool up the dual exhausts to quiet the noise. Yet with all its faults, I loved that car. It was a limited edition, and whenever I drove it, heads turned. The car even made me something of a celebrity at Rutgers University. Everyone knew my car.

It was so unique that the cheerleaders wanted to paint it scarlet, the school color, and use it during football games (I nixed that idea).

When the top was down, it sometimes came loose and flapped in the

> *"Whenever I drove it, heads turned..."*

breeze. Rather than stopping to fix it, I would continue to drive, throwing my right leg over the front seat and leaning backward to grab the top. Then I'd force a portion of it into a convenient crack and proceed on my way.

I never told Dad about the car. Since I didn't have insurance, I knew he would never let me keep it. Whenever I drove the 35 miles home from school, I'd park around the corner so he wouldn't see it.

One day I came home in mid-afternoon and pulled into our driveway because I thought my father was working—I was wrong!

### Abrupt End to Affair

When he saw the Phaeton, he almost had a fit. "Who owns that wreck in the driveway?" he shouted as he came charging into the house.

"I do, Dad," I said sheepishly.

"You do!" he shot back.

"Yes, it's mine."

"When did you get it?"

"About 6 months ago."

"Do you have insurance on it?"

"No."

"Get rid of it!"

So ended my first love affair. The next day, I called one of the cheerleaders and asked if he wanted to buy a great car for $50. When he learned it was the famous Ford Phaeton, he jumped at the offer.

Last time I saw it, it was racing around campus in a blaze of black smoke.

**REUNITED.** The Wildenberg family was back together again after Bob (with wife Esther and son Bobby above) was discharged from the service in 1946. Bob bought this Plymouth new for $750 in 1941. Six years later, he sold it for $1,450! Bob and Esther now live in Manhattan Beach, California.

## It Sounded Like a Fire Truck ...And *Felt* Like a Fire!

AFTER World War II, used cars that actually ran were at a premium. Working various jobs around my hometown of Kansas City, Missouri, I'd saved up $250 for my first car.

So when my uncle told Dad he'd found the perfect car for me, we boarded a train and rode 250 miles to rural Iowa to go see a 1930 Model A Ford with a Jeep engine and transmission.

The rear had been removed and the backseat replaced with a wooden floor, making it an open-ended station wagon. It was really a pretty sorry sight.

Even though I was very disappointed, we decided it was all $250 was going to buy (and it did run well). Back home, I found a good rear body at a salvage yard, and a nice man cut it so it would overlap mine.

I installed it with a couple hundred stove bolts, replaced the rear seat and finished the interior with blue and white oilcloth. The exterior was treated to a coat of the new black powder-puff paint (so named because it was actually applied with powder puffs).

Since there was no horn, I hung an old brass bell above the engine and rang it by pulling on a wire that poked through the dashboard. Now it sounded like a fire truck.

I replaced the 19-inch tires with

**SHAKE, RATTLE AND ROLL.** John and Elizabeth Henshall were students at Oklahoma Baptist University when John bought this Model A for $65 in 1948. The couple now lives in Kenedy, Texas, and Elizabeth says the one thing she'll always remember is how badly this car vibrated. A long trip would leave her feeling as if the whole world were shaking.

smaller wheels and fat tires to make it look like a hot rod. My friends and I had lots of fun with that car, but our favorite trick was putting an unsuspecting passenger in the backseat, crowded against the rear wheel well.

Turning a corner with a car full of kids would push the Ford's body against the fat tires, causing friction—and giving our new passenger an unexpected "hot seat"!—*Jim Sigler, Olathe, Kansas*

## Wandering Wheel Didn't Delight Everyone

ONE PLEASANT autumn day in the late 1940s, my friend and I were clipping along a straight and level concrete highway in his vintage Model A.

Just as we met a late-model Oldsmobile traveling in the opposite direction, we heard a bang, and the A's left rear dropped somewhat. "A blowout!" we exclaimed and coasted to the verge.

To our surprise, we found the left rear wheel itself was gone. This seemed hilarious at the time. We were laughing and looking for the wheel—until we noticed the Oldsmobile's driver walking toward us and shouting irritably.

It turned out that the bang we'd heard was the A's wheel hitting the Oldsmobile's left front fender and suspension! His car was so disabled it couldn't move under its own power. But no one was hurt, and, in time, tempers and machinery were repaired.

We found our wheel in the farm field it had landed in after jumping a fence. It showed no damage or even a mark from all its travels. Those old cars were as sturdy and long-lasting as hammers.

—*Dean Sill, Monroe, Iowa*

**TATERS AND TURNIPS.** These high school students in Montpelier, Idaho had a wonderful time with this Model T in the summer of 1949. Marlene Helland (sitting in car on the right) says they bought the car for $35 and, since there was no radiator cap, used potatoes and turnips to keep the radiator from boiling over. To start their Lizzie, they had to push it, then run and jump in. Marlene, who now resides in Salt Lake City, Utah, recalls that red and white curtains helped "doll" the car up.

## Pipe, Pop Bottle and Ingenuity Got Them Home

AFTER my buddy Dick and I graduated from high school in 1949, we left Staten Island, New York for a 3-day trip to Washington, D.C. On the way back home, the engine in Dick's '36 Plymouth began missing.

Halfway through New Jersey, the problem had gotten so bad that we had to stop. Somehow we had to get gas to the carburetor whenever the engine started to miss.

Our solution was to remove the hose to the windshield wipers (remember the old vacuum systems?), then crank open the windshield and run the hose down through it and under the hood to the carburetor.

Then we removed the stem from Dick's pipe and slid the other end of the hose over the opening of the pipe bowl. At a filling station, we bought a quart of gas and had the attendant put it into a soda bottle through a funnel.

For the remainder of the trip, I sat with a bottle of gasoline in one hand, and Dick's pipe, with hose attached, in the other. Every time the engine began to miss, I poured some gas into the pipe bowl and it ran down the tube into the carburetor.

Believe it or not, our system worked. We were almost out of money, but we kept 50¢ for the Outerbridge toll and a nickel to call home if we couldn't make it. But somehow we did—with a whole half-pint of gas to spare!

—*Douglas Nielsen, Syracuse, New York*

## How to Cram a Coupe

IN THE FALL of 1949, my friends and I often went to a nearby town in northern Minnesota to roller-skate. We took a 1947 Dodge coupe one of the boys borrowed from his father. Five of us sat in front, with some sitting on the others' laps.

The two smallest ones traveled lying down on the back shelf! I don't think my friend's parents ever knew how many of us crammed into that coupe. But we had good clean fun skating with

**DELIGHTED WITH HIS DODGE.** You can tell by the look on his face that Odis Prater was proud of this burgundy '48 Dodge coupe. Odis, of Madison Heights, Michigan, recalls he was just about ready to "go see my gal" when his buddy snapped this picture.

kids from nearby towns, and we always got home safe and sound.

Can you imagine anyone traveling that way today?　　—*Judy Tamminen, Forest Lake, Minnesota*

**TOMORROW NEVER CAME.** After the war, a number of independent automotive engineers set about designing the "car of tomorrow". This three-wheeled Davis was one such vehicle (the Tucker was another). With a center of gravity only 18 inches from the ground, the seven-passenger Davis was said to be extremely stable. Its top speed was over 100 miles per hour and it got between 35 and 50 miles to the gallon. Better yet, it was expected to sell for the "old-fashioned" price of $995. Art James, who provided this picture, now lives in Cambria, California and was in line to be a Davis dealer in 1948. Unfortunately, designer Gary Davis was unable to obtain long-term financing and the car never made it into production.

# Back Safely from War, Buddies Hit the Road

*By Kenneth Reiter, Wauwatosa, Wisconsin*

**FRIENDS FOR LIFE.** Kenneth Reiter (in middle of photo above left, at far right above) and his buddies enjoyed "road trips". They rented this cabin for $20 *a week*.

When my childhood friends and I came home to Milwaukee after World War II, we were ready for some adventure. So from 1946 to 1950, we pooled our money and took several trips. Some were weekend jaunts; others were longer, like the one we took to Canada and Niagara Falls in June 1946.

We usually tried to cover 400 miles a day, but that figure was optional in Canada. There was a lot of "wild nothing" up there, and gas stations were not plentiful.

The following year, we planned a trip west on Route 66. I wrote to tourism offices and chambers of commerce in every state we intended to visit. One memorable personal reply from Texas read: "Stop in Oklahoma City. Make a left turn. Head south into the greater part of Texas, where there is a lot to see."

We did see a lot on that trip and others—Mt. Rushmore, the Badlands, the Corn Palace, the Grand Canyon, Boulder Dam, the Petrified Forest, the Mormon Tabernacle and more. But one of the most memorable sights occurred when we didn't know where we were.

On the way to Yellowstone, there was a detour that we messed up on and ended up in a dark heavily wooded ravine with two dirt tracks for a road. Finally we came to a small creek with an ancient wooden bridge.

As we were pondering whether my friend Donnie's 1939 Oldsmobile convertible could make it over the bridge without crashing through, we couldn't believe what we saw coming toward us— a bearded old prospector leading a loaded-down mule!

Later that day, we reached Yellowstone, but it was too late—the South Gate had already closed. So we "bunked out" for the night amid howling coyotes. Boy, that was a first for a group of Midwestern guys!

I'm afraid all my traveling buddies are gone now, but I'll never forget the fun we had on those postwar car trips. 🐾

**THE NIAGARA WAGON.** Al Kraut (the "yawner" in top right photo) owned the '37 Ford seen in pair of photos above. This was the vehicle the group used for a 1948 trip around the Great Lakes to Niagara Falls and back. Note the trip's log written on the side of the car.

# Ancient 'Monster' Had Last Laugh

*By Walt Halstead, Aurora, Colorado*

D uring the summer of 1947, I was working at the Narragansett Inn on Block Island, off the coast of Rhode Island. My friends Doug and Frank were working there, too. We were all 17 and fresh out of high school.

Midway through the summer, I saw a 1923 Buick touring car sitting on blocks in the hotel's ramshackle garage. It was a dusty monster but had only 20,000 miles on it.

Sam, the hotel's owner, agreed to sell it to Doug and me for $25. (Frank didn't need a car since he had a new Cushman scooter.)

### Doug Was the "Brains"

Doug knew cars, but I didn't know a carburetor from a generator. To get the car running, Doug did the brain work, I did the grunt work—while Frank just laughed and told us we'd never get it home to New Jersey.

The car's accumulated rust didn't surrender easily. Even with both of us leaning on the crank, the engine remained immobile. Doug somberly announced that we'd have to remove the pan—whatever that was.

I soon found out, lying on the floor and trying to get the pan bolts to release their death grip on the block while Doug slopped penetrating oil all over the engine.

Eventually the six cylinders yielded, and we were able to turn the engine by cranking. Next, Doug tackled the electrical system. The ignition switch wouldn't respond. Our "key" consisted of two bare wires twisted together.

### The Monster Lived

One day Sam told us the real problem with the car was the starter motor. "There's nothing wrong with the starter motor," Doug countered, climbing into the driver's seat. "I'll show you."

He twisted the wires together and stepped on the starter. The engine turned over, spluttered and started running. After a stunned silence, we both blurted, "Whoopee!" We had a car that ran!

**BLOCK ISLAND BUICK. Walt Halstead and his friend Doug fixed up this 1923 Buick after discovering it in the garage of the hotel where they were working.**

There were just two small problems. First, the car had 1939 Rhode Island plates. We'd sent for New Jersey plates but didn't know when they'd arrive.

The second problem was worse—the clutch was stuck. Eventually, after some not-so-gentle persuasion with a pry bar and hammer, the multiple-disc clutch relented.

When Labor Day arrived, it was time

*"We got an unexpected request for a mission of mercy..."*

for us to head home, but we still didn't have New Jersey plates. Frank was staying an extra day to help close up the hotel, so he came to the boat to see us off—still mocking us and our car.

A hotel guest had agreed to tow the Buick to his used-car lot in Providence for safekeeping until our license plates arrived. Doug and I stayed at a nearby YMCA, close to the main post office, impatiently checking the mail at least twice daily.

On the third day, we got the registration—but no plates. I called home nightly, concocting reasons for our de-

lay. The fourth night, my mother angrily informed me that my father was on a train to Providence.

He intended to make us sell the car and return by train or bus. Somehow they'd found out!

We had 2 hours to devise a plan, so we made our own license plates out of cardboard, attached them with twine and retrieved our belongings from the Y. Now all we had to do was convince my father.

### Didn't Deliberate Long

We didn't say much to Dad at the train station. We just took him to the car. Satisfied that it wasn't a piece of junk, he relented and we started for home about midnight.

"We don't want anybody falling asleep up there," Dad cautioned from the backseat. "I want to hear a lot of chatter."

He didn't say another word until a Connecticut trooper stopped us about 2 hours later. Since we had the registration, plus a real adult in the backseat, he accepted our cardboard plates.

The hometown police took a dimmer view of those plates, though. We were grounded until the metal plates caught up with us. And then we got an unexpected request for a mission of mercy.

Frank's scooter had broken down on his way home. He wanted us to use the Buick to haul it back to New Jersey!

**CLAMBAKES AND LEMONS.** Ads like this one for the stylish 1948 Studebaker whetted the postwar public's appetite for shiny new cars. But, as buyers like Philip Horn (see his sad tale below) would learn to their chagrin, a new car often meant a new kind of "excitement"—the kind they'd just as soon have done without. There were plenty of lemons around, but very little lemonade.

## Postwar "Lemon" Was Not Hard to Part with

MY FIRST new car—a 1949 Ford coupe—filled me with excitement, wonderment, anticipation and pride. Unfortunately, the excitement occurred one night on the Pennsylvania Turnpike when the hood latch failed at about 60 miles an hour.

One minute I was following the yellow line in my headlights—the next, all I could see was my hood! Luckily, I was able to pull over and safely coast to a halt along the side of the road. There I discovered that the hood ornament had been driven into the top of the car with such force that it took three of us to pry it out.

My wonderment was about what would happen next...like the white puff of smoke from the engine compartment when the temperature gauge read "normal". I eventually learned that was caused by gasoline overflowing the carburetor and splashing onto the hot engine block.

Anticipation centered on when I'd have my next flat tire or strange accident. The strangest one was the time my *insurance agent* backed his car into mine!

After that, the driver's door could be opened only from the inside. And, of course, nothing was ever fixed properly by either the dealership or the insurance company.

Just about the only source of pride I felt with that car was when I went to sell it. I was offered (and gladly accepted!) a little more than what I'd paid for it.
—*Philip Horn, Jonesboro, Arkansas*

## Horseless Carriage Rolled On Toward the Future

IN THE SPRING of 1947, I had a remarkable visitor at the Standard service station I managed in Winterhaven, California. The man's name was J.J. Ruth, and he was driving a 1902 Sears Roebuck motor buggy.

Mr. Ruth wanted the buggy checked before he drove into the sand dunes of Imperial County. He'd received the buggy from his uncle, the original owner, in 1918. Both lived in York, Pennsylvania and dreamed of driving the buggy across the United States.

With the war over and gas rationing only a memory, Mr. Ruth had set out to fulfill that dream. He told us the buggy had gone through six sets of tires, had been driven about 100,000 miles and had its motor reconditioned once.

A two-cylinder motor under the floorboards pushed it to a top speed of 30 miles an hour. Mr. Ruth graciously answered dozens of questions and even let my assistant and me drive the buggy around the lot.

But he was anxious to get back on the road. He wanted to reach San Diego by nightfall, so we gave him a presoaked water bag and wished him well.

I never found out whether he completed his trip across the United States, but I suspect he did. Before he left, Mr. Ruth told us that the trip was not a promotion of any kind...just a celebration of the end of the war and rationing.

But, it might just as well have been a celebration of the restless spirit that created the first "horseless carriages" and, by the late '40s, had changed the face of America forever.

The last time we saw J.J. Ruth, he was waving good-bye as he drove west across the desert.
—*John Milam Wellton, Arizona*

**ENCOUNTER WITH THE PAST.** When J.J. Ruth traveled cross-country in his 1902 Sears Roebuck buggy (below), he stopped at the gas station managed by John Milam (on left below left).